MW01248858

new series HEAT, a literary magazine in
book form, publishing contemporary
Australian and overseas authors, writing
on a wide range of subjects and in a
variety of styles. The essays, fiction and
poetry featured here have been chosen
for their literary quality, and their
imaginative appeal.

Heat 1. New series

Edited by Ivor Indyk

The Giramondo Publishing Company from
The University of Newcastle
Newcastle, Australia

Published by The Giramondo
Publishing Company
from the Faculty of
Arts and Social Science
University of Newcastle
Callaghan NSW 2308 Australia

Designed by
Harry Williamson
Formatted and typeset in
11/14 Garamond 3 by
Andrew Davies
Printed and bound by
Southwood Press
Distributed in Australia by
Tower Books
(02) 9975 5566

Fire and Shadow
(HEAT 1, New series, 2001)
ISBN 0 9578311 1 0
ISSN 1326-1460

The editor acknowledges the
support given by the following
institutions, without which the
publication of HEAT would not be
possible:

The Department of English
and the Faculty of Arts and
Social Science at the University
of Newcastle

The Australian Government
through the Australia Council,
its arts funding and advisory body

Sydney Grammar School

The NSW Government –
Ministry of the Arts

Acknowledgements

Annual subscription (two issues)
$40 in Australia and New Zealand,
$55 overseas.
Institutional subscriptions
$66 in Australia and New Zealand,
$75 overseas.
Amounts are in Australian dollars.
Australian rates include GST.
Payments may be made by cheque,
money order, Visa, Mastercard or
Bankcard.

Subscriptions and editorial enquiries
should be addressed to:
HEAT
PO Box 752
Artarmon NSW 1570 Australia
TEL. AND FAX: (+61 2) 9419 7934
EMAIL: heat@newcastle.edu.au
WEBSITE: www.mypostbox.com/heat

Contributions
should be submitted in manuscript
form with an appropriately sized
stamped self-addressed envelope
and mailed to:
HEAT
Department of English
University of Newcastle
Callaghan NSW 2308, Australia.
TEL.: (+61 2) 4921 5171

All published contributions by
academics are refereed.

Contents

Prose

9   Beverley Farmer   MOUTHS OF GOLD

37   Gustaf Sobin   BASSO CONTINUO

51   Alexis Wright   A KIND PEOPLE

57   Eva Sallis   THE KANGAROO

61   Louis Nowra   CHIHUAHUAS, WOMEN AND ME

87   Suneeta Peres da Costa   DREAMLESS

111   Kerryn Goldsworthy   ALMOST AN ISLAND

119   David Malouf   THE SOUTH

133   Peter Holbrook   POETRY AND SADNESS

143   John Dale   ON SMOKING

151   Marion Campbell   GOODNESS ITSELF

163   Dorothy Johnston   A SCRIPT WITH NO WORDS

219   Alexander Pitsis   THE TERRAIN OF HIS ETERNAL AMNESIA

Poetry

46   Robert Gray

82   Antigone Kefala

106   Judith Beveridge

127   Anthony Lawrence

147   John Foulcher

149   Peter Boyle

176   Kate Camp

181   Michael Farrell

203   Emma Lew

227   Peter Rose

Literary Engagements

185   Gig Ryan   'EVIL HAS NO WITNESSES': PRAMOEDYA ANANTA TOER

205   Eden Liddelow   AN INTERVIEW WITH SUSAN SONTAG

229   Christopher Pollnitz   CRITICISM, BIOGRAPHY AND LES MURRAY

243   Fay Zwicky   PAST AND PRESENT WORLDS: ON ROSEMARY DOBSON

249   Andrew Dowling   TRUTH AND HISTORY: ON PETER CAREY

Graphics

36   Noel McKenna   60, 162, 218, 248

83   Jacqueline Rose

Beverley Farmer

Mouths of Gold

Beverley Farmer's recent books include the novels *The Seal Woman* and *The House in the Light,* the writer's journal *A Body of Water: A Year's Notebook,* and *Collected Stories*, published by University of Queensland Press.

All winter, for half an hour after sunrise on any clear morning, a stalk of sun burns along the edge of my blind on to the wardrobe door. It spreads a tall flame across the matchstick blind, like a church candle. Then the whole blind is fire and shadow, cast by the tree outside. A print, a lion face.

A slice of blood orange is a wheel of fire. The skin surrounds a smudged pith and ten radiating white veins sodden with dark red: ten segmented translucencies of red gold like a dragonfly wing, and filaments like combed hair. A segment of blood orange is a red gold mouth pressed thick on the mouth, bitter as pomegranate.

Low tide and a waveline of jellyfish like ice on the thaw, clearer than water, so clear the sand is alight.

Ship smoke hangs over the garden of this house of the edge of journeys. Some of the older houses on the bay have a widow tower where women whose menfolk were at sea would watch for a ship coming and going through the Rip. All of them have a tin roof and narrow windows in their wooden walls, hooded to keep the summer out. The rooms have tall sash windows that run on ropes and the boxed panes are made of thin flawed glass that moves along with you like a sheet of water. The boxes of window are six feet by three, the dimensions of a single bed, Grania says, or a casket. A street of caskets with glass lids.

This story in the making: more and more self-effaced, lapped in the folds of itself, as water is, and reflections on water, developing in loops rather than along a story line, and therefore devoid – or free – of narrative tension. The surface tension of water. It involves Grania and her daughter Rosalie on the day and night that the family sustains, at a remove, a violent death. To be true to its organic form, any tension there is can only be that between the current of lived time and the reverberating rings of wave made by the stone that has broken through.

Attention to what is. Because whatever is added to the image hoard of one mind is an addition to the world. Not a permanent one, needless to say. What is permanent about a grain of fire in space?

We believe in anything rather than accept that a whole world emblazoned inside the eggshell of the skull is fated for extinction. We must be more than sparks of matter, atoms of finite being. We bind ourselves to others and to the world in the three dimensions of time with silken threads of soul stuff, extrusions of the self into the void, webs of meaning which we anchor where we can and hang there. The hope of the soul is tenacious. It is inborn, in our bones.

White wings, rags, moths flapping out in the garden are irises, for the first time in years, winter irises on the cusp of spring, self-sown in a blue-flickering darkness of rosemary.

Grania squats down with a fork grubbing up weeds, old bones, chicken drumsticks knotted at both ends and baked a wooden brown, a fish spine like a white fern, washed up with stones and roots and covered again, tides of the soil and rain. The place is a midden, year after year laid down and now coming to light, a lifetime of summers, of winters closing in like nightfall, other lives, compost spread out as mulch, black potatoes, some sprouting, avocado pits and their leather skins – fork the soil over anywhere along the dunes of the coast – ashes, knucklebones, eggshells, cuttle bones, a seabird's head all beak and eyehole, oyster and mussel shells, the antiquities of untold generations of a light-footed race, all the dark dead, their bones and blood and flow of hair.

Facing the two men the woman in the dream room shakes the water off her hands, but it spots the floor at their feet, dark blood, bad blood.

Flapping at her back all afternoon, the sheets on the lines as they fill out with wind and sun, four sheets like square sails airing for the family, two double for the parents, two single for the boy. Time now to haul them down and bring them in, pulling the French window shut behind her, seeing how the sun catches her through the trees as a blur on the glass, a fleece of hair hung on branches, one arm stretched out as if to cast a spell while the other hugs her bundle. Four sheets to untangle and fold, thin old cotton sheets, warm now, and yellow in the creases, like sheets off a sick bed – but no, the yellow goes away once the cloth is hung out flat, it was only the late light pooled in them. Arms stretched and lifted, she takes it slowly, matching the hems and selvedges in the dance that mothers used to take their partners for when she was a girl, a step forward, a step back, bringing up their hands in slow pat-a-cake unison. If a corner drags on the floor and is trodden on, never mind, it soon rubs off. They fill the room with the summer breath of salt and hay.

A stored image can broadcast itself when conditions are favourable, taking form in words, in ink and paint, film, clay, stone. Images are seeds. They have latency and the power to endure. They are like stored shadows burnt on to film for a fraction of a second, decades ago, the lost negative in the family Bible of a child with the sun in her eyes, seen for the first time in the child's old age. She sits squinting white-eyed in the pram. Her eyes are crescents in a jelly of dark flesh, albuminous, as if candlelit from inside. O, let me not be blind, not blind.

The brass lamp on the mantelpiece has no shade and the globe casts a yellow wash on the pair of photos she has propped against the wall at its back, two photos already in the key of yellow. In the first, the sun through the darkness of a cavernous ruin strikes a brass candle as tall as a man and melts it; on either side of it stand her daughter and grand-son, each posed half in shadow, half light. In the other, two stocky men are smiling out of the haze. The one dusty with sunlight, his mane of hair alight, is older and heavier than the other at his side, in his shade: Tomo with his brother Theo from Australia, so close in age they might be twins. Chrysostomo, he of the golden mouth, whose speech is golden. Theodoro, gift of God.

We know when someone out of our range of vision is staring at us. We sense the gaze, we turn to meet it: but how do we, using what sense? The orb spider poised in the web sees me watching: what is her idea of me, and how does it compare to mine of her? The horse as it takes the

apple off my palm in a whiskery kiss, the octopus writhing its fiery skin in rage at the glass of its prison, perceive me – in what form do they?

Our eyes live in a head they never see on a body always more or less out of sight. What drives us all more than half blind through this world of invisibilities, and how do we find our way? The wayfarer's way of attention, observation, navigation by signs, by memory, by experience.

We know, from experience, how experience has its meaning beyond the moment, a meaning which is only ever gradually revealed and grows with the revelation. The process is always incomplete. The meaning goes on growing, like desire, like memory, in the dark. The fullness of the meaning is only to be known by its weight, its power of displacement. It is at once intimately and exclusively ours and universal; as unknowable as the dark side of the moon or, for that matter, of the brain.

Mick watching his Nan bow to the oven with a tray is always reminded of his other grandmother on baking day, how the lumps of dough swelled up, with air, she said, sliding them swollen into the oven, and the air was baked in with the flour and water and yeast. He wonders again what made the difference between heavy bread and the bread that was a honeycomb of mostly air. And whether the air stayed trapped inside a loaf as if in so many bubbles of crust, or flowed in and out, a warm wind, then cooling, the breath of the bread.

No narrative, so no current of lived time, not so much as an undercurrent. The moment itself, stopped, as in the camera, isolated, shuffled, strung – beads on a rosary.

Someone calling out in the caravan park, Are you by yourself? – the strangeness of this double exposure. I know by inference that another self does inhabit me, live side by side with me, as ever-present as the skeleton and no less hidden. It is this other who keeps the flame of my life as flesh, in a dimension outside the mind's reach where it is at home, silent and unerring, a smooth animal. I and my self, the invisible twin: shade and water to each other in a dry land.

A presence accompanies him, keeping pace, moving where he moves, reflecting his every movement, not his brother. It shrinks from the light and is himself alone, his body, transparent, all its complexities of flesh woven on bone, the image and intensification of his dread. It looks like his brother, the image, and is not him at all, nor is it the soul of one or the other of them wrenched or shocked out of the body, an emanation with a seeming life of its own. It is a self-image. What he sees is his undeniable self flayed and infused with light.

Low tide this afternoon again, and there is such a sense of access, plenitude, now that the reef – a stone reef here, not coral – is exposed again and we can walk out over the seabed, the lips of pools studded with limpets and grapeweed, so often hidden and for a time laid bare. A hot northerly is starting up. Sunsodden, the sand spreads. Its creases gather and run under the rocks, like a sheet going thin and yellow, translucent with age, weighed down with stones, sand caking and feathering, drying itself.

Dinner over, they are on the last of the Naoussa wine and Mick is in bed when the phone rings, late, a call out of a Greek day for Theo, the first of many. There has been an accident. A car crash. On the mountain, and his brother Tomo is in hospital. And the boys? Just cuts and bruises, shock. Their mother is in a coma. Then Tomo is dead. He died in the arms of his son Michali, died, yes, instantly – it was just that no one could say it straight out. The funeral is tomorrow, according to custom. Theo asks them to wait, he'll fly over. It's up to the son as next of kin, after his mother, and he says no, tomorrow. Where? Thessaloniki. No, shrieks Theo, in the village of his birth! My father lived here in Thessaloniki, Michali says, with us, and hangs up. A quarrel ignites and burns on into the night across the world, the family taking sides: fighting, her daughter tells Grania, like jackals over the body.

What we know about anything is what the mind knows. Our death, for example: we pay lip service to the impending fact. As for the wisdom of the body by which we live, it keeps its own counsel, which amounts to a working disbelief in death. Let the mind know what it knows, the dreamer in the flesh will turn a blind eye.

Ποίησιος was 'making' to the Greeks, not our 'poetry' but the plain act of making. As in honey, as in web – imparting form to whatever a given self may yield. All metaphor is ποίησις. Μεταφορά. One is transported, taken beyond. Where? All gods are metaphors, all religions. We grasp at meaning, for an insecure foothold on truth. Dream is metaphoric. Metamorphic. Visitants, spirits and the occult, the near-death experience, angels, devils, are flickers in the cave of the skull, brain events as real as the fiery after-images of contrary colour – negative colour – that visit the eye are real. Perception itself comes down to metaphor.

For in Homeric days a restlessness seems to have possessed the Mediterranean
basin, and ancient races began shaking ships like seeds over the sea.
D.H. LAWRENCE, *Etruscan Places*

There are scraps of paper all over the hearthstone that Theo must have torn up, a head, a speck of candle flame, the photos from Agia Anastasia. Rosalie is stooping to pick them up when he utters a hoarse cry at her back and swings the empty bottle. It smashes on the hearthstone in a spray of light – she has sprung back just in time, and terror invades her. She watches, still throbbing all over with it, as at a great distance he throws himself face-down on the floor, blood in the black hairs of his arm, and on the hearth, no, red ochre and drops of glass. No. Grania has gone for a walk. If Mick wakes up and comes in – what's happened? – it's all right, only the lamp, she will say, it fell and broke, now go back to sleep. Listening in to the silent house.

Relics, memorials, the tide's leavings and ours, humanity's, so few, bones and driftwood, shells, crab casts and scrawls on the sand that were wave traces and the broader ones that ended in a limpet or a periwinkle, threads each with a knot at one end. Standing stones and rune stones, crosses, middens, ruins, shards and shreds as haphazard and rifted with meaning as the elements of a dream.

Magic began it, resurrection magic to thwart death: hence the gods. Death is the secret name of God. Religion, science, art, love, as one they body forth the eternal human longing to go on being. What has made us human, *homo sapiens*, if not this most ancient dream of all? So, the rebellion against death – this is our *sapientia*? Such as it is, I think so. What sort of wisdom is that! The wisdom of folly. Paradox.

Something has woken him, a wind, hoarse and steady, which is not the wind, or not only the wind, more the sea and he is at his Nan's place at the beach, the pitchdark sleepout. He lies with his hands folded in the heat of his armpits, not daring to pull on the cord over the head of his bed and flood the walls with the salvation of yellow light. Not for anything will he open his eyes or push a hand up out of the blankets to grope in the dark for the cord.

He still has the last traces of a dream in his head. They were all back at the monastery, all of them, even his Nan. It was old and crumbling, like a giant loaf of bread with a cracked red crust, and inside it was more like a cave than a church. A saint's bones were in there. Not all her bones. There was a queue to kiss the glass case and make the cross, all old women in black monks' hoods who looked like they'd seen a ghost, like his other grandmother, but when it was his turn all he saw was himself as if underwater, afloat over a little skull the size of a monkey's, in a silver helmet, until it moved its eyes, he saw it, and then his breath hid it.

The instant of the death, the thunderbolt. And the crux, comprehension. At the snowline halfway up the mountain on a Sunday morning in the late winter of his seventeenth year Michali in the front seat of the car sees out of the corner of his eye a truck veer into their path and grind through the windscreen. There follows a long moment like flight, of freedom from any sensation, before he can free an arm, a leg, another, his own and his father's, and drag them both out of the creaking wreckage that may explode at any moment, and over on to the gravel. The head against his shoulder is stove in. It wants to speak. He leans close but no words come out. He presses a frantic kiss on the wry mouth. When he lifts his head away the jaws fall open. A mask of blood crackles on his

face. A screaming in the air, his little brother, alive, and now boots crunch and voices call out but he is too cold to respond, cold and heavy in the snow with the burden in his arms crushing down with the weight of rock. Then he is afloat in clammy air. Cold, dim. Printed in blood on his white shirt, a rough head of hair.

These are the tall white irises, fleurs-de-lis, white and gold. They have an elaborate structure of six long outer petals, three of which stand up, alternating with three that fold down, pouting bottom lips each with a beard, a yellow brush that runs from the root to the rounded tip. The effect is of three caterpillars with their heads thrust down the throat – where these three outer petals, and only these, are overlaid with an inner petal. The light pools in it as in a shaded white room, in a breath of vanilla sugar. The six outer petals rise from a pod enclosing a green-gold throat, freckled, mackerel-skinned, to become broad and filmy white with a fan of glassy veins. The inner petals are pure white with a seam down the middle, along which they are humped and thick, but pointed at the tip; after a time the tip may split into two horns. From underneath, this hump of the inner petal is divided along the seam into two lobes, overlapped by a flange at the edge of the horned tip, as if two thicknesses of skin have fused. The hood thus formed shelters the strip of beard where it begins in the depths as the rich gold of egg yolk; out in the open, where the petal spreads, the beard fades to a pale lemon, almost white, and tails off. The hood has a name, *calyptra*, from the Greek καλύπτρα, veil. What does it veil? Nothing, it seems, until you pinch open one or other of the hooded inner petals, like a snapdragon's jaws, and there it is: a little needle, with an eye and a fuzzy skin, quivering out over the bristle of beard, a stamen, otherwise so shielded and screened in folds of white as to be invisible. The outer folds are translucent, long-veined under a silky glaze, with a fine sprinkling of moisture, like mica in marble, that is not dew or rain but their own drenched flesh. They cast shapes of shadow on and through their own translucencies.

The petals spill from a green pod, itself translucent, which is one of two at the top of the stalk. The other, lost in the folds of its open twin, remains a closely packed bud, but frilled and already white, while those further down are still the faint indigo of the skin around an under-slept eye. In two or three days the twin opens up, just a chink, like a cockle shell, and then wide; the lower, smaller ones follow. Each one as it withers turns cobwebby and shrinks down to a ball in a green fist.

A child crying has woken me. I listen into the silence. I have been dreaming. No, a wail on the wind, sobbing, a child – whose? Mine, mine, the unborn.

A photograph of the iris – white on black, a sea creature, a fat tongue with a ridge of bristles, white caverns, a bonnet and mantle, shadowy membranes. Underneath is a naked woman with her back turned, a tuft of soft hair in a blur where the head should be – a shoulder and breast half in shadow, a long flank and beyond, against the darkness, a white flounce crinkled at the edge like a dancer's fan, a jellyfish mantle. Or it is her front, the second breast in shadow, and she is bent back like a ship's figurehead, a mermaid, the flesh grainy like scales on one haunch: fused thighs and an open fantail. And rising out of her is the white hood, a split tongue of white flame, nose of a white whale. Blurred pale convolutions of flesh, they drift at the edge of vision in dark water as fathomless as sleep. They look like nothing so much as the deep sea creatures that live around fissures in the seabed that vent volcanic gases – the fire drake, the kraken – white, blind, gathered at the hearth fire on the ocean floor.

It has never seemed to me that 'agnostic' need be a negative, except grammatically. The concept of αγνωσία posits a lack, a limitation and not, or not necessarily, a void. Unlike 'ignorance', whose Greek root it shares, it is a stance. A judicious suspension of belief is implied, a verdict of not proven. There has to be an element of defiance in any wilful embrace of limitation. It is like the absence of perspective in so-called 'primitive' art, which is a dynamic absence, not simply a lack, as of something missing. The art is in the distortion, disproportion; the flat figures cast no shadow and seem barely to touch the ground, bodies and robes twisted in an airy fluidity of motion set hard in gold: monu-mentally still. Gestures in this world are timeless, not natural, not caught in passing, not static either, however: in the stillness there is the illusion, the glimpse out of the corner of the eye, of movement on the point of coming to life.

Like the absence of perspective, the absence of colour – the refusal, the defiance of colour – is a freedom. Monochrome is the beauty of the bare bones stripped of flesh. The Greek word for 'beauty', for that matter, ομορφια, stems from 'form', μορφη – not so the English.

Grania on the jetty sees: two torches moving, one near the shore and one on the outer edge of the rockshelf, and shifting in a wide flare or candling underneath or awash for a moment in a pale swill; every line of light in the sea underneath is a fold over lines of shadow drawn in the sand and water, all running the same way; the moon is high and white, already half-full, like the slow lantern spinning in the light-house, on off, on off. There is a word for that, its own strange word. What word? – occult. An occulting lighthouse. Light, dark, and red gold, the heave and loud flaking over a wave.

   She turns her face towards home, her cloak wrapped around her like wings, and picks her way through the limestone ledges that throw their shadows on the sand and the pools, dragging her feet more the closer she comes. The house is under occupation. Light and noise and turmoil, the shock of a near death, burst out at her through its skin of silvery wood. She shrinks from going back in. And they are her own people, all she has in the world, dear to her. Wishing them away all the same, anywhere but here, she stares across the winking black bay.

Thessaloniki is built on layers of itself. In its buried heart not long ago a temple was unearthed and found to be a Serapion containing a marble statue of the goddess Isis, now in the Museum, as the mother holding the child Horus. Isis, Au Set of Egypt, was the Blessed Queen of Heaven, the all-holy of her day, the παναγία, all the goddesses of the world in one – and foremost, in antiquity, in that part of the world, Demeter who was death's door into the earth and out again. Before there were settlements, let alone temples, a goddess had her shrines in caves and farmhouses and tombs and at the crossroads, much as the

Panagia Maria today has her wayside chapels and blue shrine-cabinets like bee boxes with glass doors, containing an ikon, candles and matches and a glass of water with a wick like a toy wheel afloat in dark oil. The plains were sown with graves first, and goddesses, any number of holy mothers, their names lost, and those from the time before they had human names, the great black and grey and sandy golden stones that are still standing, the mother stones, their skin weathered and raddled with oil and wine, milk and honey and blood; and a multitude of little stone or clay ones, fat with child, broken or whole, often just the head, formed in baked clay or stone and left in graves to be turned up one day under the plough. A little face looking up, almost smiling – the ploughman halts the horse and stoops over the clods, his shadow slithering at his feet in a silence like water and in the hollow of his hand a stored heat, crusty out of the oven of summer.

On the floor under the lamp Theo stirs and groans. He is shiny and cold, bathed in a smell of whisky. Blood is smeared on one arm and Rosalie lifts it anxiously, but there is only the one slit, shallow, it has already stopped bleeding. She sponges it and then his breathing face, taking care not to wake him, squeezing the sponge into the bowl of darkening water and softly wiping him dry. Ελα, she says, έλα να ξαπλώσεις, come on, lie down. Παιδί μου, έλα, and at that he props himself in his sleep and lets himself be rolled up on to the futon and tucked in, it was her saying παιδι μου like that, my child, she knows, my son, my darling. She gathers up the bowl and the towel, the broken glass, the shredded photos, and leaves him to sleep it off.

The dead were in the keeping of the goddess, in token of which trust, corn was sown on graves. The dead were the Δημήτρειοι. To this day the autumn festivals of the Δημήτρια are held in Thessaloniki, in honour of the murdered patron saint and martyr known as Demetrios. The grain crops were, and are, δημητριακά. The river-flat country north of Thessaloniki is one of the rare granaries in a land of dry rock. Here as in Attica, Demeter, Δήμητρα, was providence incarnate in arable land, the ample motherly home of corn and barley and sesame. She gave mankind the plough and the threshing floor, and to all who kept the rites she granted in the flesh the fruits of the field and beyond the flesh, immortal life.

Blood of the womb fed the cornfields, as ritual coupling sowed them, and a girdle of spilt blood safeguarded them. These Mysteries were in the keeping of women. The Mysteries, μυστηρια, are simply the rites and sacraments that make a door open into the godhead: baptism, the Lord's Supper, are ancient μυστήρια. The initiates are μύστες, as they were when they walked to Demeter's shrine with a winnowing basket of the fruits of the earth, a lighted candle, a phallus; and the candidates for initiation carried a piglet to Eleusis at harvest time, purified along with themselves in the sea in slippery squealing masses of flesh, to be sacrificed to the goddess, as the sow who eats her farrow. Once, beyond memory, the victim was human, as was still the case until much longer in the cold north, Denmark, Ireland, where they would feed a man his ritual meal of all the grains that wanted blessing, throttle him or cut his throat and thrust him into her lap of bog. At Eleusis pigs were thrown into snakepits and what was left, well-rotted carrion, bone and ordure, was mixed with the seed corn for laying on the altar. Earth magic, birth magic.

The snake was always holy to the mother of earth in whose dark places he lives and on whom he flings himself winding belly-to-belly. He whose sting is death is also the master of death, sliding out of his old skin ablaze with new life not once, like the bee or the butterfly, but over and over. Under the skin, besides, the snake is doubleness itself from the forks of the tongue to the genitals; and, like earth, a store of seed, in that the female lays fertile eggs months, and sometimes years, after mating. And the snake is the shelter of the household that gives it shelter and feeds it bowls of milk.

The bee was also holy to the goddess, whose priestesses were called Melissai, bees. She was always offered honey, as were the dead and also the newborn, who, once their lips were sealed with honey, were human under the law and not to be exposed or killed. The pomegranate was hers, and the fig, those blood-red seedy fruits; her flower was the tall and golden-tongued, late-winter-flowering purple iris. But, like children, and cities, new gods grow by feeding off the old, and she went to earth, the goddess, earth to earth, biding her time.

Νυκτιπόλοις, μάγοις, βάκχοις, λήναις, μύσταις
– *nightwalking magicians, bacchantes, revellers, initiates in the mysteries...*

The widow is a Greek of different stock. Her village is not inland in the plains but due east of the city, on the top of the dark mountain that crowns the peninsula. Her village is goats, stone walls and mud streets, icicles, deep in fog the one hot eye of an oven, a smithy. On the way there Tomo always pulled up at the old monastery, its wooden bones exposed – sooty cupolas and the sun thrusting in, great fallen rafters of smoky sun. Everyone went in and lit candles to poke in plates of sand. In a glass casket was displayed, set in silver, the skull of the saint, brought here reverently from the fallen Constantinople, tiny in a lace bonnet of silver like muddy melting ice.

It sat in the bowl all winter, a durable pomegranate with its red skin fading like the paint on an old boat, no stain though, no black spots, intact – only that it felt too light when I picked it up idly one day in spring, as light as a shell, and when I cut it in half there was only here and there a glow of red, no more than three seeds left alive in what was otherwise earth, soft, acrid, brown, full of clots the size of sheep drop-pings, a dusting of pale green mould.

The rites of the Mysteries were held underground bathed in fire. The initiates took an oath of secrecy, which was kept. Only a chink or two of light has ever come down to us.

I approached the very gates of death and set one foot on Proserpine's threshold yet was permitted to return, borne through all the elements. At midnight I saw the sun shining as if it were noon: I entered the presence of the gods of the under-world and the gods of the upper world, stood near and worshipped them.
LUCIUS APULEIUS, *The Golden Ass*

Rosalie knocks and pushes her mother's door open. The bed is empty in the dark. She undresses and slips in under the covers on the far side, her father's old side. Her mother's side is as cold. Where is she? A widow and her double bed. No one is saying a word about the

widow who is their sister-in-law, the widow who doesn't know she is – who will wake out of a coma to be told her man is dead and in his grave. And the boys? she will cry out and, reassured, will undergo the first spasm, as in labour, of her bereavement. How will she bear it? Much as all the village women who have always gone on keeping house and planting, hoeing all week and on Saturdays tending the graves. Their heads are shaded under a white cloth, a τσεμπέρι; and under the hot fabric and the glaze of sweat their faces take on an intense frail pallor, a transparency in the sunlight reflected off the dry soil, as if by candlelight. Frail, and yet even the oldest, the ones whose τσεμπέρι is brown or full black, for widowhood, burn with a naked strength. A black strength in a white body. A sisterhood of the bereaved.

The eclipsed moon in its totality, its scabs and burnish clear against an inner coppery light, as in a hand held open, filling with sun, over the eye. In a deepening silence, dimmed, it made its way over the stars in a flush of blood.

The brother of the dead man lies torpid as shapes of light swim up under his eyelids, red shot with blue. The bed smells of hay and something acrid and sweet, wine in the basin. Two women are hovering over the doughy mass on the bed, one a darkness, his mother, and the other in a rim of yellow. One lifts the scrubby grey head in both hands while the other fastens a bandage under the chin, knotting it at the nape. He hears the soft lick and slop of the sponge as they lift one limp arm and then the other, one leg and the other, a line of drips as yellow as oil strung out shimmering. He is as cold as the sea. The strokes of the sponge leave a varnish of water scribbled with black hairs.

Demeter's lost child was Kore, image of her mother. Greek names take the article – the Maria, the Thessaloniki – the same as common nouns. Κόρη is the common word for daughter, as well as the mirroring pupil – apple – of the eye. It used to encompass girl, virgin, doll, so that the κοροπλάστης was the maker of κόρες, figurines for the grave, dolls of clay or wax that came fully formed out of the plaster shell. Spoken of by name, Kore is just 'the daughter', any daughter, at the same time as she is the Kore whose womb is yet to shed blood in the moon's good time and, on her resurrection, the Persephone whose bleeding has run cold.

One wild scream and she was gone. When no one could tell the mother where her Kore was, she robed herself in black and, starving, searched the land for nine days and nights by the flare of two fennel brands held high, until she came to Eleusis, 'advent': and so the pilgrims fasted and carried burning brands to the temple. The priestess of Demeter played both parts, Kore and Demeter, the daughter raped by Death, and the *mater dolorosa*. She played all three parts, it might be truer to say, since Kore as a girl torn from the sunlit fields was a world away from her later Persephone-self – Proserpina to the Romans, Persipnei to the Etruscans – the bride of Hades. The figures of Kore and Persephone stand as the two halves of the matrix split apart, two shells and in their clasp the moulded figure of the mother, Demeter – a plaster negative and its mirror twin, Day-in-Night and Night-in-Death, the one white as snow and the other white as bone, enclosing the red gold clay of Birth, Life. Or – since Persephone replaces Kore, they are never both present at once – she was the sliver of cusp, first on one side then the other, that clasps the dark ball of the moon. She was to the figure of the Mother what the glow is to a source of light, the equivalent of the penumbra around the shadow, *umbra*: she was its fullness. All three were the one goddess, as the full moon and the two halves are the one moon; and each of the three was all three, fusing and splitting like flames over water.

As long as they live, cults grow in layers of themselves, augmented by influxes, grafts, fusions. The holy ones of old Europe and the Mediterranean basin – which has no tides, or only human ones – the goddesses first, and then the gods spreading war, all migrated, divided and coalesced, shifting shape through story after story. In an oral culture they are presences as immanent as breath, having their whole being in the lived ceremony, the sacrifice, the oracle and the old wives' tale by the hearth fire. They can live on in the word, but only when given breath. Art turns them to stone. Writing is the death of them.

We, on the contrary, say: In the beginning was the Word! – and deny the
physical universe true existence. We exist only in the Word, which is beaten
out thin to cover, gild, and hide all things.
D.H. LAWRENCE, *Etruscan Places*

Rather than bring myself to eat the three red seeds I had potted them
in their skinful of earth. Now one was in leaf. I was digging a hole in
the garden for it when the spade found a lump, two water drops that
were slit, were eyes, alive, in a muddy little frog. I carried it caged in
my fingers to the safety of the long grass and knelt, hands open. It sat
in my palm staring out for a time, pulsing, spun jelly fingers strung
out wide, before it could make its leap. Then I set my pomegranate tree
in its well of earth.

Unseen horses, a chariot, the pale god of the Dead, had burst out of
the earth and seized Kore. Ruthless in her despair, Demeter let the
land fall into waste until at last she was told that her daughter could
come back, as long as she had not eaten in the land of the dead. But
Kore had. She had eaten a single seed, or three, or seven seeds, of a
pomegranate, and so she belonged there in part, and must spend part
of every year forever after with Hades. In the summer of her absence
the land would lie bare under the sun as if dead. At the time of the
autumn sowing of the stored seed corn – the old crop, and the new –
it would come back to green life.

In Attica her absence was the furnace of summer after the
harvest. Further north, it changed to the winter of ice and snow.

In the myth she has nothing to say. One scream rings out
through the earth and sea and then silence. The silence of Persephone
is the silence of the grave. Why did she eat? Did the serpent beguile
her? Did Hades force her? The lily maid pure as the snow, and the
apple of venom, meaning death – was it for the glow of red in it, a
far sun? There in the underworld gloom she finds a tree hung with
faded carapaces, little clay pots left out in the rain. One has a gap in
the bottom, a red darkness. She pulls it in half and lying in her hands
are two white lobes of honeycomb, packed with beads of shining red.
She picks one out, bites down with a shudder. What has she done?

She stares at the red ball. A thread of blood runs down her arm.

The skin of a face quaking like milk on the boil, before collapsing, and on its mouth the blood drop of a pomegranate seed. And this is what it takes to prove the right of Hades to his bride, his seal of ownership? Yes, if it stands for the show of blood between her thighs.

One of his father's sisters and her husband are looking after the details of the funeral and his mother's hospital for him. They are paying because there was no money anywhere at home, only small change. Another aunt is nursing his brother. She and the others urge on Michali the anguish of his old grandmother, who can visit the grave any time if it's in the village, in his own native soil, but Thessaloniki is too far. Again he says to leave him alone, he is the next of kin and it's up to him when and where his father gets buried. Next of kin – what about the mother who brought him into the world? And remember, in the village he will be buried once and for all and not dug up after three years. What if the bones need more time, what if the earth has not finished eating the flesh, as can happen? Think of it! Michali does. He cracks. He yells that they can have the bones when the three years are up and do what they like, eat them for all he cares, burn them, bury them. For the first time since the mountain he sobs out loud. The aunts pet and comfort him and he throws them off, burning. My mother, he prays, wake up.

I pull the lid off the compost bin and recoil from an animal nestled inside, a ball of spun white fur, long and spangled with dew, the size of a kitten. It does not move and its body, as I peer into the silvery pelt, is a raw wound. I lift it on a stick only to see it fall mushily apart, sending a sharp smell up – of course, now I remember – of rotten figs.

Almost morning when a body sinks on the bed and she gasps, but this is her mother saying go back to sleep, and she does, they both do, in the quiet bed breathing in her blood smell. The shuffle of the sea in their sleep and now and then a thud, hollow, on ribs of dark water.

The spun fur, faintly incandescent, of mould on the figs, a smell,

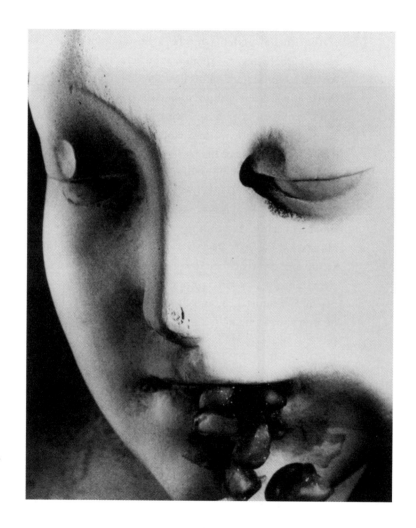

an exhalation, of alcohol – the veil that spins itself around death is what art is.

Three years after this day of the funeral the whole family will gather on the lip of the grave, all hostilities suspended for the time being, the women shrilling around the young widow, the old mother, and the priest intoning, all eyes on the shroud of dark flesh on the bones. The head on its hinge will be a broken shell too heavy for its stem of neck, like a baby's. The sexton will put aside the spade and step in to lift out the skull, greeting it by name and wrapping it in a cloth. Head first he came into the world: now the mother, not the widow, will open her hands for it and they will watch while she stands dazed turning it this way and that, as if it were a lost schoolcap and she looking for the name, who until this day of the ξεχωματα, 'unearthing', will have been hoping for a miracle, a new Lazarus, a smile as he opens his eyes to the light.

In a recurrent dream she is at a crowded beach on a hot night, a child, when an apron of water, having hollowed out a lap between knees of lifted sand, surges high up over the wave line to where she is lying, alone, she must have fallen asleep, and wakes up to find a black wave breathing in her ear, in the nick of time.

The Archaeological Museum is down the road from the graveyard of the Evangelistria, another title of the Holy Mother. On a day of baking heat, dimness, footsteps echoing in room after room, a glow on a blade of glass narrows down to fine leaves, goldfish, on a shelf, mouth-masks of pure gold – gravegoods of a kind unknown elsewhere, in an abundance so far only found in the Archaic stone tombs in and around Thessaloniki. They were only ever worn once, in death, tied on with threads passed through two small holes and knotted at the back of the head, and how they call up even in here the silence of the deathbed, the shadows of women moving around the corpse, the head lifted briefly up, as if for feeding, while the knot is tied, two working together, or else one working alone with the head held at her breasts. What were they for, these mouths? They swim in the heat and gloom with the dense liquidity of honey, but they are finely detailed, made out of hammered sheets of a soft red gold, plain or embossed with rosettes, waves, an eye, a ship with sails surrounded by dolphins, most crumpled under the weight of earth, some with an impression of the teeth. No lid for the eyes, except one woman's, and only a few full masks where the face was embedded in the gold: just this mouth of gold closed on the mouth of flesh. Was it that the dead needed to see – they had oil lamps – but not speak? All the same, food and drink were offered, as they are to this day at the funeral and all the memorial days. Maybe it was the coin for Charo that they wore on the mouth rather than in it, οι χρυσοστομοι οι νεκροι, the golden-mouthed dead, each a plumb-weight of silence at the grave-mouth, gagged under this kiss.

The mourners had left them figurines of a smiling seated goddess and such keepsakes as birds in the shape of luminous globes of sea blue glass, beads and rings and amber, phials of perfume; black iron miniatures of household goods, pans, cauldrons and tripods, sieves and copper lanterns pricked like sieves, green as mould, wine cups for the dark wines of memory. The children had clay toys, barn-yard animals as plain as the dough ones of baking days, with an odd, blind life still in them, a dog, a pigeon, a craning tortoise small enough to close a fist on, worn smooth as river stones. Soldiers had their rusty armour and weapons.

More lamps burned on the pride of the Museum, the relics of a murdered king, and on his ivory and gold shield that they found in flakes like fish scales, and on his gold wreaths. He was found in a casket of gold: a jumble of bones, brown blotched with indigo, and a crushed wreath of oak leaves and acorns, pure gold, on the skull. One eye socket was stove in. The corpse had been burnt, then the bones washed in wine and wrapped in a purple cloth that had evaporated like smoke to leave only a blue shadow on the bone. They laid the bundle in the casket in a marble tomb, in a mound. Now he lay at full length in a glass case, cracked spindles of bone, a grin in a brown shell. It was a day of blinding heat and in the marine sombreness of the hall the objects shone through the glass in drops and pools of irregular bright-ness like the sun through vents in a cave and along one wall swam speckled fish with gold-ringed eyes.

Unless — what if they had another meaning altogether? That speech, not silence, is golden? In which case the mouth, being the organ of the soul's truth, turns to gold; and the mouth-mask is more like the warrior's bronze armour in a tomb in Etruria that looked to Lawrence to be *beautiful and sensitive as if it had grown in life for the living body, sunk on his dust.*

Some say the body is in its soul. Yes, if its life, its being-alive, the quality of being animate — where soul, *anima*, is implicit in the word, enfolded and enfolding — is the soul. This mantle of livingness we move in, whose tissue is pulse, breath.

My friend with cancer has visitations. Struck down in the bathroom one night she stared up into the light to see her own mother lean out of the mirror mouthing words of encouragement.

Honey is on tap at the bulk store, in a steel drum mounted over a base like a ship's lantern where a globe is burning, loosening the flow with its warmth and at the same time candling it, like a fresh egg, so that it unwinds in a rope, every speck visible, dust motes, pollen, a white trail of bubbles, a galaxy. Here is the truth of honey laid bare in liquid fire. Grania closes the lever and a last wisp hangs like blond hairs down a little boy's nape. When it shrinks up into a neb she wipes it off with her finger and sucks a sweetness that chokes, of winter honey. Iris honey, for all she knows, though not everyone has irises this time of the year. In Greece they grow wild, ἱρίδες, or simply κρίνα, lilies, the death flower, and αγριόκρινα, wild lilies. Winter-flowering icy efflorescences. Essence of fleurs-de-lis.

So that the Nectar or liquid hony is of two sorts: one hard and white even like unto sugar, which is therfore called stone-hony, or corne-hony: the other so soft that it will runne, which therefore is called live-hony.
CHARLES BUTLER, *The Feminine Monarchie*

Here and there all over Europe the ruins of graves left over from the Stone Age lie in the long grass or snow. On a day between winter and spring, after the thaw, in a meadow like matted tobacco from the months under snow, I came across two such graves in a mound inside a ring of rocks overlooking a bright sea. In the belly of the mound they were two gashes lipped with stones and lined with splintering snow, and in the shadow of the tall rocks were huddled clumps and shreds, the only snow in sight, as if where stone was, winter still was. A low tomb lay out on its own further inland on the edge of the bare beech-wood. This was in Denmark once, not far from where the Tollund Man had lain two thousand years in the peat, his nose squashed like a baby's at the breast. The tomb had legs of stone edging a rough lintel blotched with lichen. The pillow in its lap was the last snowdrift, blue with deep shadow. A dark hole, a breath of ice.

The cave was the first temple, the cavity with a tight entrance, the stone beehive with its mouth to the sunrise, an oven, a belly: magic in the grave raised in the shape of the mother's womb, stone-smooth or furry with grass. Then as now, the bereaved set up the wail at the grave-side that we all made as babies for our mother. The dead were folded in the foetal position, hollowed out and tarred, cured, pickled, reduced to ash or jugged in the honey of immortality, set adrift in a ship of death at sea or in the earth, or in between, in bogs that were earth-and-water wombs of the goddess. They were bathed in red ochre, the blood of rebirth, for nurture and for safeguard, so she would know them for her own. They were given oil, grain and wine, milk and honey, kitchen tools, armour and gold; sometimes a slaughtered dog to lead the way, and, for a king, a slave woman to share the dark with; a siren to ferry the blessed to the islands; brightly frescoed scenes on the inner walls of sarcophagi, paradises for the soul's habitation.

A gap over the lintel of the megalithic long barrow of Newgrange in Ireland was so angled that the sun rising on the winter solstice would penetrate in a lightning thrust, a blade of gold, a glaze like candlelight along the stone walls, the reanimating fire.

Heavy lips, articulating words of honey, in the dream, the golden flow of words I understand without hearing and wake up having forgotten.

I am at a window watching snowflakes, slow and heavy, rising, blurring, a flight of white bees, some so close and slow I see the glaze of their wings. Now I am pacing along a cloister, a caged quadrangle under snow, a vault of silence. The snow is unmarked except for folds of shadow and a few dry stems poking up, each in its hollow of melt. The columns of the cloister shimmer and then fade like the skin of a caught fish. My eyes open on a sword of light emblazoned on a door.

Lucius Apuleius, *The Golden Ass*, translated by Robert Graves, revised with an introduction by Michael Grant (Penguin: London, 1990), 194.

D H Lawrence, *Etruscan Places*, edited by Giovanni Kezich and Marco Lorenzini (The Olive Press: London, 1986), 46, 50, 102.

Charles Butler, *The Feminine Monarchie* (Da Capo Press, New York: 1969), facsimile of the first edition, Oxford, 1609.

LOST DOG —

Please help !!!!!!!!!!

- Male, Border Collie — lost 27.12.00
- Black and White
- Microchipped
- Answers to Lenny

REWARD

PLEASE CALL 0417 600 160

or 91305352

Gustaf Sobin

Basso Continuo

The Past as Accompaniment

This essay deals explicitly with the themes of time and memory present in Gustaf Sobin's two recent books, the collection of essays *Luminous Debris: Reflecting on Vestige in Provence and Languedoc* (University of California Press), and the novel *The Fly-Truffler* (Bloomsbury).

1 Historians, grammarians, archivists, invariably come late to a given civilisation. Their approach is marked, already, by a spirit of retrospection: one in which the dynamic of that given civilisation has begun giving way to doubt, and doubt – ineluctably – to nostalgia. They face backwards and attempt to collect, as they do, the fading evidence of a past that – by its very evanescence – calls out for inquiry, and inquiry, in turn, for documentation. Doesn't this spirit of retrospection apply to ourselves as well? At the very gates of a new millennium, on the threshold of a so-called new age, haven't we, too, as a people, begun turning backward, growing in our innermost moments increasingly reminiscent? Victims of a 'regressive evolution' in which the immense advances of technology have all but depleted the fertile landscapes of the imaginary – that vast terrain in which we once erected the statuary of our collective referents, establishing thereby the determinants by which we might recognise ourselves – we, too, have begun gazing backwards. Tracing, resuscitating, preserving whatever we can of those lost worlds, we've taken to collecting artefact, restoring all but forgotten public monuments, recording each and every available detail (no matter how minor) touching upon each and every vestigial scrap (no matter how slight) that we've managed to uncover. We've grown greedy – it would seem – for the obliterated.

This movement was long in coming. If the Renaissance and its convulsive aftermath, the Baroque, were far too engaged in the unravelling of their own hallucinatory fabric to look backwards, their demise in the late seventeenth/early eighteenth century gave rise to a Neo-Classicism resolutely nostalgic in its *Weltanschauung*. 'All beauty of art emanates out of the Antique,' would declare Pier-Leone Ghezzi (1674–1755). His meticulous renderings of antique subjects from marble inscriptions to architectural ensembles, accompanied by his own invaluable commentaries, would herald an age of intense retrospection. Motivated every bit as much by a search for the sublime as for the underlying postulates of reason, painters, sculptors, architects, art historians and collectors descended upon Rome. The attraction of Rome, what's more, had been enhanced by the recently excavated sites of Pompeii and Herculanum. Celebrating in over two thousand plates the desolate splendour of sites such as these, Giambattista

Piranesi (1720–1778) would raise the mere fascination for *antiquaria* to an elevated aesthetic plain. In depicting broken staircases, sectioned columns, collapsed domes, all caught in the chiaroscuro of a late afternoon light, Piranesi was portraying – far more than the subjects at hand – the spiritual climate of a late crepuscular world. That light, in fact, would go on fading. And if, soon enough, it no longer struck the flanks of antique ruins but the boughs and branches of a nascent Romanticism, that Romanticism would have simply transferred the decor of retrospection from the architectonic to the pastoral.

Backwards, we gaze backwards in precipitating forwards. Or, rather, in *being precipitated* forwards. For certainly the accelerations generated by the Industrial Revolution from the nineteenth century onward would create an ever growing hiatus between our material conditions and those – ultimately far more determinant – in which our deepest psychic imperatives once found palpable expression. Looking backwards, we could only be searching for ourselves. Straying through the ruins and debris of past civilisations, we could only be hoping for glimpses – no matter how tenuous – of our long forgotten identities.

2 Freud himself called it *'eine Phantasie.'* In sending Sándor Ferenczi the twelfth and last chapter of his *Metapsychologie* on 28 July 1915, one of the seven chapters he himself would destroy soon after, he forewarned his disciple: 'I can only hope that the reader...will be indulgent even if, for once, critical spirit gives way, here, to fantasy.'[1] In an attempt to trace the origins – the aetiology – of neuroses, Freud, fully aware of the hypothetical nature of his exposé, reached far beyond the Greco-Latin mythologies to which he was deeply attached to the Palaeolithic itself. 'Under the effect of deprivations provoked by the advent of the Ice Age,' he boldly proposed, 'humanity became collectively anxious.' It is during this very period, he continued, that, due to the scarcity of basic sustenance, birth control came into practise. This, in turn, gave rise to sexual repression for the first time in human history. What Freud called a 'constitutional disposition' had been established. It would serve as the source of each and every ensuing neurosis.

Even if we can readily dismiss such a hazardous supposition

(Freud himself certainly did), this *Phantasie*, nonetheless, laid the ground for an entirely fresh interpretation of the human psyche. Inspired, no doubt, by the work of Ernst Haeckel (1834–1919), the German biologist and philosopher, Freud would apply 'Haeckel's law' to the human psyche, correlating ontogenesis (the development of an individual organism) with phylogenesis (the development of a genetically related group of organisms). The evolution of the individual, that is, could now be considered as a recapitulation of that of all humanity. Seen in this light, each of us, in our psychic development, passes through each and every stage – call it strata – of humankind at large. 'Impressive analogies from biology have prepared us to find that the individual's mental development repeats the course of human development in an abbreviated form,' Freud had already written in his *Leonardo da Vinci* study in 1910.[2] The individual at birth, according to this insightful interpretation, is endowed with a 'libidinal sediment' – a set of instincts inherited from an aboriginal past – to which new and individual traits come to add themselves like so many layers in an archaeological cross-section.

We know, of course, of Freud's profound fascination for archaeology, and the analogy he often drew between his own nascent discipline and that of archaeological excavation. Both, indeed, reach downward and, as they do, explore deeper and deeper levels of vestigial deposits. These deposits, be they those contained within an individual psyche or secreted within some richly anthropic subsoil, are charged with the history of their respective origins. Properly examined, analysed, classified, they contain the hidden history of those very origins. Here, Heracleitus's fragment 'the way up is the way down' might well be read in paraphrase. For certainly, as we reach downward through those successive strata, those impacted layers of lost testimony, the darkness therein grows luminous. Becomes lit with the light of essential disclosure.

3 Everything's there. For anyone living in an archaeologically rich milieu or, alternatively, driven by curiosity to the texts themselves and what might be called 'archival excavation,' the evidence awaits us. The past, no matter how elusive, not only underlies

the present, but – properly interpreted – comes to clarify it as well. Like the *basso continuo* of an ongoing accompaniment, its notes, often fragmentary, even illegible, lie in counterpoint to our own; establish the ground – the very *grund* – upon which our own successive substructures stand.

It would far exceed the limited ambitions of this essay to explore that ground, those successive substructures, in a thoroughgoing manner. One might, however, touch briefly upon certain critical moments in their composition. Basing our own interpretation on vestige alone, one might begin, indeed, with the eolith (*eo* for dawn, *lith* for stone). Yes, one might well begin with the 'dawn stone,' that chipped pebble dating from the Pleistocene (an estimated two million years ago). All but indistinguishable from an accident of nature, this earliest constituent artefact – the product of the first intentional artisanal gesture on the part of *homo habilis* – might be compared to the muscular twitching of an embryo in its uterus. Even the most trained typologist often has trouble differentiating, at this stage, matter from its materialisation; substance from its substantiation. This incipient handaxe scarcely shows any sign whatsoever of a separate development. It still belongs, it would seem, to the very magma out of which it has only begun to evolve.

A second chip here, a third chip there, and one reaches – a quarter of a million years later – the first discernible 'pebble cultures.' Here, at last, one can begin to distinguish with ever growing certitude the worked tool, duly articulated. Without falling into a *Phantasie* ourselves, couldn't we postulate, at least, an analogy of our own: one in which we, too, over a vast expanse of geophysical time (measured more by glacial expansions and contractions than any chronological sequence) come to individuate, to distinguish if not separate ourselves from that surrounding magma, i.e. nature itself. We go on, chip after chip, flake after flake, fashioning our tools in an increasingly complex, increasingly distinct manner. Over a million years later (circa 500,000 BC), the elegant Acheulean *biface* – an oval-shaped handaxe pressure-flaked about its edges and often compared to a limanda due to its fish-like aspect – will make its appearance. Even this highly evolved tool, however, could only have been conceived as a discrete unit: as, that is, an artefact executed in a single, all-inclusive moment of non-evolving time. It precludes serialisation. One would have to await the so-called flake-tool cultures (and most especially the Levalloisian) during the third glaciation (circa 200,000 BC) to discover the very first implements prepared in a predetermined, premeditated fashion. These flake tools (skinning knives and skin-scrapers for the most part, far more appropriate to life in cold and wet climates than the handaxe) reflect an evolving attitude in regard to time on the part of their makers. Production strategies, a growing sense of the sequential, of cause and effect, have clearly come into play. One might postulate, now, based on the execution of such artefacts, an ever-growing awareness of temporality and all that such an awareness implies in terms of psychic development.

Reading prehistory on the basis of vestige alone, one cannot help but equate 'evolution' with 'separation'; how our own gathering self-awareness as separable/separate entities in both temporal and spatial terms comes at the cost of an ever-increasing sense of rupture. In growing, we grow away. Each technological achievement generates a breach, a violation, a distance taken from the aboriginal matrix out of which all life, originally, emerged. Every instance of material progress elicits, *ipso facto*, a fresh instance of severance, 'distanciation.' Moving at a catatonically slow rate towards self-consciousness in the Hegelian sense of the word, we come, at last, to take measure of the immensities, now, that surround us.

In reaching the Aurignacian (circa 32,000 BC), we begin invoking those very immensities by means of graphic representations. Be they painted, carved in relief, or engraved upon exquisitely fashioned bone tools, these first semiotic gestures depict, almost exclusively, the animals that inhabit those surrounding immensities. They attempt to summon – graphically speaking – horse and bison, rhinoceros and reindeer, toward the proximate, the immediate; reintegrate the estranged within the innermost circles of the familiar. For a cleavage exists, now, between the 'here' and the 'there,' between what we've come to call culture and nature. Having acquired a separate status over the millennia, we feel an increasing need, now, to lure, draw, induce – by whatever means possible – what lies otherwise beyond our reach. The magical properties of graphic representation become the privileged vector, at this very time, of such an appeal. 'Art,' in its earliest, most quintessential form, emerges as an attempt to bridge the gap. 'What characterises humankind,' Georges Sauvet writes in regard to late Palaeolithic art, 'is our ability to evoke absent objects; to *re-present* them visually.'[3] Haven't we, though, become the 'absent objects' ourselves? Haven't we, in our irrepressible need to acquire such a separate status, 'broken contract' with our earliest – deepest – affinities?

The arrival of the Neolithic (circa 9000 BC in the Near East) would see a violent acceleration of this very process. In coming to control our own food supply as emergent farmers and stockbreeders, we'd take an even greater distance from those surrounding immensities. With the Neolithic, we'd begin to produce what had always been proffered; take what had always been given. Concurrently, the invention of ceramic would allow us to store such produce *against* the vicissitudes of the very milieu that had brought such produce to bear. The rupture between the 'here' and the 'there,' between culture and nature, had reached – by now – irreconcilable proportions. 'Ineluctably, a sense of alienation would arise out of that instigating moment, that act of primal violation. On a mythological level, it would find expression (at a somewhat later date) in Prometheus's theft of the thunderbolt from the gods overhead, and – in its Judeo-Christian counterpart – Adam's theft of the forbidden apple from the garden. In each case, disgrace, humiliation, would be the price exacted, what humankind would have to pay for having 'seized control'.[4]

Out of that all-critical moment in human evolution would emerge our first gods. 'A vertical typology begins to develop at the heart of the human psyche,' writes Jacques Cauvin, 'in which an initial state of anguish finally dissipates, but only at the price of an intense mental effort in an ascensional direction. That effort is experienced as an appeal to a divine instance that is both beyond and above humankind itself.'[5]

In interpreting human history on the basis of artefact alone, we might site the emergence (in the Mediterranean, at least) of carved figurines: tutelary spirits, proto-divinities for the most part, they once accompanied the dead as psychopomps. From the Cycladic idol to the Provençal funerary stele, these Bronze Age sculptures (circa 2000 BC) emerge as liaison figures between the living and the dead, the here and hereafter, earth and its freshly projected complement: heaven. Bits and pieces of such carved work are still discovered today in areas richly charged with protohistoric artefact. An eye here; a nose there; an entire torso yet there again: the relics of that evolving idolatry (and, along with it, the first instances of human figuration) can be found scattered across the surface of the ground, confounded with the flint, ceramic, serpentine, of other cultures, other epochs.

As we've already suggested: everything's there. In shattered fragments, disparate shards, vestiges emanating out of virtually every moment in human history rise to the surface, and – like some hermetic grammar – beg to be read. For read, duly interpreted, they might well tell us everything we need to know not only about human evolution but – far more immediate – that of our own individual development as well. Harping back to 'Haeckel's law,' and conflating, as he did, phylogenesis with ontogenesis, we might find astonishing parallels, most especially in terms of those successive, seemingly inexorable, stages of human severance. Be they historico-collective, proper to the entire species, or specifically individual, they trace a singular itinerary. Yes, in growing, we've grown away. We've wrested free of the matrix, be it that of nature itself or its most archaic personification: the *Mater Magna* endowed – as mother figure – with the aura of a radiant psychic investment. Driven, no doubt, by a profound anguish that knows little if any limits, we've come to establish, in ever increasing increments, our separate identity. This has been attained, however, at a terrible cost. Severance has led, ineluctably, to isolation, and isolation – more often than not – to despair. The citadels of our selfhood envelop, we've come to discover, little more than a frenetic emptiness.

In looking back, now, in crossing those elected fields in which vestige abounds, inspecting this bit of Cardial ceramic or that bit of knapped Acheulean flint, in establishing as we go – through all that disparate artefact – a viable chronology, could we, indeed, be searching for anything but ourselves? For those suppressed levels of consciousness? For those lost worlds in which we once exulted in an intensely reciprocal, if not fusional, state with our very origins?

More than metaphor, vestige represents analogy. Rising *hors contexte* to the very surface or lying in successive layers immediately beneath us, it bears witness – palpably, materially – to those lost reciprocities. Becoming, as we have, the historians, the grammarians, the archivists, of that obfuscated past, we're given – therein – a plethora of evidence. Underlying our own present-day existence, underwriting our every measured reflection, archaeological vestige serves to reminds us of everything we've forgotten. Even more, it preserves – within its own resonant depths – the dark chords of our own most fervent longings.

---

1 In 1983, Ilse Grubrich-Simitis, in preparing an edition of the Freud-Ferenczi correspondence, came upon this letter and the attached document tucked away amongst Ferenczi's papers. My translation.

2 *Leonardo da Vinci*, trans. Alan Tyson (Penguin, 1963), 136.

3 Georges Sauvet, 'Rhétorique de l'image préhistorique,' in *Psychanalyse et préhistoire*, ed. A. Fine, R. Perron, F. Sacco (Presses Universitaires de France, 1994), 84. My translation.

4 Gustaf Sobin, 'Stelae: The Emergence of Human Figuration' in *Luminous Debris: Reflecting on Vestige in Provence and Languedoc* (University of California Press, 1999), 76.

5 Jacques Cauvet, *Naissance des divinités, naissance de l'agriculture: la révolution des symboles au Néolithique* (Editions du CRNS, 1994), 100. My translation.

Robert Gray
The Fishermen

There comes trudging back across the home paddocks of the bay

pushing its way

waist-deep in the trembling seed-heads of the light

the trawler

with flat roof and nets aloft,

with its motor that thumps like an irrigation pump

and a winch triangulate

on the monolithic cloud. And this cloud is straining out the sunrise

of a Bible tract

and that shows a few lumps of islands and just the one boat

in the blazing sand-box of the sea,

while close-up the edges of such a volatile kind of grit

are being swept ashore.

It's all noticed by a cyclist on the wet asphalt, who takes a corner

above the banksia scrub,

by someone in pyjama stripes and venetian slats of light

among the wide bungalows,

by two early walkers going down a track

onto the dunes,

from where they will watch the baggy sea, that is practising its

ju-jitsu on the kelp.

Only the harsh approval of the gulls

that the fishermen are back, the small boat

swimming exhausted with nose up; back

from a night far out on the weird phosphorescent plain, in that
    seething culture
of the hatching snake eggs, or from deep
in the icy slush
of moonlight; the sea corrosive-smelling
and raw
like rust. Back from the cobra-flaring,
gliding and striking sea, goaded it would seem by their being there,
who tear
up by the roots the nets and the lobster traps.
Back from a sea sweaty with stars, or from one black and flowing
    like crepe.
From a sea that erupts
and falls on them so hugely that only the radio mast could have shown
in the foam, if they'd had one. The fishermen have been taught,
by each other, that if swept off
in such a sea, without a jacket, which they don't wear in their work,
to swim straight down and make an end of it,
since they will never get back.
They live inside a dream
out there, everything they know about is in shadows,
who sometimes see a liner,
further off, that goes drifting past them like a town
on the moon,
and who see the ocean vomit a black whale
like its own tongue.

ROBERT GRAY

But you have come back, the two of you, to a morning world
of newspapers and washed cement,
of swollen, damp
milk cartons, of car fumes,
of a train going to the city, through the small town, moving off again
    with stiff spine,
to the old wooden tenements, with sand hung
in their eyebrows, near the line,
and a sky like bacon.

One of you has a wife, and she is brusque, earth-bound, and
    unforgiving still.
She loves you, you can tell, by her sullen glances.
Her humid-smelling nightgown, and the smoky
curlicues of hair about her ears, in the streaming light –
'Don't empty those boots there!'
'Mum Mum Mum Mum Mum Mum…'
'Why must you always have this bloody soup for your breakfast? Look,
I'm burning it again. Do something:
watch it. No,
that toast is for the children!'

Who can know how strange the land is for you, the place where you
    come to sleep?
You have watched the single mass of the mountains slowly worked loose,
that goes down aslant into the Underworld, and alone then in the bows
    have seen the bear-paws

48

of the ocean idly claw for you.

You see now, half asleep, the children eating – the grains come undone
    in their mouths;

you don't speak, and you watch your hands, you once slapped one

like a wave.

           And then you wake,

and all is silent. You stagger, scratching

at your underwear. The little cells of the screendoor,

in the afternoon sun,

are sealed with dust. Those big lemons, breast-tipped,

are new for this young tree, out alone in the concrete yard. On
    the table

the shopping lies agape

like a mouth of grief – the cans of tomatoes, red molars; the pot-
    scourer; the foamy bread.

You give up, quite soon, tinkering with the bath heater

and write on the back of a note

a note, with a pen that half works. You walk through the glare

like someone taking a sick day, to the pub, and again you share the dark

waters there; you and they launch out from the Pier Hotel,

travelling together glass by glass.

The school kids come out shrieking in the sun;

such animals, you see, as you have released from your body,

in the hope of a little comfort, a home. What mad delusion was that?

Children were to keep a woman busy

until you got back. In the pub, you stagger before you can walk again
    on the water.

It is time to go out

with this bastard, your old mate.

You look up at him, where he comes to get you – that face

might have been some woman's nightmare;

a breath of sour acids,

and never a tender intonation to his voice.

You take your mate's hand, that is hard as a damp stone,

reached to you on the floor,

in the gutter,

in the sea. Through his broken teeth he tells you

to hold on, you'll be all right. He pulls you into the boat

or he'll come out himself.

It can never be said, but you think, Where

have you found a love like this? In the morning you will part from

    him again

with a curt word, at the jetty. You'll turn and walk inland

and give life another chance.

Robert Gray's poetry books include *New Selected Poems* (Duffy & Snellgrove, 1998), and the collections published in the UK, *Lineations* (Arc) and *Grass Script: Selected Earlier Poems* (Carcanet, 2001).

Alexis Wright

A Kind People

from *Carpentaria*

Alexis Wright is a
member of the Waanyi
people of the southern
highlands of the Gulf of
Carpentaria. She is the
author of *Grog War,* and
the novel *Plains of
Promise* (UQP, 1997).

The day, all action packed like it was, was now all said and done. The
men of Mozzie Fishman's dedicated convoy to one major dreaming
track stretching right across our stolen continent, were now sitting up
there on the side of the spinifex hill – like rock wallabies, looking
down at what was left of *Gurfurritt* mine. Just looking, AND turning
the sunset crimson with their thoughts.

What a turnout. Gee! Whiz! We were in really serious stuff now.
We were burning the white man's very important places and wasting
all his money. We must have forgotten our heads. We were really
stupid people to just plumb forgot like that because the white man was
a very important person who was very precious about money. Well! He
was the boss. We are not boss. He says he likes to be boss. He says he's
got all the money. Well! We haven't got the money neither. And now,
all it took was a simple flick. A flick, flick, here and there with a dirt
cheap, cigarette lighter, and we could have left the rich white people
who owned *Gurfurritt* mine, destitute and dispossessed of all they owned.

Straight out we should have been asking ourselves – Why are
you not hanging your head in shame to the Whiteman? We were
suppose to say, Oh! No! You can't do things like that to the, umm,

beg your pardon, please and thankyou, to the arrr, em, WHITEMAN.

Somehow though, everyone got carried along the humpteen tide of events, like we must have swallowed one too many sour pills that morning for breakfast. Now, we were looking at the world like it was something fresh and inviting to jump into and do what you jolly well liked. That was how our dormant emotions sitting down inside our poor old hearts got stirred up by the Fishman when we listened to him talking in that fetching, guru type voice of his, saying we gotta change the world order. Change the world order? Mozzie Fishman! He is sure enough a crazy man. Oh! We said that. But he goes on and on in his satirical slinging voice about what happened ever since that mine came scraping around our land and our Native Title! 'Well!' he says. Us? He wanted us to tell him what that turned out to be. We were a bit cross with Mozzie standing up there, Lord Almighty like on top of that rust bucket of a Falcon station wagon of his. All its crucifixes hand wiped over that white coloured car through the stains of red mud.

'You know who we all hear about all the time now?' he asked us. 'International mining company. Look how we got to suit international mining people. Rich people. How we going to do that?' Now, even we, any old uneducated buggers are talking globally. We got to help United Kingdom money. Netherlands lead air problems. Asia shipping. United States of America industry, and we don't even know German people. 'I says,' he says like he is singing, 'We mobs gots to start acting locally. Show who's got the Dreaming. The Laaaw.' He liked to emphasise 'The Laaaaw,' whenever he was heating up around the ears on the subject of globalization.

We whispered among ourselves – Ignore him. Clap your hands over your ears to put an end to his *blasphemy*. Don't listen to him. Everybody knew he always had plenty going on in his big head. We would always say to him – Ah! Yea. Pretend we were listening. Or else, we'd say, Oh! Well! Then. Or – Whatever. Or else – What can we do? Still, he was not finished with us. What happened to those three little petrol sniffing boys must have really split his head open. Poor three of them – Tristrum Fishman. Junior Fishman Luke. Aaron Ho Kum. All finished up under mysterious circumstances together, right in the Police Station, under the White man law.

He goes on ignoring our pleas and we say that we were not rebellious people. Nevermind, in the end he demanded things of us. His voice was soft as silk, he knew who he was playing with. All satiny voice, he said it was time now to end our cowtailing after the white people. It was finale time – Hands up. Who we got to follow? The Whiteman, or the Fishman? This was the ultimatum. Well! He made us that wild. Of course, we got no choice – we got to go with culture every time. We should have known he was leading up to all of this destruction. But we? We were like following dogs, and we were happy to do it, not even giving any of it a bit of extra thought, because we were acting solely and simply on pure rage.

The sound waves coming off the explosion in the aeroplane hangers at the biggest mine of its type in the world, *Gurfurritt*, were just about as tremendous a sound you could ever expect to hear on this earth. Like guyfork night. Booom! Booom! Over and over. But one hundred times more louder than that. Ripped the lot. We were thinking, those of us laying on the ground up in the hills smelling ash – what if our ears exploded? What would deafness sound like? We should have thought of that first.

Sometime during our precious time on earth we could have asked a deaf person what it was like to not hear the sounds anymore, before we go around deliberately destroying our own good hearing on wildness. Oh! But there was no going back because no one was going to reverse where the rotten hand of fate was heading. So, even though we were shaking in our old work boots, thinking we got busted eardrums, we watched the fire rage like a monster cut loose from another world. It might even have come from hell. Even the devil himself would have least expected us weak people to have opened the gates of hell. But we watched full of fascination of the fire's life, roaring like a fiery serpent, looking over to us with wild eyes, pausing, looking around, as if deciding what to do next. Then, we could hear it snarl in an ugly voice you would never want to hear again, *All right, watch while I spread right through those hangers like they were nothing, hungry! hungry! Get out of my way*. It did that roaring along, exploding through walls and rooftops which looked like toadstools bursting open, then once those flames shot outside, going a million miles an hour up into the sky, sparks just landed wherever, like a rain shower, out in the grass somewhere around the back.

The fire spread out the back of the hangers in the dry grass, and then it came burning around to the front again, fanned by a gustily south easterly wind. Then, the monster smelt the spilt fuel on the ground. It raced through that, quickly spreading itself over the ground weeds, until it found the fuel bowsers, then it paused, maybe the fire had thoughts of its own and could not believe its luck. The fire just sitting there was as awesome a moment you could experience for the men waiting in the hills, sneaking a glance from over the boulders they were hiding behind, peering through the black smoke, thinking maybe their luck had run out and what next.

It looked as though the fire was going to peter out. Mind you, wind fires are naturally unpredictable, and the fire was just sitting, smouldering, not knowing where to go next because the wind was not blowing strong enough to fan it in the right direction. Then, our men looking from the hills continued staring at the little flame flickering there, fizzing out. What could they do? It looked like defeat was imminent. And, that same old defeated look, two centuries full of it, began creeping back onto their faces. But, it was too late now, they had a taste of winning, so they started projecting their own sheer will power right across that spinifex plain, calling out with no shame, *Come on, come on,* willing the little flame not to fizz, believing magic can happen even to poor buggers like themselves.

Somehow, someone started yelling, 'Look, look, it is starting to move,' and can you believe it was happening? The unbelievable miracle came flying by. A whirly wind, mind you nobody had seen one for days, just a matter of fact sprung up from the hills themselves. It had swirled straight through from behind those men, picking up their wish and plucking the baseball caps which came flying off their heads, and together with all the loose balls of spinifex flying with the dust and baseball caps the whole lot was moving towards the fire. When it passed over the open rubbish tipsters the mine had lined up along the side of the hangers, it picked up all the trash, all the cardboard boxes, newspapers laying about and oily rags, and spirited the whole lot across the flat towards the line of hangers on fire.

Bloody hell, there was nothing else the Fishman's foot soldiers could say while they watched incredulously as the flames shot up the whirlwind and the fiery vortex headed straight for the bowsers. Talk about lucky.

It happened so fast when the fiery whirlwind shot into the bowsers and momentarily, lit them up like candles. Well! It might even have been the old Pizza Hut box someone had left on top of one of those bowsers that added that little bit of extra fuel, you never know, for the extra spark, or it would have happened anyway, but the wick was truly lit.

The finale was majestical. Dearo, dearie, the explosion was holy in its glory. All of it was gone. The whole mine, pride of the banana state, ended up looking like a big panorama of burnt chop suey. On a grand scale of course because our country is a very big story. Wonderment was the ear on the ground listening to the great murmuring ancestor, and the earth shook the bodies of those ones laying flat on the ground in the hills. Then, it was dark with smoke and dust and everything turned silent for a long time.

"You think they heard it in Port D'Arcy?" some young lad whispered carefully through the settling dust, because he did not want to frighten anyone by making the first sound of this new beginning. It was so uncomprehendingly silent he needed to speak to hear himself talk because he was thinking of his family and the noise of his memories of them was the only sound he could hear.

The sound of this young voice being the first sound was a relief for the others who had been thinking they were listening to the sound of their own deafness. However relieved and pacified we were to hear speech though, it was not enough. Everyone kept listening, listening for what else remained missing – Ah! It was the noise of the bush breathing, the wind whispering through the trees and flowing through rustling grasses. We needed to hear birds chirping, the eagle hawk crying out something from the thermals high above, but the eery silence lingered on. The birds were nowhere to be seen or heard, not even a singing willy wagtail lightly filtering from rock to rock wherever anyone walked, or a miner bird haggling at your feet. They looked into the dust and smoke darkened skies and saw no twisting green cloud of budgerigars dancing away in thin air. The wind had completely dropped. Silent clouds passing overhead cast gloomy shadows over the peaceful trees, while grasses and spinifex stood stock still as though this world had become something false almost reminiscent of a theatre setting. The men floated somewhere between the surreal stillness and the reality of the ants, lizards, beetles and other insects moving through the rocky ground as though nothing had happened. No one else spoke or answered the boy, because they guessed the explosion must have been heard on the other side of the world, let alone Port D'Arcy.

One will never know what really happened that day. Fishman never stopped smiling about it. He said his recipe was top secret. We regarded him with awe whenever he came into our presence. It was a privilege to know the Fishman. We respected what he had inside of his head. Too right! Nobody could know highly confidential material in case someone like Mozzie had to do it all over again some day. Some ignorant people would always ask though, *How did you stop the mine?* And, he would look at them for a long time with his steady eye, like he was making up his mind whether you were worth letting in on the secret. Finally, he would say, *I have decided to give you the truth*, and the truth was the very same words he had always used about what he would do to the mine from the day it got set up on our traditional domain. "I put broken glass bottles on the road to stop the buggers – that's what I did." Somehow, this was the truth. Truth just needed to be interpreted by the believers who could find the answers themselves about broken people just like the Fishman had done. At the same time he offered another piece of advice, which was, a smiling man would live for a very long time. And he did.

Eva Sallis

The Kangaroo

Eva Sallis is author of the prize-winning novel *Hiam* (Allen & Unwin) and the critical study *Sheherazade Through the Looking Glass: the Metamorphosis of the 1001 Nights*.

Amin and Zeen invited Samir and Ilham to go for a trip to Berri. They had relatives in the Riverland and all were excited at the adventure such an unprecedented trip would be.

'Just for fun!' they said to each other. 'Just for a drive! What a surprise we will give everyone. Why didn't we think of it before?'

It would be like going up to the village in the mountains. It would be all family, a real get together. Both Ilham and Zeen dressed carefully for the trip and the arrival.

They set off in high spirits in a suitable country car, a white Valiant borrowed from Uncle Mahmoud. Zeen and Ilham sat in the back; Amin and Samir in the front. Ilham wore a hat and Zeen wore the latest Candy Frost lipstick. They consulted the map carefully, surprised to find there was only one road so getting lost was impossible. Who would have thought you can just go there, on these lovely, civilised new roads, seeing the Australian countryside as you go. Zeen wound down the window and let the breeze blow her hair about. No wonder the Riverland relatives had been urging them to come up. It was so easy. Not even snipers to worry about and no roadblocks.

The heat of the day intensified and the landscape became too much to look at and comment on. At a sign from Ilham, Zeen wound the window up. Ilham pulled out the cards and dealt and they played a ragged game of *tahneeb*, couple against couple, made more difficult by Amin having to concentrate on the road and keep eye contact with Zeen through the rear vision mirror. They entered mallee country, noticing briefly that there were now straggly grey trees everywhere, dappled in white light; then returning to the game.

Suddenly Amin said, 'Look, Look! Oh Lord!' and they all looked up.

A red kangaroo was bounding down the centre of the highway towards them. It didn't deviate off the white lines, just bounded hypnotically, its powerful toes planting regularly about every third or fourth strip. Uncle Amin slowed the car right down, waiting for the animal to sheer off to the side and bound away into the bush. It got larger and larger, and then, at the very last minute, it swerved as if suddenly magnetised, straight into the roo bar of the car. Its red form filled the windscreen and everyone screamed, leaned back and pushed their feet hard to the floor. There was a slow, almost elegant impact. The kangaroo disappeared and the car slid sideways down the road, on and on. The *tahneeb* cards flew around the cabin like wheeling seagulls. Everyone sat still, staring at the slowly crazing windshield as if at the movies in a particularly tense scene. The car stopped.

The sun beat down, the mallee trees shook in the breezes, a bird flew by. Everyone breathed out in unison and relaxed their taut bodies.

'Praise be...' Ilham began. She stopped. The car had begun to shake. It was as if something had the car in its teeth and was throttling it. The Valiant gave little irregular shudders and then sharp lopsided jerks. Ilham began to wail in a high voice just as something outside began to roar in heavy gasps. Zeen stared ahead, white as a wedding dress, her short hair rising.

The kangaroo suddenly stood up, shaking the car heavily as it rose. It stood a good two metres above the bonnet and leered through a bloody eye at them, bleeding mouth open, showing enormous yellow rat teeth. Samir, Amin, Ilham and Zeen screamed and slammed back rigid in their seats. The kangaroo raised its fists and began beating wildly at the bonnet. They could feel it kicking and tearing at the radiator.

Amin gasped. 'The poor thing. Oh my God. I have to do something!'

Ilham shrieked, 'Stop it from destroying the car! Quick! Quick!'

Amin bashed the driver's door open with his shoulder and got out.

No-one could quite explain what happened next, it all happened so quickly. Amin walked up to the distressed animal, hands outstretched placatingly, although what he was going to do, no-one was quite sure. The kangaroo turned to face him, rose up high above his head and grabbed him from behind the neck with a huge black fist, sinking black claws into his nape. It wrenched his body around into a headlock, threw its head back, and with its nose pointed to the sun and roaring, began to jump about, tearing its hindlegs against the body in its embrace. Amin disappeared from sight behind the bonnet. Then, before anyone quite registered what was happening, Zeen was outside, hauling her patent leather stilettos off her feet. She rushed up to the animal, brandishing the shoes above her head and screaming. She thwacked it across the head with one heel and then the other.

Zeen and the kangaroo fought. The kangaroo dropped Amin and faced the shoes. Zeen balanced lightly on her stockinged feet and had to spring at the tall beast with her feet together, for her pencil skirt could not be rucked above her knees.

She held the shoes by the toes and beat the kangaroo to death. The car was spattered with blood, and Amin, standing by with his shirt shredded, looked on in shock. He staggered over to the driver's door and sat down.

Zeen screamed with each blow, 'Kill my husband? Kill him? God is GREAT!'

When she finished she crisply vomited onto the road and then climbed shakily back into the car.

'What sort of animal was that?' she asked, her chest heaving. Her clothes were speckled, her stockings torn and the shoes broken and bloody.

'A kangaroo,' Amin whispered.

There was a silence. Everyone stared ahead, the car ticking slightly in the heat.

Louis Nowra

Chihuahuas, Women and Me

Louis Nowra is a playwright, novelist, and screenwriter. His memoir
The Twelfth of Never was published by Picador in 2000.

She had eyes as black and shiny as fresh grapes. Her head was shaped like an apple and her ears were shaped like a bat's. She was so small that she could fit into the breast pocket of my leather jacket. She was Ren, my black and tan chihuahua.

The last time I saw her my marriage was ending. My wife and I had been separated for a short time and so things were raw and bruised between us and trying to find common ground to talk without accusations was difficult. We met in Rushcutters Bay Park where we used to take our two chihuahuas for their evening walk. As we sat on a bench under a giant fig tree, plump white Plugger sat dozing at his mistress's feet while Ren excitedly scanned the park for any signs of other dogs, regarding them as intruders on a territory she thought of as her own. Her ignorance of her owners' turgid attempt to find some sense of detachment in talk of divorce and property settlement was contrary to the anthropomorphic sentimentality of dog owners who believe their dogs sense emotional upheaval in their owner's lives, and instead, was closer to the truer representation of dogs in Renaissance paintings where, as a duel is fought or Christ is about to be born, a dog sits in the corner of the picture scratching itself or licking its balls. And yet, when it came time for my wife and I to part, Ren looked up at me with what could almost be described as a frown, slightly puzzled that she was being called to follow her mistress rather than the four of us returning to the apartment together.

I watched my wife walk over the storm-water bridge and occasionally Ren turned back to look as if half tempted to run back and join me. Then the trio headed around the sports oval and Ren with that upright bouncing gait common to the breed grew smaller until she resembled a bouncing dot not unlike those cheerful bouncing dots indicating rhythm and tempo that once accompanied songs on the cinema screen. And then, as my wife was about to disappear with the dogs behind a row of fig trees, I was struck by a visceral sense of déjà-vu. That was not my short, black-haired second wife walking away with my chihuahua but my tall, strawberry-blonde-haired first wife, and instead of heading off in the opposite direction I am hurrying towards her as she walks through the Exhibition Gardens in Carlton. And trotting beside her is our young chihuahua. I laugh because he looks so small, almost as if Sarah is being accompanied by an orange with four toothpicks as legs.

When I finally catch up to her, having been delayed by a phone call, Iggy, hearing me approach, spins around. He is so excited that he wraps the leash around his neck several times almost choking himself. I unfasten the clip that attaches the leash to his collar and he's off joyously running through the thick carpet of brown, yellow and red autumnal plane tree leaves, alternatively vanishing below them and then resurfacing like some rabid squirrel. I hear a couple laughing and pointing at Iggy, *Oh, look at the rat!* Sarah and I are used to this abuse because it seems that most people regard a chihuahua as if it is some freak of nature rather than a real dog.

Yet I asked for this. I could have bought any other breed of dog for Sarah's birthday but I had my heart set on buying her a chihuahua. There was nothing in my past to suggest I would ever buy one. My family liked dogs and we had several over the years. There was the white German shepherd dog that guarded my parents' trucking company. It was always filthy because it liked to roll in the oil stains. There was a fat beagle that spent hours on its back waiting for its mottled warm belly to be rubbed. A Cocker Spaniel that went so mad it used to jump through closed windows if it saw anything of interest on the other side. And a Pomeranian so randy it was called Phillip after Prince Phillip.

My knowledge of chihuahuas was limited. When I was learning the clarinet I liked to watch Hollywood musicals on television, and the first chihuahua I ever saw was in a 1940s MGM musical featuring the Cuban bandleader Xavier Cugat who popularised the mambo and the rumba in America. While he conducted his orchestra he held a baton in one hand and a chihuahua, about the size of a tea cup, in the other. So identified was he with chihuahuas that the cover and the text of his 1948 memoir *Rumba is my Life* is filled with drawings of the little dog.

Cugat is credited with popularising the breed and yet it is women who seemed to be attracted to them, especially actresses. The love of Lupe Velez, the so-called 'Mexican Spitfire', for her chihuahua Chips was returned so fervently, that the dog would often turn on her lovers with a ferocity that belied his smallness. Marilyn Monroe had chihuahuas, but it was Jayne Mansfield who adored them so much that she was once caught trying to smuggle two of her tiny dogs through Heathrow customs where she was spotted by one transfixed officer who noticed that her huge breasts were not bouncing so much as squirming. There is also the infamous photograph of the car crash that killed her. In the foreground is the gruesome sight of her dead whelping bitch lying on the road, surrounded by her mistress's blonde wigs and bottles of whiskey. Billie Holiday's chihuahua Chiquita was photographed many times at police stations being cradled by her mistress as the singer was booked for heroin possession.

Lapdogs and women have seemed a perfect canine and human match for centuries. Film stars and idle, wealthy, kept women have been especially identified with small dogs, such as the woman in Chekhov's *Lady with a Lapdog*, although in the story it is a white Spitz, a favourite dog also of Queen Victoria. Of course it has to be said that Sarah was not wealthy nor was she idle. She was a composer and, at the time, was struggling like I was to make a living from her creative work, and we were forced to supplement our paltry income by performing in nightclubs with our band, which had a transvestite. A chihuahua would suit the cramped narrow house where we lived behind a boot repairer's shop. However, there was a couple of other reasons why I wanted to buy one: it was not only its peculiar appearance but there was something strange about a dog that had abnormal appeal for a Cuban bandleader, a junkie singer and blonde bombshell actresses. It wasn't your normal run of the mill dog. It was weird.

Chihuahuas were hard to find in the middle 1970s. I tried to buy one puppy but the owner's children cried so much I had to return it. Eventually I found a breeder who sold them out of the back of her car. We named him Iggy, after Iggy Pop the rock singer. In some ways he was to change my life more than Sarah's. Fawn-coloured with intelligent eyes, he was not the timid, yapping thing most people imagine chihuahuas to be. He was robust, proud, very intelligent, with a profound dislike of being laughed at which is common to most chihuahuas and which unfortunately goes with the territory of being one.

Because they are lapdogs I was to learn that chihuahuas, unlike a lot of other breeds, like eye contact. Iggy had a fervent desire for eye contact and would sit on my lap as if trying to mesmerise me, then, after staring into my eyes, he would at odd moments jump off my lap and run around the room as if looking for something to do. It was only after several weeks that I realised he believed that somehow I was communicating something important to him when I winked. In order to test my theory I placed a bowl of milk in front of him, made him sit and then I winked. At first he was confused and then he realised that the wink was a yes. Over the next few months he learnt to obey several codes of winking that ordered him to bring his bowl over to me, made him jump up on the chair and place the bowl on the table, and gave him the command (three winks) to drink his milk. He could do this in any sequence and became especially excited when visitors came because he understood that the both of us would be showing off his wide selection of tricks and he would end up with a bowl of milk. The trouble was that he grew so adept at obeying my winks that if I accidentally blinked he would hurtle off my lap and rush to pick up his bowl. His intelligence was such that I believed he thought he was training me, and sometimes he would run to the fridge and look back as if trying to train me into giving the required number of winks to open it. In his own way Iggy also trained me to like chihuahuas, not only as an odd even amusing looking dog but also as a smart and devoted animal. He made chihuahuas essential to my life.

By the time we shifted to Sydney Iggy became pushy and grumpy if I didn't wink at him, and in order to stop him from fixing me with a stare as if demanding me to wink I had to look away from him so he couldn't read my eyes. In our house in Sydney he would jump up on the arm of the couch I was sitting in and trot backwards and forwards behind my head and peer around at my profile, satisfied at being able at least to wait for one eye to wink. Melbourne may not have put on my plays or played Sarah's music but Sydney was different and Iggy liked us being successful because it meant more dinner guests and visitors and that also meant many more chances to cadge food. Although his bug-eyed hypnotic stare unnerved many people, he had also learnt new tricks, including a dance, which gained him many a titbit from impressed guests.

During the early eighties Sarah and I spent two years in

Adelaide working for Lighthouse, the State Theatre Company of South Australia. Besides directing and writing I was also Associate Artistic Director so I was spending an inordinate amount of time in the theatre. So involved was I that I failed to realise that although Sarah was composing music she was lonely. I only realised this when I picked up some photographs from the photo shop. The first group were of Sarah in a bikini standing in a dam. She is laughing because she has just carried Iggy out in the middle of the dam and has released him to swim back to shore. There is a look of abject terror on his face as he frantically paddles towards land, his muzzle straining to lift itself out of the water. The next photograph is also of Iggy and Sarah. She is standing in a doorway, holding him in her arms. She is trying to smile but has an aura of desperate unhappiness about her, while Iggy looks pensive. The rest of the photographs were of Sarah smiling glumly or not even pretending to be happy but allowing herself to be photographed as if too unhappy to complain about being photographed. I had been so caught up in my work I didn't realise how unhappy and lonely she was. My solution? Another chihuahua. This one was extremely tiny, or as the Americans say in the dog ads, 'a tea cup chihuahua.'

The first photograph I took of Patsy (my musical tastes, as revealed by the names of the chihuahuas, were as diverse as Iggy Pop and Patsy Cline) she is fastidiously trying to nibble at a bone held by Sarah which is twice as big as her. Patsy was so tiny that she was easy to sit in the palm of a hand. One day as I was walking down the corridor into the kitchen, holding her in my hand, she fell. She hit the floor with a soft thump and lay still, not breathing. Before that moment I had never understood or experienced shock. I was paralysed by the thought that I had accidentally, carelessly, killed her. It was up to Sarah to rush to her and revive her. In a couple of hours she was bouncing around Iggy trying to make him play with her. As usual, he walked away believing play was beneath his dignity – he was never a playful dog – and, of course, he was jealous that he no longer received his owners' undivided attention.

I decided it would be a nice idea to cast Patsy in a play I was directing. It was the Australian premiere of Beaumarchais's *The Marriage of Figaro*. I thought it would be a splendid touch to have the countess carry around a chihuahua with her so as to indicate her vapid, pampered life. On the first day of rehearsal the actress accidentally dropped Patsy, nearly sat on her twice in the bedroom scene and barely missed stamping on her when supposedly annoyed with the count, her husband. During the lunch break as I was holding the traumatised dog the vastly more experienced stage manager came up to me and said: 'She's gonna kill that mutt because there's no way she's gonna let a dog upstage her.' I saw the wisdom of what he was saying and realised that if I continued with the idea Patsy would be dead by the end of the day. After lunch I told the actress the news. She could barely hide her satisfaction. 'That's good,' she said, pretending she was thinking of Patsy, 'cos that absentminded cunt of a stage manager is likely to drop her.'

A few days later Sarah found Patsy in the back garden under a flowering almond tree foaming at the mouth. We took her to the vet who thought she had eaten some snail bait that probably came into our garden from the next door neighbour's after the unnaturally heavy rain which had put a stop to his and his girlfriend's adulterous and strenuous sex sessions outside on his back lawn. Patsy was so small that her internal system broke under the strain of trying to combat the poison. Patsy was quickly followed by Lulu, who was a dumb as Iggy was smart, and I think Iggy never really got over the feeling that despite all his tricks, eye-reading and dancing, all Lulu had to do was sit before us with her constant stupefied gaze in order to get snacks.

After completing my contract in Adelaide it was back to Sydney where we bought a house in Sydenham, but something had irrevocably changed during our time in South Australia. The more Sarah's unhappiness grew, the more I retreated into my work. Iggy, however, was becoming more interested in Lulu, especially when she came into season for the first time. We decided to separate them, worried that Lulu was too small to have puppies. But Iggy was frantic and spent all day trying to mount her, and at night he whined with sexual frustration and scratched at the door of the laundry where Lulu slept. What made it even more frustrating for him was that he could poke his muzzle under the door, but could not squeeze through, no matter how much he tried. Several times I found him stuck under the door, whimpering with desire. I read all I could on the subject and constantly came upon the euphemistic description of chihuahuas as 'sturdy stud dogs'. Tiny rapists came readily to mind as I watched him feverishly pawing at the door. The only time he ever tried to bite me was when I pulled him off Lulu when he tried to mount her while she was sleeping on my lap. I began to worry about him. He was losing weight and becoming red-eyed with a lack of sleep. Then one morning I came out into the laundry to see him contentedly sleeping next to Lulu. He had eaten his way through the door.

Soon Lulu was showing signs of pregnancy and she began to resemble a football on four pegs. The vet told us to watch for the signs that she was about to give birth because he would have to perform a caesarean on her. The time came late one evening when, after several glasses of wine, I was about to sit down and watch the FA cup final and Lulu began hobbling around the room in distress. We rang the vet who was at home having a wild party, if the cacophony of music and laughter in the background was any guide. We rushed to the animal hospital. The vet was already there, a little unsteady on his feet, apologising for not having a nurse because she was, as he said, 'pissed as a fart.' Sarah and I were there with our goddaughter, Juliet, and he asked the three of us if we had ever given a needle before. We shook our heads and he pointed to Sarah. 'You'll do,' he said, believing women were better at this than men. As the two of them were tying Lulu down on the operating table Sarah went white and, looking as if she were going to faint said, 'I don't think I can do this,' and with that went out into the corridor.

'It's up to us boys,' said the vet cheerfully. Lulu, looking like a bloated toad, was on her back with her four legs tied to the four corners of the table, as if taking part in a canine sado-masochistic ordeal. The vet instructed me where to put the needle, which had to be done while he was cutting her open. He made an incision down her belly and then pulled apart the two flaps of skin. Standing on the opposite side of the table to him I was expecting a calm, wise remark about what he saw. Instead, I heard a gasp of 'Oh, my God!' It sounded like a scientist in a horror movie who cuts open a pregnant woman only to find a demon in her womb. It turned out that she had four pups, which he had never seen in such a tiny dog. I felt a tinge of male guilt. There was Iggy back at home, probably fast asleep, while the object of his brief sexual passion was near death carrying his pups. Each pup the vet extracted, removing the thin membrane that shrouded their bodies, was not breathing, and at the same time Lulu was dying. 'I can't do two things at once,' he said, motioning to fourteen-year-old Juliet. 'You'll have to suck the mucus out of their noses, that's why they're not breathing.' 'You mean I have to suck our their snot?' asked an incredulous Juliet. 'Don't worry, it's sterile,' he said. So while the vet and I attempted to save Lulu, Juliet picked up the first unconscious puppy, which was the size of a mouse, and gingerly sucked at its nose. The pup was so tiny that it needed Juliet to give just one strenuous suck for her to swallow it. Eventually after clearing the nasal passage she whooped with delight. Its tiny heart was starting to beat. Sarah joined in and one by one they breathed life into the pups. By the time all four were breathing so was Lulu.

Back home we placed Lulu and the four puppies in a cardboard box in our bedroom. Iggy trotted in, took one sniff of his offspring and left the room, never to show any interest in them again. Because Lulu was recovering from her operation Sarah got up every three hours and fed the puppies with an eyedropper. We didn't intend to have children and yet Sarah was as devoted to the puppies as any mother. To hear the alarm go off in the early hours of the morning and hear her get out of bed and return from the kitchen with warm milk for the puppies and feed them one by one was curiously affecting. In a way it was the chihuahua puppies that temporarily brought us closer together.

As if to reclaim our attention Iggy's back legs started to hurt him. If he were a human he would have been called a sook and a hypochondriac but the vet decided to operate on him, telling us that any normal dog would take only a few weeks to recover the use of his legs. But Iggy, appalled by the idea of even the slightest twinge of pain, decided he wouldn't use his back legs at all. He took to walking on his front legs like some sort of canine acrobat. To see him hopping down the back steps on his front legs was to marvel at his skills but also his sheer stubbornness. Now we had six tiny dogs, five of whom would rush everywhere together. Iggy only deigned to become part of the mob if food was in the offering, and even then he would barge between his offspring and Lulu, sending them scattering because he carried a large plastic bowl in his mouth. Afraid that we might step on the pups we put bells on their collars, only to take them off a few days later when the sounds of loud arrhythmic tinkling began to get on our nerves.

But even the chihuahua pups couldn't stop the inevitable and Sarah and I separated. She stayed with the dogs and I shifted into an apartment. When we got back together to talk about our future it was the dogs that preoccupied us of course. After giving away two pups we kept the parents and Candy and Brutus, the largest of the four pups. Candy was the smallest of the litter and although she had the slight dazed expression of her mother was extremely cute. She was named after Candy Darling, one of Warhol's transvestite stars and I wanted to give her fifteen minutes of fame.

I wrote a television movie called *The Lizard King* and demanded that the character of the barmaid in a country pub carry her when working behind the bar. In order to humour me the producer Jan Chapman agreed, and on the first day she was required, there was a knock at the door and a uniformed chauffeur asked for 'Miss Candy'. 'I'll just put her in her box,' I said to the bewildered man. When I returned with Candy in her carry pack he was stunned. He quickly got into the spirit of the thing and for the next two days allowed Candy to sit on the front seat of the white limo so she would get the benefit of the air conditioning. I went to the set on the third day. The director was using an old Balmain hotel as the set for the country pub. It was so hot that the actors' make up was dripping off them. There was one old rattling fan on the bar but no-one got the benefit of it because standing in front of it was the chauffeur holding Candy whose eyes were closed with pleasure and her two bat's ears shaking slightly with the force of the breeze.

The barmaid was played by Clarissa Mason, the widow of the famous James Mason. She was a strong-willed woman whose smile sent a shiver through me. 'The dog's a treat,' she barked in her husky voice. I could tell she didn't like the idea of having a cute chihuahua to compete with her and yet as I watched take after take she didn't make a fuss. It was only after we saw the rushes that I realised how cunning the old pro had been. Knowing how much the camera was framing the top half of her body she would lower the hand carrying Candy so that all one saw at the bottom of the screen was something that looked like two flickering razor blades.

My last attempt to promote Candy came when the director Neil Armfield wanted her for his bawdy and infamous production of *The Country Wife* at the Sydney Opera House. I have never been so proud as when, on opening night, I saw Kerry Walker come onto the stage carrying my chihuahua. Candy was so docile in any situation, compared to her hyper father, that she always seemed to be soporific. So lazy was she that when Kerry exited, Candy, having become bored with the play during the many rehearsals, jumped on her train as if hitching a ride, and so she left the stage to huge laughter and applause. 'I thought it was me they were applauding,' said a slightly miffed Kerry afterwards, as I cradled the sleepy, tiny star.

I returned to the house and the dogs while Sarah went to live with a painter. Iggy liked my new partner, Justine, because for the first time he was allowed on the bed, and since he was the only one capable of jumping from the floor onto the bed now that his legs had completely healed, and the others had to be lifted up, he always got the best spot, which was her lap. Photographs from the time show Justine sitting up in bed while the sheets seem to squirm with rodents. 'Well, you think an Aboriginal like me would be surrounded by dingoes, but here I am with these tiny things,' she once said, marvelling at her own attraction to a dog she would have once dismissed as a joke.

A few years later I was briefly living in Melbourne, while Sarah cared for the dogs. Iggy didn't like Sarah's new boyfriend and often took the opportunity to piss on his leg, knowing that the new man in his mistress's life didn't like dogs, especially small dogs. I had grown very fond of Candy and once settled in Melbourne rang Sarah asking her to air freight the dog down to me. The next morning she rang to say that Candy had died overnight. I made a joke that she shouldn't have told Candy that she was going to Melbourne, but I was devastated. Then Iggy, in ill health and ill humour died aged fourteen, and Lulu quickly followed suit two days later as if bereft or at a loss to understand the world now that her grumpy guide had gone. I vowed never to have a chihuahua again.

Back in Sydney I often talked about them to my eventual second wife, Gerri, so much so that she joked to people that the reason why I liked her was that she was small like a chihuahua. One Christmas night, after we had had our customary Christmas drinks party, she said she was going to visit a mutual friend who lived a few doors down in Elizabeth Bay Road. She returned half an hour later with a brown paper bag and said, 'This is your Christmas present.' I looked in the paper bag and saw two tiny furry animals with bright black eyes and apple shaped heads staring back at me. I thought I had had too much to drink but no, my Christmas present was two black and tan chihuahuas. They were adorable and cute and the size of a tennis ball. There was only one problem: animals, of any and every description, were forbidden in our apartment building. 'We'll teach them not to bark,' said Gerri cheerfully. Overwhelmed by the fact that they were illegal, and afraid that if I fell in love with them either the Board would hear about them and force me to get rid of them or else they would die young like Candy, I went straight to bed unable to cope with the responsibility of them.

Once they were on the bed Christmas morning, staggering around, their tiny insect legs finding the thick doona as treacherous to negotiate as newly fallen snow, and peering curiously at me with their gleaming black eyes, I fell in love with them. At the time my favourite television show was a cartoon called Ren and Stimpy. Ren is a psychotic chihuahua and Stimpy his fat docile friend is a cat, so naturally I called the bigger chihuahua Ren, especially as her slightly lazy eye gave her a disturbing similarity to the psychotic cartoon chihuahua, and the other one I called Stimpy. Gerri wouldn't hear of it. I couldn't name a chihuahua after a cat, so after much deliberation we called it Holly, after Holly Golightly from the Capote story.

Not long afterwards there was a ghastly coincidence when both dogs broke a leg. Chihuahuas hate children and Ren had every reason to have that attitude reinforced when a child demanded to hold her after the mother proclaimed that 'she's good with dogs'. Ren tumbled from the child's clumsy grip onto the floor and yelped in excruciating pain. Later that day Holly fell from a chair. For the next month the dogs, each with a leg encased in a cast, hobbled around the living room looking like more like cartoon dogs than real ones. Because I had to search for film locations in Ireland I went away for two weeks and while I was away Holly died. According to the vet, she was so tiny that survival into adulthood was always going to be difficult. Twice, while I was separated from them my dogs had died. It seemed to me that being apart from them I was somehow partly to blame, as if some sort of crucial psychic bond had been broken by distance and that if only I had been with them maybe their deaths might not have occurred.

We bought a new dog, a white chihuahua, who had a slight medical condition in that one of his balls had failed to appear and was still lodged inside him. As the famous Australian Rules star Tony 'Plugger' Lockett had a groin injury at the time, the new dog was christened Plugger in his honour. From the day of his arrival he was an amiable slow-thinking dog who seemed in awe of the highly strung Ren, who, like her namesake, had a demented intelligence that made simple things arduous. It was easy to teach Plugger to sit because it was a comfortable position that didn't require much energy but Ren seemed to require a reason for it and found it difficult to get the point of why, after having proved she could sit, she had to remain seated. Her curiosity was boundless but Plugger's was tightly circumscribed by the amount of effort it required. Once the doorbell buzzed Ren would rush excitedly down the hallway to greet guests, while Plugger remained in the living room, knowing the guests would eventually end up there anyway. Plugger would wait patiently to be lifted up and placed on my lap but Ren would leap up onto my ankles and then crawl up my legs like a salmon struggling upstream. If I didn't pay attention to her, she would gain my attention or that of a guest by jumping up from a standing position. Her back legs were extremely powerful, as she had come from what the breeder had said was a 'long line of jumpers'. Many a guest sitting in the living room was disconcerted to see what looked like a crazed large rat momentarily appearing in their eye line before vanishing, only to mutely reappear with increasingly frenzied expressions of demand.

Of course, there was the problem of how to hide the dogs from the rest of the apartment owners. Although chihuahuas are regarded as yappy dogs they proved easy to train to be quiet, especially Ren who seemed to sense that there was something important about being silent. Both dogs seemed to understand from the first time we stuffed them into a handbag and took them down in the lift and through the apartment foyer that it was important that they did not bark or move, which they never did, even when someone unexpectedly entered the lift.

Recently I read a survey in a tabloid newspaper that said a marriage was in trouble if the couple allowed a dog or cat to sleep with their owners. Ren and Plugger were introduced to our bed soon after we got them. This step was not so much our doing but Ren's, who demanded to sleep with us by jumping up and down for hours on one spot next to my side of the bed with a demented and increasingly exasperated desire to be on the bed. The dogs quickly grew more attached to one of us than the other, so while the lazy, shuffling Plugger took to sleeping on my wife's side of the bed, Ren liked to crawl down under the sheets to curl up at my feet or else, if it were too hot, curl on the pillow beside my head so that sometimes when I woke up I would be shocked to see what looked like a black fetus on my pillow. Plugger was content to sleep all day, Ren saw it as her duty to wake me at the same time every week day. She was as regular as a clock and if I took too much time to get out of bed she would show me what to do by jumping onto the floor and hurrying towards the bathroom. If I did not follow her immediately, she would repeat this endlessly until I did as instructed, then worn out by her efforts to get me up, she would jump back on the pillow and contentedly fall asleep now that she had completed the job she had assigned herself to do. If I decided to work on a Saturday Ren, who hated disruptions to her routine, would mope and look at me with what I can only describe as a sad hope that I would take her to my office, a place she seemed to regard it as a privilege to be, especially as I took her and not Plugger. Of course, on the way she liked to canter along the slippery floors of the Edgecliff shopping centre as if knowing she was the centre of attention, especially from old ladies and the woman newsagent who liked to cradle her and whisper sweet nothings in Greek into her ear. Chihuahuas generally dislike all other breeds except for their own but Ren disliked all other chihuahuas except for a grizzled ancient chihuahua who arthritically followed in his blind owner's footsteps. Tied to a short leash, and at the mercy of his owner's limited vision which frequently had the both of them bumping into benches and shop windows, the dog gave up trying to pull away from constant and imminent danger and was content to be dragged on its back across the shiny floor by its owner, who was oblivious to the fact that her dog had given up walking. Ren became so possessive of me that if Plugger somehow ended up in my lap Ren would jump up and head-butt him off. Plugger would tumble onto the floor and sleep where he fell.

The chihuahuas took over other aspects of my work. They began to appear in my fiction and my screenplays. Any film that had even a fleeting image of a chihuahua I videoed or hired out and soon I was able to discourse to dinner guests on the way chihuahuas have been used in movies, either as a prop to indicate homosexuality as in *The Third Man*, or as a leitmotif in Tim Burton's films, where they are used to suggest Bela Lugosi's remoteness from the real world in *Ed Wood*, or the weird and absurd humour of *Mars Attacks!* where aliens genetically splice a chihuahua with a woman. Then there are the many full-length cartoons, like *Oliver and Company* where the chihuahua is portrayed as a hyper, highly strung character with a high pitched Hispanic voice.

In fact the more I looked for chihuahua references and portrayals the more I found. It seemed that in the 1990s the chihuahua's time had come. The dog was on greeting cards, its image was used to sell mobile phones and insurance and even featured on the covers of such novels as Laurence Shames' *Sunburn* where an an old plump chihuahua is wearing sunglasses and using a Zimmer frame. Chihuahuas feature in many of the urban myths written up in the books *The Mexican Sewer Rat* and *Pelicans and Chihuahuas and other Urban Legends*. There are many such urban legends, some of which had been told to me as fact, including that of the American couple who bought a Mexican sewer rat believing it was a chihuahua, and the common Australian urban myth of an old lady walking her chihuahua along the beach when it is scooped up by a pelican and the last she sees of her dog is the leash hanging outside the bird's beak as it carries the chihuahua aloft. But reality proved worthy of these urban legends. In 1999 Californian newspapers ran the continuing saga of how a three-metre long boa constrictor had grabbed a chihuahua called Babette whose cautious seventy four year-old owner had briefly allowed it outside to 'go potty'. No charges were laid against the owner of the snake but Babette's distraught owner did get compensation when she appeared on a television court show presided over by former New York mayor Ed Koch.

I also set out on what has proved to be a never-ending quest to buy any ornament, toy or paraphernalia that has something to do with chihuahuas. I have several large boxes of towels and T-shirts with images of the dog. There are key rings, statues, coffee mugs, drink coasters, socks, book covers, advertisements, and even a music box on top of which sits a carved chihuahua with one foot resting on a large red ball. When wound up the music box plays 'Friends'. To others this is probably a pitiful obsession but then – what would they know of the love and obsessions a chihuahua can inspire?

I have found myself at chihuahua shows, earnestly discussing the merits of the normal chihuahua compared to what is called 'the Bambi', a chihuahua favoured by the Americans. If there is a generalisation to be made about chihuahua owners it is that, yes, many of the women are fat and the men thin, with disturbing shifty eyes. The last time I went to a show one of these men was hoping his chihuahua would win in memory of his male lover who had hanged himself from a tree the week before. But even the breeders and exhibitors know little about the origins of the breed, except to claim it goes back to the ancient Olmec, Toltec and Aztec civilisations. Carvings and even toys from the period seem to indicate that there was a chihuahua-type dog. Many Spanish chroniclers, writing about South America and the Caribbean at the time of the Conquest, refer to small dogs which the Aztecs sold in the markets or the Incas venerated. Acosta writes about mute tiny dogs that 'were for the amusement of the ladies, who carried them in their arms.' Probably most of the references are to the Mexican hairless dog rather than chihuahuas who seemed to vanish from Mesoamerica only to reappear in the late nineteenth century when the breed was saved by American tourists. Because of its rarity and exotic looks it soon became highly sought after and was quickly associated with upper-class women and courtesans. In *Punch* there is a cartoon entitled 'Dog Fashions for 1889' which ridicules the taste for new dog breeds. It shows a wealthy woman walking in a park with several weird hybrid dogs and leading them in a prancing gait is an extremely tiny chihuahua labelled 'Bug Dog'. It was around this time that chihuahuas broke into show business. A British performer, Rosina Casselli, had a group of at least a dozen chihuahuas in her stage act performing 'all manner of tricks'. Yet, although it is easy to trace its history since the late nineteenth century all the reading I have done, including such splendid histories as the Varners' *Dogs of the Conquest* and Marion Schwartz's *A History of Dogs in the Early Americas*, still refuses to throw up information that would definitely confirm the existence of chihuahuas as we now know them. Gradually I developed the theory that the chihuahua may be the hybrid of a dog native to the Americas and a later imported European dog.

What set me on the path of this theory is a stunning painting by the Venetian painter Carpaccio (1460?-1525). Called *Waiting*, it consists of two panels, one entitled 'Men hunting on the Lagoon' and the other 'Two Venetian Ladies', which shows two upper class women waiting for their men to return. One of the women is clutching the paw of a small white dog who stares directly at the viewer. There is no mistaking its similarity to a chihuahua – the apple-shaped head, bat-like ears, prominent eyes and small size. The likeness is uncanny. Its possible that this typical Venetian dog was taken to colonial Mexico where it was interbred with a local variety. The notion obsessed me so much that when an Italian film company asked me to write a film partly set in Venice I agreed in the hope that I could prove this theory correct. The director, who was much more interested in Venice's huge empty tobacco factories, found my interest in visiting every art gallery mysterious and tedious and soon gave up accompanying me. What I discovered confirmed my suspicions. There is a popular eighteenth-century Venetian genre painter Pietro Longhi, whose rather stiff but cheerful works have an undeniable charm. What fascinated me is the leitmotif of a small white dog, not unlike the one in Carpaccio's masterpiece, that occurs in many of his paintings, appearing at the feet of plump children, beautiful women in gorgeous gowns, and in one delightful example, sitting on a stool gazing in bewilderment at a violin trio playing from sheet music spread out on a piano top. The film director grew increasingly annoyed with my absences from location-hunting but I was spending my time searching for paintings and images that featured this little white dog that looked for all the world exactly like Plugger. I irritated library staff wanting reproductions of the paintings or secretly filmed the paintings with my digital camera. In a way Iggy had lead me all the way to Venice. The film didn't eventuate, as I knew it wouldn't, but I had uncovered enough information to think my theory had some sort of credibility.

My own credibility however was losing ground with friends who thought that what was once an amusing interest of mine was becoming an obsession, yet around me the chihuahua was becoming ubiquitous in films, advertisements and television commercials. I have no doubt that part of its growing attraction was its idiosyncratic appearance. In advertisements such as the Orange Internet promotions, the chihuahua is deliberately made to look bizarre. It seems to me that one of the reasons for its rise in popularity has been the contemporary fascination with aliens who are generally seen as small odd-shaped creatures with appealing large bright eyes. But if there was one thing that caused the chihuahua to become extraordinarily popular it was the Taco Bell dog with big brown eyes, quivering body and deep voice that did for the chihuahua what Lassie did for the Collie and what *101 Dalmatians* did for the Dalmatian.

The fast food company Taco Bell brought out a series of commercials which feature a chihuahua who hangs out with Generation X-ers, climbs fire escapes and roams the desert to convert hamburger loyalists into taco lovers under the banner of the Taco revolution and is given to loudly demanding, 'Yo Queiro Taco Bell!'. The ad agency that came up with the idea decided that the chihuahua was their idea of 'A nineteen-year-old guy in a dog's body who primarily thinks of food and girls.' In other words, for the first time in popular culture, a chihuahua was considered, as one reporter remarked, 'a cool dude'. There were of course criticisms from various Hispanic organisations who thought that the voice given to the chihuahua was demeaning to Hispanics, but the Hispanic actor who voiced the dog put these criticisms down to the fact that Hispanic men didn't think a chihuahua was macho enough for them. For breeders there were both good and bad aspects to the rapid popularity of the breed caused by the advertisements. Because the demand was so great unscrupulous breeders sold inferior dogs; but the thing that made many chihuahua lovers despair was that the Taco Bell dog is an anomalous example of the breed. It is too tall, too heavy, too leggy and the head is not round enough and its muzzle is too long. Chihuahua purists feared that children especially would be demanding a chihuahua that looked like 'this freak', as one breeder called it, and force them to cultivate substandard dogs.

Frankly I didn't care about the fuss and on my visits to LA I was always thrilled to see the many huge billboards featuring the Taco Bell chihuahua. An insomniac, I would spend the early hours of the morning in my hotel room sipping gin and channel-surfing in the hope of seeing the Taco Bell commercials. My love of chihuahuas was being vindicated; they were now considered cute, funny, and hip. The Taco Bell advertisements were so successful that Taco Bell in Australia held a search to find an Australian chihuahua to use in the local commercials. Without a skerrick of shame, but on the contrary with a pride that is common to stage mothers, I entered Ren in the contest. A few weeks later we turned up at the Taco Bell restaurant in George Street Sydney on a hot humid night with nine other chihuahua owners, all of whom were women of a certain age and bulk. The restaurant was filled with photographers and television cameras. Ren and I were to audition last but as we watched the others I realised that every dog before us was white. The judge was a blonde, voluptuous TV celebrity who was a part of a long line of attractive blonde chihuahua lovers from Jayne Mansfield and Marilyn Monroe right up to Madonna. By the time our turn came to parade I realised that black and tan Ren would not win against the white chihuahuas. However, in a pathetic attempt to gain Ren an advantage I grabbed her after she had done her tricks and placed her on the celebrity's lap before she knew what was happening. With a stage mother's cunning I wasn't aware I possessed, I knew that dark Ren would make a wonderful photo opportunity as she sat on the white frock of a beautiful woman. And sure enough, photographers literally elbowed me out of the way in order to get the picture, one of them so furious that I had impeded him that he snarled, 'Out of the way, cunt'. But my cheap stunt wasn't enough. During the presentation of the prize (private limo to photo shoots, five hundred dollars) I vainly wished I was in the US and could cite prejudices against blacks in giving the prize to a white dog. I suspect Ren realised I was disappointed because in the taxi trip home she was very affectionate, and spent the time snuggling up to me and licking the back of my hand. As a consolation prize I gave her more cheese than usual and was later gratified to discover that the winner never appeared in any advertisements.

It was around this time that my marriage began to dissolve. When the atmosphere in the apartment become tense and strained I would take Ren out for a walk late at night, but unknown to my wife, we did not go down to the park, instead we headed up the street to the Sebel Town House hotel where, after hiding her inside my leather jacket to sneak her past the concierge, we would slip into the tiny bar. The barman knew us and without a word he would pour me a dry martini and give Ren a champagne glass full of salted peanuts. After stuffing Ren into the top pocket of my jacket I would sip my martini and she would dip her head out of the pocket and daintily pick up a peanut at a time. I could always tell the alcoholics at the bar because they pretended they didn't see what looked like a large rat eating peanuts out of a champagne glass.

And then the events that helped break up our marriage become a blur. Once the marriage was over my wife and I would meet on the neutral ground of Rushcutters Bay park to discuss our future. Because I had shifted out and was settling into an apartment of my own Gerri kept the two dogs. We didn't discuss their future because it was fraught with a major problem. Ren was my dog and Plugger was hers. And even though I wanted Ren I didn't want to separate them – dogs can get terribly lonely. Our last meeting in the park settled nothing and after watching my wife and the two dogs head off back to the apartment I went on my way.

When I shifted into my new apartment it took me quite a while to unpack all the boxes of my belongings. Eventually I came upon several photograph albums from the past two decades. Curiously, although I had several studio photographs taken of me with my chihuahuas, amongst the hundreds of social photographs there were none of me with them. All the photographs of chihuahuas were with the women who had been a part of my life: Sarah walking Iggy, Sarah with the tiny, mouse-sized puppies, Justine beaming as six chihuahuas swarmed over her, countless pictures of Gerri with Ren and Plugger – even at our wedding there is a photograph of Ren, who had to be sneaked into the reception room, sitting in the hand of a beautiful actress, her blissful face turned towards the last rays of the setting sun.

I heard that my wife was working briefly in Brisbane and had the two dogs. A couple of months later I was in the Edgecliff shopping centre buying a newspaper when the Greek newsagent said sympathetically, 'I'm so sad to hear about Ren.' It turned out that Ren had died in Brisbane. For the third time my separation had resulted in the death of one of my chihuahuas. I was distraught. She meant much to me. I held my own wake at the Sebel Town House bar where the barman placed a champagne glass full of peanuts next to my martini for 'Ren's ghost'. Some days later I received an e-mail from my wife. Ren had been run over outside a veterinarian's surgery when, on getting out of the taxi, she smelt the horrid odours of a place she had always hated, and blindly bolted across the street. My wife buried her in a friend's backyard and on the grave placed a cube of cheese, for which she always had an inordinate if not fanatical craving. I felt guilty. If only Gerri and I hadn't separated then Ren would never have gone to Brisbane and would be alive today. The death of my marriage had also resulted in the death of my beloved chihuahua.

Antigone Kefala

Summer at Derveni

We sink in light
disappear in the silence
nothing but
the slow folding of the sea.

*

Afternoon heat
empty of voices
on the foil surface
heads drifting
like heavy ornaments.

*

At dusk
the fishing boats
massive dark stones
planted
in a field of moonstone.

Winter Afternoon

She was smoking
stirring her coffee
giving me her news.
A detached observer
presenting a life
unconnected to her
that left her
indifferent.

Through the glass
the sea green with the wind
and the seagulls
icy white with red eyes
shrieking above the beach.

Antigone Kefala's *Absence: New and Selected Poems* was reprinted recently by
Hale & Iremonger.

Jacqueline Rose

Josephine's Song

Josephine the singer is the mouse-heroine of Kafka's last short story, written in 1924, the year of his death. What is remarkable about Josephine is how unremarkable her singing skills are. She squeaks no better (even a little more weakly) than the other mice. It is the intensity with which she performs her squeaking which sets her apart – she does what all mice do, and yet by making a theatrical performance out of the mundane, thoughtless act of squeaking, she raises it into an art.

Of course it is squeaking. How should it be anything else? Squeaking is the language of our people; it is only that some squeak their whole life through without knowing it, whereas here squeaking is freed from all the trammels of everyday life and so, for a short while, sets us free too.
FRANZ KAFKA, *Josephine the Singer*

So there she stands, the delicate creature, shaken by vibrations especially below the breastbone, so that one feels anxious for her, it is as if she has concentrated all her strength on her song, as if from everything in her that does not directly subserve her singing all strength has been withdrawn, almost all power of life, as if she were laid bare, abandoned, committed merely to the care of good angels, as if while she is so wholly withdrawn and living only in her song a cold breath blowing upon her might kill her.

FRANZ KAFKA, *Josephine the Singer*

Josephine's Song
Artist's Proof (Detail) 2001
Soft ground etching and aquatint
Plate: 60 x 80 cm
Printed by John Loane, Viridian Press,
Melbourne
Courtesy of Christine Abrahams Gallery,
Melbourne

Suneeta Peres da Costa

Dreamless

Suneeta Peres da Costa was born in 1977. Her novel *Homework* was published in the US, UK and Australia by Bloomsbury in 1999.

For a brief interval of my life, I did not dream a single dream. If I had dreamt and forgotten, it would have been another matter, but as it was I was convinced I could not dream at all. When this happened to me, I had just moved from one country to another, one continent to another. In fact, my world had literally been turned upside-down because these two continents were also in different hemispheres, such that I would sometimes wonder, like Alice as I fell into my albeit much more desolate abyss of sleep each night, 'Might I reach all the way to the other side of the earth like this, might I reach home this way?' I had been reading *Alice in Wonderland* while waiting at a real estate broker's office in the new city to which I had moved. I had bought the copy of *Alice in Wonderland* for a few dollars on the street before I went in to meet the broker; on the first pages, as she plummets towards Wonderland, Alice guilelessly remarks, 'How funny it'll seem to come out among the people that walk with their heads downwards! The Antipathies, I think…' And as I had read her words the slip was very poignant to me because it was with some bad feeling that I had left my own antipodean home.

Before I left, I had written a book, a book that had meant a great deal to me at the time that I had written it; the book was about many things, but mostly it was about madness. Sometimes, while writing it, I would become so absorbed by the story's sadness, so consumed with its reality, as though in the throes of a terrible nightmare, that tears would be rolling down my face without my even being conscious of them. When I arrived in the new country, the book was about to be published, but the feelings of importance I had had for what I had written had now turned to indifference and perhaps shame.

When people questioned me as to whether the story was auto-biography or fiction, I offered convoluted arguments of form, though what I really wanted point-blank to answer was that to me there was really no difference between these concepts. If there was a difference, it was as difficult to distinguish as that between my actual face, the face that I knew so well, and the angry wounded face reflected in the blurry bathroom mirror of the new apartment I had illegally leased. (As it happened, the broker whom I had gone to see had told me that it was too difficult to find me a home as I did not possess an adequate 'credit history': in realtor vernacular, a euphemism for the fact that I had no finances. Actually, if I had been in serious debt, he pointed out, if I had a record of bankruptcy or bad debts, this at least would have constituted a history of a kind, but as it happened I had no history at all.) What I wanted to answer, when I was questioned about the reality of what I had written, was that reality could be darker than Dostoievskian realism.

I was thinking of Dostoievsky because as I lay down on the sofa-bed which I had bought with my last savings from a charity shop in my new neighbourhood, I was trying to read *The Brothers Karamazov*, but so insensible was I to his terrifying hallucinatory universe, that I found myself turning back every few pages, able to take in only little of the story. The words swam before me with little purpose or distinction; the fate of each character was numbingly predictable. Indeed I felt bored by Dostoievsky! I was not tired, but reading *The Brothers Karamazov* this evening – it was early dusk – on my tattered, perforated sofa bed, I fell asleep.

In the beginning, I could fall asleep at any moment. I could nod off without any trouble at all, and when I awoke after sleeping for twelve hours, I was the most tired then; not tired in my bones as though I had slept too deeply or too much, but weary with a vague feeling of disgruntlement. I should say that this weariness was something I had never known before. My whole life, I had woken in earnest and with an uncanny conceit about my place in the world. In the world, if people were distinguished by their night and morning sensibilities, I would be a 'morning person', by which I mean that I rarely hesitated about the importance of getting out of bed.

There was a writer, Jean Rhys, who lived earlier last century and whose work was so ahead of its time that she remained until her death quite unrecognised. It should cause no sadness that her fame was largely posthumous; what is remarkable is that anyone achieves fame before their life is finished. Reading her work, which speaks with honesty, with a brutal kind of candour about not feeling in place anywhere in the world, I would have the feeling that her words had no skin, no surface, and these open wounds that were her words would cause me to sigh. I thought about Jean Rhys now when I awoke, tired and disgruntled. I thought in particular of one of her late stories, 'Let Them Call It Jazz', written from the point of view of a West Indian woman who is evicted from her London flat; her destitution, her solace in alcohol. Jean Rhys was an insomniac, she was an alcoholic and, although for a long time she was forgotten by the world, she was prolific. In many of her novels, she wrote about women not wanting to get out of bed of a morning. I thought about her because in order to write as well and as much about women who did not want to get out of bed of a morning, Jean Rhys would herself have had to have risen pretty early.

At the time that I stopped dreaming, I believed the feeling of numbness that hit me in the morning when I awoke with the sun on my face – I had not bought blinds or curtains because I had very little money and many debts; I was waiting for the money for the book which I had written, but the money was very late in coming – I believed the nihilism into which I woke had more to do with my forgetting my dreams than not having any at all. I was not tortured by this forgetting because I supposed that it would pass sooner or later. When I woke up, I would not dwell on my amnesia, but remembered that I had many bureaucratic feats to perform, such as getting a bank account for the little money I did have; important purchases to make, like getting an answering machine. I would try, to the best of my ability, to think about the future, but the future stood before me as a void.

When I went outside, it was strange to see the trees in full foliage in the middle of the year. The colours on the billboards and in shopfronts were so gaudy that I was at once drawn to and nauseated by them, as a child towards a fun park ride. It was unnerving to see taxis speeding by on the opposite side of the road; it was perturbing that all the doors, except for the revolving ones, which I found absurdly existential, opened outward. I enjoyed the feeling that no one outdid me in my estrangement, that no one surpassed me in my alienation. I fancied my malaise was not dissimilar to that of the autobiographical narrator of Rilke's *The Notebooks of Malte Laurids Brigge*, a book which I had in my possession and which I would read on public transport, wondering how it was possible that Rilke's poetry was so much superior to prose; wondering how, when his verse was in formal German – a language I had to read in translation – I still found the cadences absolutely and unspeakably stirring.

And yet, it was the narrative disruptions of *The Notebooks* which I now admired. The frequent discontinuities of the prose seemed suggestive of my metaphysical state: I was moving on public transport; the subway or bus, as it happened to be, stopped to pick up other passengers and to carry us to our varied destinations; my momentum and thoughts were frequently interrupted and in continual renewal as the vehicle was reinhabited from the inside. This was a mimesis uncharacteristic of the Rilkean poem whose internal state is far more static, whose metaphors are always tightly sealed, whose structure is unbreachable even as its subject implores transfiguration. Rilke's prose was not perfect, my predicament was not perfect. I was not in Paris. There were children selling plastic trinkets on the subways; there were tramps and beggars all about me, but I was not in Paris; there was no one shouting a dissonant *chou-fleur*.

In the country to which I had moved it was hot because it was midsummer. I didn't know quite how hot because the temperature was calculated in Fahrenheit and Fahrenheit meant nothing to me. I felt giddy constantly; I wanted to drink litres upon litres of water. I took my clothes off piece by sweat-soaked piece while I cleaned my dirty apartment, for which purpose I had bought an inordinate number of bottles of pine disinfectant.

At the supermarket to which I had gone to buy the pine disinfectant, I had needed to buy a number of other things too, but as I entered the aisles, each one burgeoning with food and produce and household utensils, I became stupid and forgot the logical location of things. The simplest mental associations – that milk would be found in the same place I might find cheese – eluded me entirely. I sought cheese where the meat was kept and milk where the fruit and vegetables were. The supermarket itself appeared to me labyrinthine. My hunger was for the most basic nourishment: bread and oranges; coffee, cheese and some plain crackers; milk and fruit juice; shampoo. I searched for these items but because to me coffee meant Vittoria, and juice Sunburst and shampoo Pears, I immediately felt cheated by the fact that they weren't there; I imagined at once that the new and unfamiliar product names contained ersatz commercial goods, that I was being set up or duped.

My paranoia was fuelled by the fact that, even though I spoke the same language, some very basic things could cause bafflement and bewilderment to the people around me. One example of this was the word 'trolley'. It was difficult to believe that the word 'trolley', whose meaning I took quite for granted, could arouse such sighs of frustration and head-shaking confusion. As it took me some time to find that a 'trolley' was called a 'shopping cart', I carried the things I had wanted to buy cumbrously in my hands until I turned a corner and saw the trolleys, jammed, as you find them everywhere in the world, one inside another.

It was surfaces that were befuddling; it was the forms the groceries took, rather than the contents themselves, which appeared to me distorted. Under the garish lights of the supermarket each object, from the packets of soap to the tins of pink salmon, was monstrous, a mirror that mocked me, a mirror in which I could not see myself reflected back without being overcome by a feeling of disquiet. And yet, when I returned to my dingy apartment, the grocery bags lost this exaggerated quality; later, when I placed each item in the refrigerator – the light of which was broken – the groceries took on their familiar, utilitarian forms.

When I returned to my apartment, I wasted no time uncapping the pine disinfectant and scrubbing the blurry mould-mottled glass of the bathroom mirror; I wiped the grime that had become congealed with stale morsels of food on the hot-plates of the stove; I scrubbed the old, unfinished parquetry floor and the two streaky windows with a fastidiousness I did not know I possessed. I washed the bathroom tub and tiles. Finally, I sat down under the naked light globe in my kitchen. When I tore open the crackers and the cheese and began eating, I was eating to fill a hunger for which it was irrelevant what was fraudulent and what wholesome, a hunger that came from a place more primitive than the names of the foods that would satisfy it, a hunger, I suppose you could say, without a name. And every few hours this hunger would return, for even though I may have lost my dreaming ability, I had not lost my appetite.

In order to open a bank account and buy an answering machine, the two feats which I believed would place me in the present, provide order and institute habit in my new life, I had to go out into the world, I had to come face-to-face with people. My trepidation was not unfounded, for everywhere I went to apply for a bank account I had to wait in a long queue to talk to the authorities. I had credentials, letters attesting to my legitimacy to be in the new country, but like Kafka's K., a stranger in the town about the Castle, I was continuously delayed and denied entry, I was continuously subjected to interrogations. Made patient to maniacal point, I felt I was losing my mind.

All the authorities to whom I had to speak seemed impossible to locate. If I did locate someone, they seemed menacingly listless or, like the Landlady in *The Castle*, they stared at me with vacant eyes before launching into a series of impossible questions and interdictions. For the most part, I was left alone while people disappeared into nearby rooms, to forage in deep filing cabinets, while someone called someone else on the telephone and spoke about me as though I were not there. At one time, someone sat before me but stared at a computer monitor without saying a word for an hour. Soon I began to wonder whether the heavy-duty air-conditioning systems, whose effect on someone like me who had just come in from the outside was to make them shudder with cold, had blasted the eardrums of the authorities.

I confess that part of the difficulty communicating was on my side: when I was admitted after a great wait and sat down to explain my situation, I opened my mouth to speak and my words would either pour out as volubly as water or I would speak in incomplete sentences, which would include tautology after contradiction. Sometimes, a word, after it was spoken, would hover, with all the potential and poise of a new idea; then it turned soft and ineffectual, and then, before I knew it, it assumed the fragile properties of glass and promised to come crashing to the ground about me. My panic about this splintered glass would then cause me not to speak at all. Eventually, I got some answers, accomplished, as they say, the bare essentials, but these achievements seemed as much a part of chance and the indiscriminate bouts of pity that the authorities took on me, as any action I had brought about myself.

I could not dream and therefore I could not write: it took me a long time to make this deduction, but when I did I could see that good writing emerges from a sort of death, a sort of darkness; it requires an annihilation of space, an annihilation of time and that these annihilations have their phantasmagoric corollary in the dream which casts light on what the mind diurnally conceals. The resemblance between the dream and writing is in a sense that between what is original and what is plagiarised; there is always something inferior in the copy, something which betrays it as a copy as such, but the inferiority in time can come to be seen as an aesthetic virtue; the faults in the bastard text can make it in its own turn original.

I could not write. I could have imitated someone else. The writer Janet Frame came to mind. I was reading her novel, *Yellow Flowers in the Antipodean Room*, a novel about life-in-death and death-in-life. Frame loves in her novels to play with such juxtapositions and paradoxes; she loves to toy with dialectics of interiority and exteriority. It made me wonder, reading her novel, what part her misdiagnosis as a schizophrenic had played in her faith in language. For since her misdiagnosis as a schizophrenic Frame has written about people who, in one way or another, would rather be incarcerated than live in a world which, if not for psychiatric institutions, could be regarded as a psychiatric institution in its own right. I could not imitate Janet Frame: she was truly inimitable. When I say her literary output would not have been the same if she had not written because of what had happened to her, I am trying to say that my own world, my waking world, would have had a huge hole in it too.

Now that I had invested money in an answering machine, I kept looking to see whether the answering machine was flashing at every moment. In this way, the answering machine became the only reference point for my earthly significance. I was quite aware that my family and friends were on the other side of the world – when I was awake they would be asleep and vice-versa – and still I made this demand of the answering machine: to account for my life, to register my gains, my losses. After a few days of seeing it blank, I began to wonder whether there might be a fault with the answering machine, and so I went downstairs to a public phone booth to test it. Though the thought crossed my mind, I did not go so far as to leave a message on my own answering machine; I simply hung up, as I had on so many machines before.

Each evening, as I became more terrified that my sleep would be as empty as my answering machine, I would blink away my fatigue. And soon enough this took on the proportions of a kind of self-induced insomnia. Outside my tiny window I saw the moon, always waning it seemed. I looked at the clock, a wall clock so worthless it had been abandoned by the previous tenants (their leaving this particular plastic clock, repulsive to the eye, above a refrigerator whose light was broken and which leaked erratically, could only be a sign of their meanness, not of their largesse). If it was late enough, I knew I could call my family on the other side of the world. I was supposed to be asleep when they were awake; between us there were thirteen hours, which now seemed like all the time in the world to me. Now I could not see the space between us as a distance that could be calibrated. I could understand time – after all, time is the vector by which an insomniac measures her abnormality – but it was as if I had been flung into another galaxy in which, besides gobbling his fledgling children, Cronus had wolfed down space itself.

If it was not late enough to call my family or friends, I would lie flat on my back on the kitchen linoleum and go on like this, cataleptically, eyeing now the clock, now the moon, in whose expressions I was seeking, like a daughter in her mismatched parents, common guidance or a sign. The stars were seldom visible in the city to which I had moved; someone had told me you had to squint to see them. But even when I squinted and squinted, I saw nothing but blackness and smog and skyscrapers forever. We say forever, imagining it is a time, but in fact forever is a space eternally empty of presence. It was not the calling long distance itself, but my ability to close the distance if I so wanted that comforted me more than the voices of those whom I had left and for whom I longed, because, it has to be said, I had left because they could comfort me no longer and, as for longing, one longs only for what is impossible, for what is irrecoverable.

It could be said that a person as cruel and bitter as I, deserved nightmares, not dreamlessness, not a comatose-like insomnia. What I wanted was the power of choice, distinction, the right of refusal, all of them egoistic and childish desires. I had been called these things – egotistic, childish – before I left my home by a friend from whom I had become estranged. Notwithstanding our estrangement, this woman had given me as a farewell gift a book of poems by a famous poet of the country to which I had come. The poet was not a poet that I admired; his verse was secular and imbued with an idealism I considered naïve. Although I did not believe in God, I loved poems that mourned the absence of God; I loved poems that spoke of the centre not holding. If I suspected that this sometime friend suffered a narcissism which she confused with mutual harmony, the fact that she chose this book of all the books she could have given me, was an innocent but telling example of her misreading of me. And yet, as I had very few books to read, one night I read from this book of poems, lines in fact about somnambulism and death, and I found them so beautiful and hypnotic that I chanted them aloud to myself: 'The wretched features of ennuyees, the white features of corpses, the livid faces of drunk-ards, the sick-grey faces of onanists/…The newborn emerging from gates and the dying emerging from gates,/ The night pervades them and enfolds of them.'

So moved was I by these lines, that I was overwhelmed with regret for the friendship which I had abruptly severed. I decided to call this old friend. I had her telephone number written somewhere. There was a time I would have been able to recall it by heart, but now I had to search for it. She was a social worker and, after we had talked for some time, she told me, only half-jokingly, to see a psychoanalyst. It didn't do any good to counter that I was not depressed, only homesick. She was very good at convincing people that she knew them better than they knew themselves. She remarked that the city to which I had come was the world's psychotherapeutic capital and we both laughed and I continued laughing even when I hung up, but I was laughing at myself for my situation seemed so grotesque: I had no money to see a psycho-analyst even though there was a surplus of such people in the city to which I had moved, there was a surplus of people who specialised in mental problems, there was a whole industry devoted to disorders.

The city to which I had moved was a monolith on a piece of land so tiny that it felt at any moment that it might disappear like Atlantis. It was clear that no one cared for anyone else; it was clear that people were dreadfully alone and empty, whether rich or poor, young or old –

and the new city was full of piercing contradictions. To say that the degradation and inhumanity did not attract me would be a lie; no one had forced me to move to this new city, I had come of my own accord. The new city was extreme; its intensity delighted me because this intensity in all its manifestations, but especially when I walked its streets at night, imbued the new city with the quality of an illusion.

When I was a child, there was a cliché of the city to which I had moved that said that it was so energetic that people had little reason to go to bed. A cliché often has a lot of truth to it, a truth so hackneyed we forget to take notice. But in the case of this cliché there was little truth: the building in which I lived was always very quiet when I came in late, and I was sure that everyone was fast asleep. What's more, by day, the people in the elevator looked tired and irritated and, occasionally, as though they wanted to kill someone. When I looked at their faces, I had the increasing sense that their faces were my face too.

One of the first things that I did when I received the money on which I was waiting was to buy a bed for myself. I had wanted to buy myself a bed on my birthday, but I didn't have the money and I was worried about buying such an expensive thing on credit because until I had the money I didn't believe I would get it. This was a good principle, it seemed to me at the time – to only spend what you had – but in fact it is impossible to live this way; my mother lives this way and it reduces everything to its most literal meaning. It is impossible to live this way because living beyond one's means, not lavishly, but beyond what is easiest and most reasonable and fair, is often where love begins, despite what a psychoanalyst will tell you. And yet, this living beyond one's means, this yearning for more, is what makes us wretched and hateful.

The gift of the bed that I bought myself did not seem less important because I had bought it on any other day besides my birthday. I knew I would not have bought such a bed for myself if it was not *for* my birthday, but I did not delight in my new bed any less because it arrived more than two weeks after my birthday had come and gone. The day that I bought the bed I had gone out intending to buy only a mattress to replace the threadbare battered sofa bed on which I had been sleeping. I knew that an old man sold cheap mattresses of reasonable quality on a street corner not far from where I lived. When I went to his mattress shop, he painstaking instructed me about the quality and texture of certain mattresses. I was so excited that I made the decision to buy a mattress very quickly. He would not accept a credit card and I had not carried my money with me because, unused as I was to having so much at once, I was concerned that I might lose it. The nearest bank was about ten minutes' walk away and, while walking towards it, I caught sight of the bed that I ended up buying.

My bed, a high, Mexican sleigh bed of rosewood and wrought iron, was on display in the front window of a shop into which I would never have ventured except that the signs all about announced that a clearance sale was on. The bed was so significantly reduced that the cost of its delivery was almost as much as the bed itself. I pointed this out when I paid for it – and I paid for it on the spot because I could not help myself, with my virgin credit card – I pointed out, not stridently, but good-naturedly, that I lived very close by and that perhaps I should be eligible for a discount on the delivery of the bed. But the sales assistant would brook no contradiction about the delivery costs, which she said were standard.

The two men who were assigned to the delivery of my bed were from the same town in the hinterland of Venezuela, a tiny town in which everyone, it was said, knew everyone and yet they themselves had not come to know each other until they came to the city in which we all now dwelt. They had come for better opportunities, but because the degrees they held were quite redundant in the new country, they made their living moving furniture. They asked me what I did and, when I told them, without wincing, that I had written a novel, we began to debate whether it was possible to write without a home, how the writing about one's home is often distorted both there and away from it. One of the delivery men launched into a laudatory speech on Joyce, who, he claimed, perverted the irregularities of history, of language, irregularities by which all three of us had come to be in the world. He was so compelling in his discourse on Joyce that we got lost and once went through a red light. Now it occurs to me that I often got lost precisely because the city, laid out on a grid, was one of the most easy to navigate.

When I was able to dream again, I was happy. I didn't know what involuntary part of my psyche's impulses had set my dreaming to stop, but I was happy that my dreams had come back. In an effort to understand what had happened, I read Freud's entire *magnum opus* on the subject, but even then I could only grasp how the dream worked, not why, not why not. Since there were no condensations, no distortions or displacements to speak of, I wondered whether my dreaming insensibility mirrored my waking insensibility. If, as Freud says, the dream resembles a translation to which we must apply a waking hermeneutics, it was as though when I woke up I had never known the original language, never been a native speaker. My sleep had been more akin to a blank page, rather than an indecipherable script. When I began to dream again, it was hard for me to recall that grief I felt when I had been unable to do so. In fact, I had the impression that a joke was being played on me by the capricious gods: I had been unable to dream and could not remember what that dreamlessness was like.

It was sometime after I began to dream again that I slept beside a man who had lost his family when he was young. He slept fitfully and often, soon after closing his eyes, would cry out so plaintively that he would wake himself up. When I asked him what he had dreamt, he would say only that he had dropped something or slipped over. Sleeping beside this man, I had odd pleasant dreams which would come back to me wistfully during the day; then and there, thinking how comforting it could be to lie beside him, I would want to summon him to me again. I began to imagine that my sleeping beside him was natural and therefore imperative. My pleasure in sleeping beside him was so total that I could not think of a time when I had slept alone. It is easy to accustom oneself to what is comforting; what is difficult is to get used to what is unpleasant. This is never a revelation, yet each time it has the shape of revelation. What is difficult is to do something with the pain that comes when you lose that to which you have, rightly or wrongly, but usually very easily, accustomed yourself.

This man was someone who, not really under the influence of any soporific, was always sleepy. During the day, if he answered the phone at all, it would be somnolently and to say that he was taking a nap. If we met in a public place, he had the habit of dropping off.

While I left him for a few minutes at the entrance to a museum or requested he wait outside a movie theatre so that I could go to the toilet, he would fall asleep leaning against a graffitied wall. He was infatuated with graffiti; graffiti was to him what hieroglyphs or ancient Greek tablets are to some curious and fanatical historians. How one could be so curious about the scripts of dead people I did not know, but I too had necrophilic predilections, I too was taken by the Dead Sea scrolls and by cuneiform. Because the meaning of what is undeciphered is yet to be revealed, always latent, it gives us hope. Illegible, unknown, it is like a disaster that is indefinitely deferred. Perhaps it is this paradox that piques our curiosity. I don't know.

All I know is that I could not understand my lover's infatuation with graffiti. The graffiti which he brought to my attention through-out the city – and it was a new city for him too, and also a new language; the language he spoke was an ancient one, guttural, full of fricatives, and he often reverted to it when we were making love, such that it had an onomatopoeic effect – the graffiti he brought to my attention was repetitive and hectic; nothing was indelible about it, not even its urgency. He tried to tell me that the graffiti amounted to an *effacement* of meaning, that the graffiti was anarchic precisely because it refused to be remembered; if it were erased by the city authorities tomorrow, this would not only be expected, but a testament to the graffiti artists' mastery. I did not refute him; I did not say that by objectifying the graffiti, by *liking* it, he, too, was missing the point. Rather, I thought, as he explicated the aesthetic principles of graffiti, that he had lost his family when he was a young man; he hated testi-monies and memorials because they gave meaning to loss, exalted loss, when the hardest part of losing for him was the state of profound meaninglessness which was his life.

My favourite time to be with this man was night-time because he was most animated and alert then. Eating, to a gluttonous degree, appeared to fill him more than his actual hunger and, while watching him eat, I could forget that he would be falling asleep at any moment. One night after we had eaten dinner, he found among a pile of books on my coffee table the copy of *Alice in Wonderland* that I had bought months before when I could not dream, and we began to talk about this

book, a book that we had both read as children, he in the city that had
been his home and from which he had exiled himself because there was
too much hate, too much incivility, too little peace. I had read *Alice in
Wonderland* in my home too, a place unravaged by war but a place that
nonetheless caused me anxiety when I thought about it. He then gave
me an improvised translation in his language, full of fricatives and
gutturals, of the Jabberwocky's poem, a performance so enchanting
that I asked him at the end to repeat it. There were other moments
like this in which it seemed we were reconciled by something larger
than the languages we did not share. I had loved enough people who
did speak the same language to see that knowing someone, which
often involves loving them in a hopeless capacity, has little to do with
sharing a language.

I think that he could not bear to see me go away and so when he
heard that I was going away for a short while he decided that he would
absent himself first. The uncoupling of these two notions – parting,
returning – begins at a moment when we are still helpless and quite
vulnerable and it goes on and goes on quite unswayed by the arguments or muscle of our will. It does not take us our whole lives to work
out there is no such thing as the beginning, no such thing as the end,
often no end in sight at all. When the man who was my lover told me
he wanted to end it, he drank a lot of coffee; he chain-smoked until my
apartment was so filled with tobacco fumes I went to the bathroom and
threw up, after which I came out to find him reading the newspaper,
another narcotic habit of his which caused us to argue even more. He
had been a political correspondent before he left his country, a country
that manufactured large-scale horror by way of a war with the people
of a territory it had long ago annexed. The war was the largest industry in the country from which he had come, an industry that kept the
mass media enthralled. We did not disagree on these points of argument, we did not disagree at all. Some things are irreconcilable: he
wanted to end it, I did not want to end it and so it was not a question
of disagreement; it was not a question of persuasion.

I was going away for a short while to promote my book and,
when I was in the airplane, at an appropriate altitude to see things,
I wondered whether he had read my book – he had not said anything

about it – and that this was why he was leaving me. When I got off the airplane, I was taken to a convention centre where I drank a lot of alcohol. There was a party of sorts, but I spoke only to one woman who had come to promote a book that she had self-published with her husband, a how-to book for children on the subject of writing thank-you cards. I did not need to prompt this woman to tell me about her book; she did not stop for breath; and, when her husband came towards her, she continued her story with even greater élan. When they had got married, she said, they had stayed at a small coastal resort. There were such terrible storms that they had been flooded in for the first three days of their honeymoon. They were not made miserable by the rain, however; they were quite good at entertaining themselves, and, one of the activities with which they entertained themselves was the writing of the three hundred and fifty thank-you notes for the wedding gifts they had received. Such was the reward for their ingenuity, resource-fulness and self-discipline: the how-to book on writing greeting cards had brought her by popular demand to a national book festival.

After I went away to promote my book, I went again, on a longer trip, a holiday. A holiday was something I had not had in a long time. I was going to holiday in the village in which my father was born. A village is a small thing, barely a smudge on the map of the world. At the time my father was born, the village and the territory in which the village was located was a part of Portugal. It was only when he was a young man that it ceased being so. On a particular day when he was a young man some soldiers from the larger land-mass which shared its borders took over the territory in which my father's village was located. There was no war, few reprisals and recriminations; very soon it was said that the territory, including the myriad villages such as the one in which my father had been born, had been 'integrated' with the larger sub-continental land-mass that adjoined it. But this integration in words amounted to very little in the minds of people such as my father.

The historical fate of each person is inexorable but varies in its degree of tragedy and comedy and farce. My father was an interpreter of the Portuguese language. Neither Portuguese nor English were his native tongues and it was a constant source of humour to me that it was by trading in these two languages – English and Portuguese, languages which had been used by colonial administrators centuries before to subjugate my father's ancestors – that my father had made his living. He did not get exciting literary commissions. He translated birth certificates and marriage certificates. His efforts were often directed at jobs as prosaic as translating the written components of the driving test to Portuguese native speakers. The one question which would time after time floor the examinee was that about blood alcohol levels. There was an irony in this because on more than one occasion, having been called upon to interpret at the trial of a Portuguese native speaker charged with drunk driving, my father had recognised the defendant as someone who had, years before, nudged him to get the answer to the blood alcohol question at the Roads and Traffic Authority.

A village is barely a smudge on the map of world but the village of my father's birth to which I was going occupied a mythic place in my imagination: its whitewashed gothic church, its green rice fields. When I thought of seeing my father's village, I wanted to capture with words my feeling of elation and sadness to be seeing it again. A place such as the village of my father's birth which had been brought under the sway of now one impostor, now another, could hardly be said to exist except in language: the church, built on the ruins of desecrated temples, the rice fields irrigated by landless aborigines – how else but by language could the violence and betrayal which was the history of the place of my Father's birth be recalled? I was not taught the native tongue of my Father; I was not taught Portuguese; and yet I had an intimation of *saudade*, that melancholy for lost things, often confused with nostalgia. *Saudade* is a melancholy with no object, a melancholy whose object is the insufficiency of language itself and, in this sense, it does not lose much in translation. The Italian writer Antonio Tabucchi has written novels and stories in Portuguese for the very reason that Portuguese offers him a posture of reflection and mediation he cannot find in his native language. His novel, *Requiem*, which I am re-reading because I admire it so much, is the stream of consciousness of a somnambulist in Lisbon, a man who walks back in time toward his past and to the past of Portugal and indeed the whole history of Europe, all of which is staged as a wild reverie. The distinction between philosophy and fiction collapses around the autobiographical in

Tabucchi's work to produce an uncanny, revelatory inventory of the possibilities of knowing oneself in an adopted language. For while language is not everything and is often nothing at all, it is all the same an entry point into the world without which we are dreamless, without which we are dispossessed.

Just before I was to go away, the post office lost a certified letter that the consulate of the country in which my father was not born but by which, by the vagaries of history, the village of his birth had come to be administered, was returning to me. The letter contained the passport of the country in which I was born; the visa enabling me to be in the country in which I now lived, as well as the visa allowing me to travel to the village in which my father had been born. The passport and visa to my father's place of birth were technically easy to obtain again, but it seemed impossible to obtain at such short notice another visa to be in the country in which I now lived. What's more, after making the necessary inquiries, I discovered that, without this visa, I would be able to exit the country in which I now lived, but I would not be able to re-enter it. This was a situation that seemed laughable at first and very serious after a few minutes' thinking about it. I went to the post office, I went to the two consulates, that of the country that had issued me with the visa to travel to the village of my father's birth, as well as that of my own country of birth, the country whose passport I had lost. I went to these consulates four and five times, for interviews, for questions, and after many long distance phone calls and much currying of favour, I found a way to leave with the guarantee of returning, a guarantee that is always fantastic anyway.

The dream is not a rebus awaiting resolution; the dream, however we try to reduce it, is as incomplete as it is irresolvable. Just a few days before I left, I had the following memorable dream: the lover who had spurned me had come with me to the house in the village in which my father was born. There were many people there, many of whom I had not seen since I was a child. The many languages they were speaking at once constituted a veritable Babel. When I made to introduce my lover to them, I forgot his name and, hoping he would not notice, called him by a made-up name. Of course, he did notice the nonsensical name and, taking offence at it, went to sulk in the room where the family portraits hung. After some time, I remembered his correct name and, in order to make amends, went to address him by it, but he did not forgive me now, anyway.

When I woke up, I was crying. I knew my tears were for something else besides the certified letter, but it was the first thing that I remembered having lost. 'The dream is, as it were, centred elsewhere,' Freud writes. The recognition of the metaphoric displacement, of the condensation of my larger loss into the tangible-intangible 'certified letter', comes only now that I, too, am 'elsewhere'. To know that I had lost much more than the letter, I have had to remember what I had forgotten was gone, and that recovery is as difficult and necessary as that of these pages which I lose every time there is a blackout here in the village of my father's birth (where I dream, where I see the stars) and where my battery-less lap-top frequently dies.

Judith Beveridge
The Dice Player

I've had my nose in the ring since I was nine.
I learned those cubes fast: how to play a blind
bargain; how to empty a die from my palm
and beguile by turns loaded with prayers –
then sleight-of-hand. Ten or fifteen years
and you get wrists like a tabla-player's, jaws
cut and edged by the knuckles and customs
of luck and deception. The fun's in sham,
in subterfuge, in the eyes smoking out
an opponent's call. I let my thumbs stalk
each die, get to know which edge might
damage probability's well-worn curves.
See, all dice are cut on the teeth of thugs,
liars and raconteurs. I've concocted calls
those dealing in risk and perfidy, bluff or
perjury, would envy. But I've never stolen
or coveted dice fashioned from agate
or amber, slate or jasper, or from
the perfumed peach stones of distant shores.
Some think fortunes will be won with dice
made from the regurgitated pellets of owls:
or from the guano of seabirds that ride only
the loftiest thermals. I've always had faith
in the anklebones of goats, in the luxated
knee-caps of mountain-loving pugs. Look,

I've wagered all my life on the belief that
I can dupe the stars, subtend the arcs, turn
out scrolls, louvres, pups, knacks, double
demons – well, at least give a game rhythm.
I know there'll always be an affliction
of black spots before my eyes, that my face
has its smile stacked slightly higher on
the one side, that the odds I'm not a swindler
are never square. But Sir, when some rough
justice gets me back again to the floor,
then watch me throw fate a weighted side.

Pedlar

Sure, I've haggled on corners with fruiterers,
barrowboys raising phlegm. I've gone on
day after day, putting forward a face I know
to be long ago cashiered of its gloss. Some
days I've buffed my face with a less penniless
tarnish, and walked out into daylight's lucrative
polish. These days who knows what's delusively
real from what's genuinely ersatz. I've carried
the faked weight of my voice through these
streets, pretending it were one of time's carats,
making claims not worth a tinker's cuss, but
smiling as if all work were illustrious. I'm sick
of the moon whose far-side no gold can limn,
of the brass sales of my neighbours' shops,
of tipping dreams into bargains and watching
the stars sharpen to jewels in the lapel-pins
of usurers, smoothing a look in the demoted
lustre of my pots; life declassed of its sheen.
But I'll go on no matter how the world glints
my loss, or the spokes of my wheels mint
out their counterfeit suns. I'll just spruik up
a mock brilliance, prink up another day in
the dull patina of my pots, and call out iron,
scraps – as if I still believed in my own finesse.

Saddhus

Some chew necrotic weeds. Some sleep
in charnel fields. Some are purified
by the putrifactive quality of time
and happily multiply in eternity's folds.
Some dig ditches and like refuse
throw themselves in. Some don't mind
the urine of town dogs. Some don't
mind their buttocks becoming sharp
as heifers' hoofs. Some are ever-walkers,
men of good sense but small gesture,
small-moment journeymen wearing
out their feet with stones. Some find
no answers in the ever-commuting sky
and lie still on bramble palliasses,
or they become ever-sitters and vow
not to straighten their limbs. Some
make leashes of their penises and walk
chastity's heavy stones. Some are lost
to an ever-administered distance,
clouds and wind their error of alliance
and so they never find peaceful homes.
Some come down from the mountains
into the searing belly of the wind,
and sit between six fires, then turn,
already blind, towards a seventh fire,

the sun. Some live sting by sting,
ache by ache, and wait for the smells
the tidal breezes bring, still not knowing
what is gathered, what is won
beyond the vermin, beyond the dung.

Judith Beveridge has published two volumes of poetry, *The Domesticity of Giraffes* (1987), and *Accidental Grace* (1996) which have won, between them, The Dame Mary Gilmore Award, the NSW and Victorian Premiers' Awards, and the Wesley Michel Wright Prize.

Kerryn Goldsworthy

Almost an Island

Kerryn Goldsworthy's most recent books are her critical study of the work of Helen Garner (OUP, 1996) and the anthology *Australian Women's Stories* (OUP, 1999)

Somewhere in the world there must still be at least one book, probably a school textbook from the 1960s, with my first-ever address on the flyleaf:

Box 31,
Curramulka,
Yorke Peninsula,
South Australia,
Australia,
The World,
The Universe.

What I liked about this address was the way it zoomed in and panned out between two extremes of darkness. At one end there was the small cube of black air behind the thirty-first locked door in the wall of post-boxes in the foyer of the Curramulka Post Office. At the other end, there was infinite space.

Of the terms in between those two extremes, all but one seemed an inexact way of saying where we actually were. 'Curramulka' was somewhere that we were not, a couple of miles away, for we lived in an outlying farmhouse and not the town itself. 'Australia', and even 'South Australia', were much too big and abstract to grasp all at once; I knew them only as shapes and maps that we drew at school again and again, using little plastic templates and spending careful hours shading in the blue fringe of coast. The World was a massive and shadowy idea.

But if you went to visit the farmer up the hill and climbed onto the roof of his barn on a clear day, you could see the blue lines of ocean on either side: the east and west coasts of Yorke Peninsula.

Sixteen years ago David Malouf published an essay on Brisbane, his home town, called 'A First Place'. Each of us, he says, has one place, our 'first place in the world', that we know better than any other, 'from inside, from my body outwards'. Starting from this premise and from the idea that it might be an appropriate time for Australian writers to move beyond the idea of 'Australian writing' and to look more closely at their own personal bits of the landscape, he argues that the unique features of your first place in the world – its topography, its architecture, its weather and colours and cosmic mood – can shape personality, and ways of seeing, and habits of thought.

Malouf was and is fortunate in the luxury of his location, in the tropical colours, dramatic landforms, unique architecture and material density of detail that go to make up urban and suburban Brisbane. But to try to think in such a way about Yorke Peninsula is to address yourself much more to absence and lack: to think about place-names (Curramulka, Warooka, Koolywurtie, Minlacowie) recalling the Aboriginal people who are no longer there; to divine the varied and implicit meanings of fence-lines and tree-lines dividing one space from the next; to consider the drama of a single farmhouse dwarfed by a wide sweep of wheat. No city, naked or otherwise, with or without a million stories; no river deep, or mountain high, or any other geographical sublimity to provide a map for the scope of Gothic emotions.

Only distance, and eventually, always, the sea. The people who get their living from the sea or the shore watch the ocean, and every direction is seaward but north. The farmers, and the townspeople whose businesses and professions support the farmers, watch the weather, or the horizon, or the weather on the horizon; the finely tuned timing of rain or the absence of rain can mean disaster. Yorke Peninsula people aren't much given to extremes of feeling; more to the watchful appraisal, the considered observation, the long-distance sailor's stare.

Yorke Peninsula is boot-shaped, roughly thirty five kilometres across at the ankle and one hundred and fifty from boot-top to heel: not the elegant high-heeled high-arched pointy-toed boot of Italy, but a large square-heeled flat-footed working boot. It does not lie at Italy's elegant angle but stands upright and foursquare, its foot firmly on the ground, its toes pointing west, as though Italy has been shrunk to a quarter of its original size and rotated clockwise through forty five degrees.

Yorke is the middle peninsula of the three that form the fringe along the South Australian coast. To the east there's the smallest: the fertile, populous, Tuscan-looking Fleurieu, Adelaide's rich hinterland, with its French name and its world-class wines and its Impressionist colours and light. To the west, there's the biggest: the harsh and mysterious Eyre, named for a reputedly murderous colonial adventurer turned vice-regent. This is an isolated, rugged peninsula shaped like a fat India with a hammer head, its colours the grey-green of scrubby bush and the bronze of ripe grain, known for heartbreaking droughts in the summer and fabled monster sharks in the surrounding waters. Yorke Peninsula is like the middle child, a mediator with the characteristics of both siblings. Its eastern coast is bounded by the Gulf of St Vincent, a calm and sheltered triangle of water across which, on a clear night, you can see the lights of Adelaide as a soft bright glow on the horizon. The western coast, the Spencer Gulf side, is wilder and stranger and more dangerous.

Our place (in the country you say 'our place', not 'our house') was in the middle, halfway up and halfway across, as far inland as it was possible to be. Yorke Peninsula wasn't a map, or an idea, or a town you didn't live in. It was the real thing, a landform on a human scale: something on which the body could locate itself, and a sight that the eye could take in. From the barn roof on the hill, you could see the lines of its parallel coasts and look at the shape that it made on the map, the shape that it made in the world.

The peninsula at its southern end is stony, salty, ancient, bleak. Rock-coloured, rock-shaped sheep graze there, but not much grows. The unsealed roads really are made of rock, top-dressed with dust and rubble. Near the southern coast, at the boot-heel, you'll see the occasional black and stunted tree, permanently bent over at the waist like a witch in a fairy tale from the endless wind off the sea. Down here it's windy all the time: the struggling little trees, the stoic sheep, the secret beaches at the bottoms of cliffs, everything is pounded by the gales off the Southern Ocean and the unrelenting sea-light. You should come here alone, or with someone you don't mind seeing your face the way it really looks, because there's nowhere here that a person could hide any kind of secret.

But drive north over the ankle and up the shin, and the land gets rapidly richer and less rocky. The sheep look softer and happier and the wind feels more benign. The paddocks roll more gently, under the ripe wheat. My home town lies in the shelter of a hollow – nothing as definite as a valley, more just a sort of saucer – in this landscape. If in January, after harvest, you drive over the crest of the hill on the road from the sea, you will find yourself looking down at the little town with its coloured roofs, surrounded by paddocks full of stubble bleaching in the sun: an egg with coloured speckles in a nest of straw.

When we inscribed our addresses on the flyleaves of our schoolbooks, did we write down our exact, elaborate locations in infinite space in order to reassure and steady ourselves? Or was it the expression of a childhood confidence, now long lost, that we knew exactly where we were? I miss the days when I didn't yet know that 'Curramulka' might not, after all, mean 'emu water-hole', depending, like so much else, on what it was that the founding fathers had thought they were hearing the Aboriginal people say. I miss the days when I didn't yet realise that the border of South Australia was an arbitrary phenomenon and not a natural one, a geopolitical entity whose shape could yet be altered or destroyed. I miss the days when I didn't yet understand that no coastline ever stops changing.

But while I was still living there, none of these things had yet come unstuck, and there were further points of reference and anchorage. One set of grandparents lived in Adelaide, the other set in an idyllic little town called Arcadia Vale, on the central coast of New South Wales. Paradise, and the City: these were the two places on the globe, apart from home, that my body understood. They put the peninsula in perspective on a map of Australia for which my coordinates were family, a map built up around the routes of those two seasonal grand-parent journeys: one made every spring and autumn, up the coast to the top of the Gulf of St Vincent and then back down the other side, south towards Adelaide and through its maze of coloured lights; the other – always in the clear heat of January, in the days before air-conditioned cars – over to and through the Riverland, across the blistering Hay Plains, up the steep winding roads of the Blue Mountains and down again, east to the sea.

Other, older features on that family map: the bones of my great-great-grandparents, resting under weathered white headstones in the Curramulka Cemetery, a pretty, tree-sheltered little place a mile out from the town in the middle of the wheat. They emigrated in 1847 from Cornwall, itself a peninsula only half the size of the one I think of as mine, and, like mine, sticking out an adventurous toe into a cold wild ocean. After a few years of work on the waterfront and a string of babies, they moved to Yorke Peninsula as pioneer farmers, two decades before Curramulka was surveyed and named.

And I wonder, thinking about them now, whether they missed the sea-light of their own first place, and found themselves in quest of geographical *heimlichkeit*, unconsciously heading for the kind of land-form that reminded them of home. Is there such a thing as a psychogeographical comfort zone? After I first saw Tuscany, I used to say that from now on my two points of reference on the map of the world would be Florence and Curramulka. This was usually offered and always taken as a joke about ludicrous contrasts, but in fact it was a serious private observation about towns in the middle of sunny, fertile, boot-shaped peninsulas: about feeling instinctively at home at certain points on the face of the earth.

After we moved to Adelaide in 1966, my new friends at high school would tell of having been taught as toddlers to recite their street addresses in case they got lost. As a child living on a farm I had had no street address; but in and around Curramulka everyone knew who you were anyway, and outside the town where the land had been cleared all round for wheat and sheep and barley, a lone child in the landscape was visible for miles.

Our address cited no house number, no street, no suburb. It was silent about our house, and about the road that ran past it, a hundred yards up the track. It was a classic Australian farmhouse, and all the houses of everyone we knew were variations on the theme: a stone box, with four rooms of equal size and a wide hall or passage down the middle. That was the original core; everything else had been added later, usually one addition at a time. New rooms were built on at imaginative angles, in whatever shape and style the builder fancied and whatever materials happened to be available, sometimes up or down a few steps. There were inner outbuildings, like the stone laundry and garage built onto the side of the house, and outer outbuildings, like the sheds 'down the back' that housed poultry and pigs.

I lived in that house for the first twelve years of my life but could not now draw even the roughest floor plan of it; the spatial relations between some parts of the house always remained mysterious, as though there were secret passages and I was not allowed to know where they were. The best diagram I could manage would be only a coded cognitive map that might hint at emotional currents and undertows. Arrows, say, might show how I would be drawn into the privacy and quiet of my parents' room, with its bright north-facing window and high wide bed and the faint smell of Elizabeth Arden's Blue Grass. Or how I would come when called, taking my seat at the green laminex kitchen table, to a hot lunch and the trumpet fanfare of the ABC's midday news, music I associate to this day with corned beef and carrots. Or how I would drift for no good reason past the piano, across the lounge-room and on through the door with the bookcase on it, down the three steps past the vague and looming shapes of my father's banjo-case and my grandfather's travelling-trunk, into the bright room for sewing and ironing where my mother taught me to read.

Like so many of the houses in the district and the township, ours had a high, wide front verandah and a heavy ceremonial front door that was never used: it is a defining characteristic of Australian farmhouses that strangers never quite know where or how they are to be broached, what path or track to follow, which gate to go through, which door to knock on or call at through the fly-wire. Our house had three different 'back' doors, two of which were actually 'side', facing south off different chunks, from different architectural eras, of the house. The third was the main traffic thoroughfare; friends and family knew it, and other locals found it easily by instinct. These, too, were standard Yorke Peninsula arrangements; perhaps farmhouses throughout Australia, or indeed the world over, are the same.

David Malouf muses about the typical Brisbane house, the breezy Queenslander with its mysterious and suggestive 'under-the-house' spaces and the sorts of psyches they might produce in children who grow up there. If, as he hypothesises, Queenslanders visualise the unconscious itself as the space under the house, full of stored belongings, sexual mysteries and animals nobody recognises, perhaps the farmhouse psyche is one firmly centred in foursquare stone, but otherwise unknowing of its own haphazard architecture, and boasting an embarrassment of ambiguous doors. And what of the difficulty encountered by strangers in broaching such a house, after it looked so easy and straightforward from a distance? Might that shape the pattern and direct the flow of relationships and communications with other people, or require that there already be a sense of shared community understanding about the conventions of visiting and the inner lives of houses?

And out in the country, if the house (or the self) was in an ongoing state of haphazard expansion, there was no surrounding suburb to contain or circumscribe it, to colour it with connotations and assumptions. In conversations with urban friends about growing up in cities, the discussion turns again and again on suburbs. You need to have lived in the city concerned to understand what is really being said when someone says 'I grew up in Marrickville'; what micro-nuance of vowel sound and plosive will identify an ingrained Medindie accent to an Adelaidian; why either a childhood spent in Peppermint Grove (on the one hand) or a childhood spent in Altona (on the other) might produce an adult in whom certain kinds of anxieties cannot be allayed. Suburbs, like all nations but the island ones, have borders, and the self is defined by identification of its difference from what lies across them.

But the word 'peninsula', says the OED, means 'almost an island'. 'A piece of land that is almost an island, being nearly surrounded by water; hence, any piece of land projecting into the sea so that its boundary is mainly coast-line.' And islands have no borders, only coasts. An island produces a strong clear sense of identity, of the boundaries of self, but without the aggression and rejection implicit in the identification of difference. As the islander's skin is to the body, so the beach is to the sense of local identity; ego boundaries are benign and clearly drawn, and the associations are with peacefulness and play.

Peninsulas, as the dictionary says, are almost like this. But you're not quite 'insula', never actually cut off. It's a pleasantly ambivalent state, a balance of security and independence; you have those clear aquamarine boundaries and that autonomy of being, but you can still claim to be mainland. It's like being a breathing newborn babe whose umbilical cord has not yet been cut. To get to Adelaide from Yorke Peninsula, you follow the clear black line on the map that marks the coast road north to the apex of St Vincent's Gulf, and then you turn around and head back the way you came, down the other side of the gulf.

And, as with the hidden mysteries of farmhouse doors, there's something inherently comic about having to drive over two hundred kilometres in order to get to a place less than a third of that distance away across the water. A clear and secure sense of absurdity, I sometimes think, is Yorke Peninsula's defining legacy. You grow up safe in the knowledge that you are firmly connected by that strong black thread of road to your fellow beings, to the city, and beyond that, to the great world. But that security is coloured by a cheerful acceptance of the fact that you'll always have to go the long way round in order to get where you want to go, and that, when you do arrive, you may not be able to get in.

David Malouf

The South

David Malouf was
recently awarded the
Neustadt International
Literary Prize. His latest
book is the collection of
short stories *Dream
Stuff* (Vintage).

On a soft, sunlit morning in March 1959, just a few days before my
twenty-fifth birthday, I stood at the rails of an Italian liner, the
Fairsky, and after a five-weeks sea-voyage that had taken me via
Singapore, Colombo, Bombay, Aden and Port Said, saw the Bay of
Naples open before me, and utterly familiar in the distance the dark
slopes and scooped-out cone of Vesuvius – all just as I had always
imaged it, like the breaking of a dream.

I had come from the actual south, and for all those weeks had
been sailing north-north-west up the globe. But geography, even when
we experience it as day after day of looking out on empty ocean and sky,
so that distance brings itself home to us as time measured out as
children express it, in sleeps and mealtimes – that sort of geography is
less convincing somehow than the one we carry in our heads. For me,
arriving in Naples after all those weeks of travelling north, was an
arrival at last in the *south*, the true south. Not the city I had grown up
in, down there below Capricorn, which was really just another version
of Dundee, but the south that Goethe was in touch with when he
tapped his poems out on the shoulder of a girl he had just spent the
night with. The naked south. The classical south. The pagan south.

That south of the spirit, at the furthest pole from Brisbane or Dundee, where the body rules – that ideal state we call 'Italy'.

I had already been there in books. In Forster's *Where Angels Fear To Tread* and *A Room with a View,* in Norman Douglas's *South Wind,* and in poems by Shelley and Keats and Byron and Auden and August von Platen – whose poems I knew through an essay of Thomas Mann. I had caught the breath of it in the works of composers from the deep north, pieces in which lives lived in the cramped world of trolls and kobolds and cod-liver oil and clocks, and the severest notions of discipline and duty, had for a time moved to a more exultant rhythm – pieces called *Souvenir de Florence* and *Harold in Italy* and *Aus Italien.* Now, suddenly, there it was to be walked into, a world of vines climbing up ten-foot poles, oranges hanging among glossy leaves, 'das Land wo die Citronen blühn'. All open and inviting – dinning with car-horns and voices out of Donizetti, and the promise of a naked shoulder in bed to tap out poems on, the dactyls and spondees of pagan elegies beyond the reach of hymns.

The world of the south, through the long dark period of Christian fear and loathing of the flesh, had somehow kept touch with a pagan view of the body as essentially innocent and good, and it was this that Goethe discovered and had taken home with him from his Italian journey, to quicken the expectations but also the senses of his compatriots. Armed like him with a sketchpad (Goethe had brought back over a thousand drawings of what Italy had revealed to him), they set off in their hundreds for Florence, Rome, Sicily and a world they believed where pleasure, spontaneous joy in the flesh, was legitimised by a tradition going back, on the same soil and under the same blue skies, to remote antiquity.

One gets a good idea of what they were fleeing from in Grünewald's great altarpiece at Colmar, one of the most impressive but also one of the most extreme expressions of Northern feeling. The big-boned bulk of the crucified Christ, with its ape-like arms and taloned, immense feet, is half shaggy brute and half grounded sky-creature that has been spread-eagled and plucked, its dark meat already rotting. Nowhere in Italian painting do we get such a view of the body, such disgust at its grossness, such a violation of its grace and dignity. Italian

Christs are lean Apollonian figures or classical athletes. The men who are nailing them to the cross are ordinary workmen. Not grinners and sadists but fellows doing a job and with their own sober dignity. The body is never brutalised or mangled, it is never dead meat. In its composed agony it glows from within with the assurance of resurrection. The proof of the body's triumph is that even on the cross its beauty, which is the visible form of its innocence, remains of its very nature inviolable, untouched.

So there it was, Italy: still there, even in 1959. Laid out in all its seductiveness before yet another pilgrim from the world of gloomy fogs as Goethe puts it – even if, in my case, the fogs were metaphorical. With its stacks of oranges and lemons in dark little caverns off the steps in every side-street, its up-turned flagstones and war-time rubble, its barefoot urchins selling dirty postcards from Pompeii and contraband Lucky Strikes, it was utterly of the moment, the Here and Now, no missing that. But it was also, since that is what I, along with Goethe and so many others wanted it to be, the fulfilment of a dream, another and freer mode of being. It was second breath, a new life. Most of all, it was the centre of things, the Mediterranean, the shining middle-point of our world; the world, I mean, of the imagination – Venus Andomene rising naked from the sea, the *fons Bandusiae* and the fountain of Arethusa, the entrance to the underworld out by the lake of Avernus (a place you could take a bus to), the cave of the Cumean sibyl, and the sort of frenzied dance that can cure a spider's bite.

Ten years later I published a set of poems on the South and what it meant to those of us who had come, early and late, from the real or notional north. This is one of them. It is called 'After Baedeker'.

Descend out of the mist, hangover
of a decade of divisions, let it be holy wars, the break-up
of a marriage, a career. Step
through to a middle period like Goethe's, putting the nine points of
   the Alps
      between
you and the wolves

and sad-eyed *Wunderkinder*. You must break
all ties with the gothic
north, its kobolds, drill-squares, pogroms,
baths. The first lake
offers you yourselves
in a summer breathing-space, the spider's poison
will teach you to dance.
Here time is another country, old age
is possible, tombs
are a form of architecture. Enter their silence
in groups: a wall of pious skulls that glow, deep cellarage
under vines and barley-sheaves,
the heels of children playing at blind-man's-buff,
a nave stretching from Dante's
exile to the opening of *Hernani*. Shake
the dust from your clothes and screw
your eyes up in the sun. Take a glass
of grappa among pimps and lemon-squeezers, the passage easy
here into afternoon or an old man's passionate lyricism.
On their climb to Fiesole
the Germans capture nothing
with their sketchpads of the play
of light on terraced hills. Twelve years later
in the blue dusk of Hamburg, the whole unlikely organism
flares, the landscape shimmers and ascends in an unsheathing
of wings. Posing on worn sarcophagi
among poppies, we have the look
– unbuttoned, ill-at-ease – of the eternal
tourist. The long-jawed locals do it better
in their dark museums. On terracotta couches two by two
between meals, they smile at something over our shoulder:
the present. Un-otherworldly.
At any moment poised for eternity.

Later again I owned a small house in Tuscany – Southern
Tuscany, the wild, unfashionable bit – and learned a little of what it

was like to test my dream of the south against the reality of living with it for seven days a week, among *contadini*, small land-owning peasants, who turned out to be even less Catholic and more pagan than I had believed, but also more earthily unromantic. 'Maladetti Toscani' as Malaparte called them, 'bloody Tuscans', with their wickedly reductive sense of humour and a good strong dash of cynicism about such matters as the durability of love, the importance of money and the good intentions of ordinary men and women as opposed to saints, about whom they were on the whole humorously condescending. This was the real Italy.

There's a delightful moment early on in Donizetti's *The Elixir of Love* when Italian attitudes to love and living are set sharply against the more sentimental and – as the generous-spirited but hard-headed little heroine of that opera, Adina, sees it – bizarre views of the north.

She's reading an old book of romances. She bursts out laughing. 'Goodness me,' she exclaims, 'what a silly story!'

'What is it?' the other girls demand. 'What's the joke?'

'It's this story I'm reading,' Adina tells them. 'Of Queen Iseult and Tristan's magic potion.' Adina is too down-to-earth, too ironical, too *Italian*, to take such stuff seriously. Love philtres, love deaths.

Of course there are forces in the world that really do work like magic on people and change the way they feel. One of them is money. Nemorino, the naïve young peasant of the opera, who is in love with Adina, is astonished to discover how attractive he has become after drinking just a few drops of 'the love potion of Queen Iseult', as he calls it, that he has acquired from the travelling quack, Dulcamara – in fact, it's a quite ordinary bottle of Burgundy. Suddenly every girl in the village is in love with him.

What he does not know is that news has arrived that his uncle is dead. Nemorino, his heir, has become a rich landowner.

That's one elixir. Another, as Adina tries to tell him, is soft-headed dreaminess and wishful thinking. But another again, as she herself discovers, is real sympathy as it lets itself out in a tender glance, a smile, a furtive tear. Genuine feeling can be unexpected, it springs straight from the heart, but it also keeps its feet on the ground, and it proves itself, not in extravagant gestures like the threat of suicide or by rushing off as a soldier to seek an early death, but in the living. It might make a nice demonstration of the difference between north and south in these matters, the real south, but also the north as the south conceives it, if opera companies gave Donizetti's warm-hearted and clear-headed little comedy, and Wagner's soulful study of the joys of dissolution, on alternate nights.

The Alps, that giant wall of rock and ice thrown up by a beneficent nature to divide the continent, seems less like a barrier between warring empires than a demarcation line between modes of being, forms of feeling, that are very nearly irreconcilable. 'Love is not the same in Bologna as it is in Königsberg,' writes Stendhal in his wonderful *Life of Rossini*. 'Love in Italy is more dynamic, more impatient, more violent, less dependent on dreams and imagination. It is not a gentle and gradual tide which sweeps slowly, but for all eternity, into the farthest reaches of the soul.'

This comes from the part of his book where he is attempting to define the difference between Rossini's genius and Mozart's. Mozart's music is essentially melancholic, a matter of soul, with the power as Stendhal puts it, 'to sweep away the dreaming, contemplative spirits of this world…and fill their souls with sad, haunting visions; the soul seems directly invaded, drenched as it were, in wave upon wave of melancholy'.

'Soul' is not a concept we need to invoke in speaking of Rossini. Rossini's sphere is the social, he is always good company – spirited, light, amusing – and Stendhal loves him as we all do. His lightness is tonic. We need him. But he has none of the 'profound spiritual qualities' we find in Mozart.

What Stendhal is pointing to is the very German inwardness of Mozart's music, its reaching always for what is authentic and eternal in the realm of feeling. What is 'amusing' in Rossini is his free-handed rejection of seriousness. What is miraculous in him is the way his inexhaustible energy and invention raises what in others would be merely superficial to the level of pure spirit. It is this Italian genius for mercurial lightness and inconsequence that the great Mozart lacks.

What then of the collaboration between Mozart and his Italian librettist da Ponte? Doesn't that strike the perfect balance, isn't it the perfect marriage, not simply of words and music but of the otherwise irreconcilable spirits of North and South?

Perhaps. But not quite perfect, surely, when we consider the lengths opera directors are forced to, in the case of *Cosí Fan Tutte*, to gloss over the heartlessness of da Ponte's libretto and make tolerable its 'happy' ending.

Da Ponte's plot is a machine for demonstrating the fickleness, the superficiality, not simply of women's affections but of lovers in general. Feelings, even the strongest, are in their nature volatile and not to be taken seriously. Love is essentially ridiculous.

All this will do very well for the cynical Don Alfonso, and for Despina, and might do well enough for Rossini; but a world of feigned feelings and self-deception, or at the best, sentimental self-delusion, will not do for Mozart. He is incapable of writing an aria that *feigns* feeling. From the first breath a singer takes the feeling is real. It ravishes, it wounds, it expresses the whole person. A Fiordiligi or a Fernando are changed forever by what their newly-discovered feelings reveal to them. Living as Mozart conceives it is continuous. What has been felt, taken into the soul, has a continuing power, and consequences that cannot be dismissed. Let in true feeling, as Mozart does, let in the irrationalism of real sexual attraction, and da Ponte's comedy, which is intended to be painless because nothing in it is really *felt*, becomes a work that can have no satisfactory ending – and certainly not the one that da Ponte planned. The characters have learned too much, about themselves and one another, about the true nature of feeling, to go back to being the conventional couples they were at the start.

Da Ponte lived for nearly fifty years after the time he spent as Mozart's collaborator (he did not die until 1833). He had already lived a good half-dozen of his nine lives before they met. Born a Jew and converted in his childhood to Catholicism, he had been a priest and a professor of literature in Italy, and had established himself in Vienna as a poet and Casanova-like libertine. Constantly making and remaking himself, he slipped from one life to another in the early years of the new century, in London, in Holland, in London again; then, in 1808, took the big leap and emigrated to New York where he was for a time a grocer. (Can we imagine a similar transformation for his great collaborator? Mozart as an immigrant iron-monger in Baltimore?) At last, in 1825, he became the inaugural Professor of Italian at Columbia, and when opera arrived in New York, in the form of a company led by the tenor Manuel Garcia, it was on da Ponte's advice, as the local expert, that the first work to be performed professionally on American soil was the *Barber of Seville*, with Garcia singing Almaviva, as he had done at the première nine years before. Rossini, not Mozart.

What are we to make of this odd disloyalty? Was da Ponte being modest? I doubt it. Or had he recognised in Rossini that true spirit of lightness that his poor friend from Salzburg had somehow failed to catch?

Speaking of migrations – I have long since returned to the *actual* south where I began.

In these last decades, virtually everywhere, from Toronto and Stockholm to Sydney, has taken as its model of the good life some version of Mediterranean, though clearly it is a style that suits some places better than others. My hometown no longer feels like Dundee.

A hundred and fifty years ago, the first Governor of the new state of Queensland, Sir George Bowen, a scholar of Greek who had climbed all three classical peaks, Etna, Parnassus and Olympus, regularly presented his southern fiefdom to his masters back at the Colonial Office in classical terms. '*Your* town,' he writes to Lord Cardwell, 'lies in a position analogous to Thermopylae; that is, at the north end of the Australian Epirus.' The climate of his little capital at Brisbane he recommends as being 'very like that of Naples'. It is, and so these days is the city itself, at least to the extent that its citizens have become coffee- and wine-drinkers and like to eat their pasta, and drink their *lattes* and *macchiatos*, at sidewalk cafés under umbrellas in the sun. No need any longer to take a six-weeks sea-journey, or even a twenty-two hour plane trip, to find the spiritual but utterly pagan and fleshly south. It has come to us.

This is the slightly modified transcript of a talk given on BBC radio on 8 August 2000, in the interval of a London Proms concert, in a series under the general title of 'The South'.

Anthony Lawrence
Gathering Pine Cones

Below where the yellowtailed wind has come through,
beaked and seasonal, loud and crested with intention,
we stand in a panel of early coastal light, on a carpet
of amber needles. Ignoring the possum skull I hold aloft,
you proffer two cones – one sealed and green,
the other open, grey, your fingers working deep
between its weather-telling scales. You study them
in turn, as if the decision to keep or discard
were an act of balance, weight, asperity.
    I have no measure of the calm deliberations
            you bring to the earth's found poetry.
When you say the only name you have for me,
with its rising inflection that never fails to disarm
and engage, when you offer up both cones, understanding
dies out like the nerve-ends of pine stems overhead.
Driving here, I saw how a single crow can change
harrowed, alluvial soil, giving its peaks and hollows
the shape of wind-blown, inland water. I told you this,
and you responded with your face pressed hard
into travelling glass, watching the crow fall and settle.
Now, when I ask if you can hear the waves, you turn
and point to the dunes before moving towards them,
dressed for the cold in a swagger that would be
at home on deck, on a solo cruise, in big water.
I have used the voice of a teaching man too often.

When I reach you, my hand is taken, and I lose
the need for description, breaking open, without warning,
into one part of the long preparation for our lives
– to be honest in each moment – and you go with me,
looking into or beyond me, one hand in the air,
one hand tugging at my trousers as I cry.

The Sleep of a Learning Man

When I woke my body
    was idling, my teeth
vibrating like small change
    in a truck ash tray.
There was much to consider
    lying there in the dark
beside my son, who was
    sleeping with his legs
tucked under his chest
    as he did in the daguerreo-
type images we saw
    of someone doing a knee-tuck
under a shifting film
    of blood grains.
Too late for sleep, I tried
    to imagine other positions
a scanned and floating boy
    might assume, and why
I was humming to my bones
    in bed. I turned over
to the right shoulder, lifted
    my head, and looked into it.
I saw a puzzle of coils.
    I heard a valve pump
labouring to clear

its body-feeding lines.
Whatever my son said then
    as he breathed and moved
into another position
    and name for sleep
held words of comfort,
    and I found myself
drifting from thoughts
    of a troubled heart
into what his first sentence
    would sound like, what
it might contain, and when
    it would surface, there
on the open border
    of his second language –
words with the ability
    to calm himself and the fitful
sleep of a learning man.

Hill End, 1963

What I remember most is the terrible thirst, in that heat
    crackling underfoot and in the air,
the rocks and trees shape-changing as I went among them
    with my father and his brother –
one a classer of wool, inspector of wheat and manager
    of rural personnel – the other
a retired professor of things earthed and aerial – shells
    and minerals, birds, the under-
sides of enemy planes. It should have been enough
    to follow them into the open-
plan maps of their prospecting heads, to find the exposed
    dry ice of quartz, to watch
as they scraped and levered, unearthed and made ready
    to enter the stone for what
it might contain. I went with them into the Latin names
    for dead and living things,
hearing stories of free-standing nuggets, of how luck
    is a science demanding years
of study, how gold can be found where the trained eye falls.
    And when they hammered
pegs into the earth, and fenced the claim with string,
    the sky over Hill End
came close,with trees dissolving into it, their branches lit
    with a loud second-growth
of cicada wings. Around me, voices and wind, the tread-
    marks of boots, the uncertain
tap of hammers on the skins of stones. I waited for thirst

to leave me, but each thought
turned to water until, with the stroke of the sun in my head,
    I sat down, within and beyond
myself, and I saw how my father was gesturing in silence
    from a square of pegged
and gleaming ground, his face now furred, now feathered.
    I've been told a number
of versions and times of what happened out there
    in the bush at Hill End –
how we staked out a claim with potential for gold,
    how my father discovered
a true friend in his brother…Now, I know more
    of what occurred that day:
something announced itself and set snares behind my eyes –
    something formal and free,
troubling and instructive. Thirst was all that mattered, then,
    and need was a fearful thing.
It still is, though it has other forms and names, and I
    summon them when I can,
from the mapless regions of the head. When I say *heat*,
    solitude, gold, amazement,
I return to my body with the makings of new poetry.

Anthony Lawrence's most recent collection is *Skinned by Light: New & Selected Poems.* His first novel, *In the Half Light,* was published by Picador in 2000. These poems are from a sequence that won this year's Josephine Ulrick Poetry Prize.

Peter Holbrook

Poetry and Sadness

With rue my heart is laden
For golden friends I had,
For many a rose-lipt maiden
And many a light-foot lad.

By brooks too broad for leaping
The light-foot boys are laid;
The rose-lipt girls are sleeping
In fields where roses fade.

A.E. HOUSMAN, *A Shropshire Lad* (1896)

Somewhere I acquired the belief that the truest poetry is the most sad – that it is what Milton called his elegy 'Lycidas': a 'melodious tear'. Shelley said: 'Our sweetest songs are those that tell of saddest thought'. I agree with Shelley. In fact, I find it difficult to think any other way about poetry.

My mother used to read aloud Alfred Noyes's 'The Highwayman'. No doubt its tender, tragic atmosphere helped form my notion of poetry. The highwayman passionately farewells 'the landlord's black-eyed daughter', Bess:

He rose upright in the stirrups. He scarce could reach her hand,
But she loosened her hair in the casement. His face burnt like a brand
As the black cascade of perfume came tumbling over his breast;
And he kissed its waves in the moonlight,
    (O, sweet black waves in the moonlight!)
Then he tugged at his rein in the moonlight, and galloped away to the west.

Later 'King George's men' shoot the highwayman dead when, suicidally, he returns to Bess.

With its inn, red-coats, and so on, this is a very English poem. But I'm struck by how natural 'The Highwayman' appeared to me in Melbourne's southeastern suburbs in the 1970s. Perhaps it chimed with the vaguely 'poetic' pathos that often pervades adolescence.

The Melbourne of that time is rapidly becoming a period: turning into The Past, fragmenting into images and sensations – Sunday afternoon's tedium; wandering for hours through quiet streets; smouldering autumn leaves in gutters. My father had an excellent voice, and on summer nights in our garden or on the verandah would drink a lot of beer, wine, or brandy, or anything else he could find, and recite poems and sing 'Danny Boy' and other songs. Sometimes his sister sang 'The Linden Tree'. In the dark it was hard to see Dad – as if he were becoming invisible, being taken away on the powerful current of some black destructive river, and his voice and the tip of his cigarette were like signals from afar. 'Danny Boy' recalled his brother Jacky, killed in action in New Guinea. This brother haunted our house. At my grandmother's, photos of he and Dad, both in uniform, made a miniature Shrine of Remembrance on top of the pianola.

'But O the heavy change, now thou art gone,/ Now thou art gone, and never must return!' Those lines from 'Lycidas', about a youth 'dead ere his prime', sum up my conception of poetry. Poetry and loss go together – people often mean by 'poetic' a feeling of gentle sadness. I at least can't think of anything more poetic than the high, doomed eloquence of Richard II:

Let's talk of graves, of worms, and epitaphs,
Make dust our paper, and with rainy eyes
Write sorrow on the bosom of the earth...
For God's sake, let us sit upon the ground,
And tell sad stories of the death of kings...

The key thing for Richard is not to *do* anything – it's lovely instead to give oneself up to such sadness. Of course, his outpouring here strikes many as hysterical and self-indulgent. In Chaucer's *Knight's Tale* 'Olde fader Egeus' strikes a graver note: 'This world nys but a thurghfare ful of wo,/ And we been pilgrymes, passynge to and fro./ Deeth is an ende of every worldy soore'. That's better, perhaps: weightier, more philosophic than Richard. But both characters utter the tragic wisdom which for me, like it or not, is poetry's 'essence'.

At first glance Wordsworth doesn't seem to fit very well into my roll-call of poetic sad-sacks. He is so healthy-minded, in William James's sense: believing in the essential goodness of things. (James compared healthy-mindedness with the outlook of the 'sick soul' in *The Varieties of Religious Experience* [1902].) Wordsworth is totally unneurotic. Like Montaigne or Nietzsche he sees nothing to regret in his life and is full of thanks for the blessings bestowed on him. But he is sensitive to pain and his happiness (as in the 'Immortality' ode) often boils down to fortitude in the face of loss, a will to find compensation: 'The things which I have seen I now can see no more./...there hath pass'd away a glory from the earth./...We will grieve not, rather find/ Strength in what remains behind.' Just as Shakespeare associates music with sadness ('I am never merry when I hear sweet music' – Jessica in *The Merchant of Venice*), Wordsworth couples poetry with it. In 'The Solitary

Reaper' Wordsworth hears a farm girl's simple song. He can't discern its content, but it stays with him. He wonders whether it concerns 'old, unhappy, far-off things' or 'Some natural sorrow, loss, or pain, / That has been, and may be again'. In 'Resolution and Independence' he famously links the poetic career with catastrophe: 'We Poets in our youth begin in gladness;/ But thereof come in the end despondency and madness'.

No matter how much my father had drunk, he never muffed a line when reciting Edgar Allen Poe's 'The Raven'. In many ways his life was unhappy. He was a part-time actor but his career never took off. He did a lot of radio drama in Melbourne in the forties and fifties and, later, got small parts in TV crime shows like *Homicide* and *Division 4*, as well as doing lots of TV ads that brought in plenty of 'dough', as he called it (Dad loved the lingo, dress, and manner of Hollywood tough-guys like Humphrey Bogart.) However, he never became the person he wanted to be: a fine, acclaimed actor. I'm not sure why he didn't pursue heart and soul what he should have done – being an actor – or why he settled for a crushing, dull job he hated. But I do know things hadn't turned out the way he wanted. He lost an adored brother and throughout his life struggled with alcohol. (He once did an ad for Fosters beer having only recently left a drying-out facility.) So I think that when Dad recited 'The Raven', the dramatic intensity with which he imbued Poe's words about hopeless desire and sorrow came in part from his own disappointment:

...vainly I had sought to borrow
From my books surcease of sorrow – sorrow for the lost Lenore –
For the rare and radiant maiden whom the angels name Lenore –
Nameless *here* for evermore.

Edmund Gosse said A.E. Housman (1859–1936) was the poet of 'the unconquerable longing for what is gone for ever'. I didn't read Housman until after leaving home, even though he was one of my mother's favourite poets. But when I encountered him I found a melancholy I recognised at once. Orwell said Housman was an adolescent's writer, so his poetry may simply have reminded me of being a teenager. But he is also an exceedingly sad poet – the saddest in English. He only wrote, he said, when 'out of sorts', which means he subscribed to what I'll call the 'Ivanov Theory of Poetic Creation', after Chekhov's despairing neurotic: 'The only thing left for me' says Ivanov – he shoots himself at the end of the play – 'is to write poetry'. Housman's topics, not least dead young soldiers, were familiar to me:

East and west on fields forgotten
  Bleach the bones of comrades slain,
Lovely lads and dead and rotten;
  None that go return again.

One can escape the pain of loss through alcohol. But in Housman it's as if death is the cure for life itself, which is by nature tragic. When his sister's son was killed in Flanders in 1915, Housman sent her a poem depicting a soldier in his grave:

Oh dark is the chamber and lonely,
  And lights and companions depart;
But lief will he lose them and only
  Behold the desire of his heart.

And low is the roof, but it covers
  A sleeper content to repose;
And far from his friends and his lovers
  He lies with the sweetheart he chose.

In this poem 'lads are in love with the grave'. The soldier's 'sweetheart', 'the desire of his heart', is death itself, which is darkly seductive – notice the echo in 'love'/'grave'. Housman thought poetry should 'harmonise the sadness of the universe': see it as beautiful and deep rather than just repulsive, silly, or wrong. We can call this very well-known, morbid attitude Hamletism: we love Hamlet *because* he is a failure, and are bored by Fortinbras's success. (Walt Whitman declared *Hamlet* unsuited to a democracy because it slackened the nerves and encouraged defeatism.)

Recently, in *Death, Desire, and Loss in Western Culture* (Penguin,

1998), Jonathan Dollimore argues that Western civilisation has made a fateful equation between profundity and melancholy. Dollimore notices the oddity of something we rather take for granted: that 'the most revered of all Western aesthetic genres' – tragedy – provides 'metaphysical reassurance that…failure is ultimately inevitable'. His analysis recalls William James's, who thought the sick soul identifies sadness with wisdom, supposing that 'the evil aspects of our life are of its very essence, and that the world's meaning most comes home to us when we lay them most to our heart'. To this type 'healthy-mindedness pure and simple seems unspeakably blind and shallow'. Reading Dollimore makes you realise how much of its metaphysics the sick soul derives from the Bible and tragedy. (Years ago G. Wilson Knight condemned Hamlet as a 'soul…sick to death'; Dollimore shows how the play – like Keats later – eroticises death as 'a consummation devoutly to be wished'.)

Housman, too, is in love with 'easeful death'. His most recent editor, Archie Burnett, has shown the presence in Housman's poems of the wisdom of Ecclesiastes and Job – the view of life that issues in the desire for death because 'all is vanity and vexation of spirit'. The Chorus in *Oedipus at Colonus* expresses the same wish (I quote from Housman's jaunty translation):

Thy portion esteem I highest,
    Who wast not ever begot;
Thine next, being born who diest
    And straightway again art not.

(Note the suppressed rhyme 'rot' in these terminations of Housman's: we are begot, rot, are not.) Dollimore sees the Western (Christian) desire for 'eternal life' as a concealed longing for death: that is, for cessation of that very mutability which is life. That longing is central to Housman.

In a lecture, 'The Name and Nature of Poetry', Housman invoked the lyrical, sad Shakespeare of the songs as a touchstone for determining poetic merit. His own poems often allude to *Cymbeline*'s 'Fear no more the heat o' th' sun':

Fear no more the heat o' th' sun,
    Nor the furious winter's rages.
Thou thy worldly task hast done,
    Home art gone and ta'en thy wages.
Golden lads and girls all must,
    As chimney-sweepers, come to dust.

According to Burnett, Housman thought this a peak of 'lyrical achieve-ment'. Certainly Shakespeare specialises in a line of quaint, picturesque sadness Housman liked. Writing in 1858, Walter Bagehot recognised a 'constitutional though latent melancholy' as Shakespeare's 'excep-tional characteristic': 'all through his works', he wrote, 'you feel you are reading the popular author, the successful man; but through them all there is a certain tinge of musing sadness pervading, and, as it were, softening their gaiety'. Housman's own effect of comely sadness owes something to Shakespeare. Think of Cordelia in *King Lear* –

          You have seen
Sunshine and rain at once: her smiles and tears
Were like a better way. Those happy smilets,
That play'd on her ripe lip, seem'd not to know
What guests were in her eyes, which parted thence,
As pearls from diamonds dropp'd. In brief,
Sorrow would be a rarity most beloved,
If all could so become it.

– or Leontes's reconciliation with Polixenes in *The Winter's Tale*: 'their joy waded in tears'. Housman admired the sweet, 'poetical' pathos of the songs: 'Come away, come away, death/ And in sad cypress let me be laid'; 'Take, O take those lips away'; 'Let us all ring fancy's knell: / I'll begin it – Ding, dong, bell./ *Ding, dong, bell.*' There's no such thing as the 'essential Shakespeare' – he is myriad-minded, as Coleridge said – but, like Housman, I find delicate pathos a Shakespearian signature:

        She never told her love,
But let concealment, like a worm i th' bud

Feed on her damask cheek. She pin'd in thought;
And with a green and yellow melancholy
She sat like Patience on a monument;
Smiling at grief.

Viola's speech gives *Twelfth Night* one element – exquisite melancholy – in its rich atmosphere. I take this melancholy to be identical to Housman's melting sadness, though it must never be forgotten that there is a mordant strain in his verse as well ('A lad that lives and has his will/ Is worth a dozen dead' says a successful lover of his dead rival). What's more, Housman sends up his own 'moping melancholy' at the end of *A Shropshire Lad*: 'But oh, good Lord, the verse you make,/ It gives a chap the belly-ache'.

Because he writes so perfectly you're disposed to give in to Housman's serene lulling pathos. But I now think his poetry is the siren's call. Indeed, his own example of 'perfect' poetry is Samuel Daniel's 'Ulysses and the Siren', first published in 1605. The Siren urges Ulysses to cease striving:

Come, worthy Greek, Ulysses, come,
    Possess these shores with me:
The winds and seas are troublesome,
    And here we may be free.
Here may we sit and view their toil
    That travail in the deep,
And joy the day in mirth the while,
    And spend the night in sleep.

Compare *Shropshire Lad* VII – one of the most sinister poems ever written. Early one morning the speaker strides out whistling 'to ploughing… / beside [his] team'. But a 'blackbird in the coppice', eyeing him,'replie[s]' to his whistling:

Lie down, lie down, young yeoman;
    What use to rise and rise?
Rise man a thousand mornings

Yet down at last he lies,
And then the man is wise.

The ploughman sees the bird's 'yellow bill' and angrily flings a stone at it: 'Then the bird was still.' But –

Then my soul within me
  Took up the blackbird's strain,
And still beside the horses
  Along the dewy lane
  It sang the song again:

'Lie down, lie down, young yeoman;
  The sun moves always west;
The road one treads to labour
  Will lead one home to rest,
  And that will be the best.'

Frightening it may be, but the poem is also extraordinarily self-conscious, commenting on Housman's own Hamlet-like weariness of life. Like the ploughman, Housman's poetry has internalised the blackbird's wish for release from existence. In *Shropshire Lad* LXIII he declares his unfashionable poems are 'flowers' that go 'unheeded': their 'hue was not the wear'. Nevertheless, 'luckless lads will wear them/ When I am dead and gone.' This is terrible – as if Housman is cursing his own readers.

Housman's charming, song-like poems express a dreadful resignation:

And bound for the same bourn as I,
On every road I wandered by,
Trod beside me, close and dear,
The beautiful and death-struck year.

(Burnett notes the echo of *Hamlet*: 'The undiscovered country from whose bourn/ No traveller returns'.) In Housman, death is 'The Merry

Guide' and 'the land to which I travel,/ The far dwelling...' His 'Athlete Dying Young' is now 'Townsman of a stiller town'. And the dead in his poems look funny and stiff as they 'lie' (his invariable word) under ground. Human existence is inescapably unfulfilling; death a welcome relief, a calm dark quiet house, with a 'sill of shade' and a 'low lintel'.

Housman lets us look back and indulge our feeling for what has been lost. And this loss – 'The happy highways where I went/ And cannot come again', or 'hearts of gold' left behind – is always mixed with the quaint pretty Shakespearian melodiousness. Here is one of my very favourite poets – but I have come to be wary of him.

I'll close with Montaigne, who refused to think melancholy deep:

No man is more free from this passion than I, for I neither love nor regard it: albeit the world hath undertaken, as it were upon covenant, to grace it with a particular favour. Therewith they adorne age, vertue, and conscience. O foolish and base ornament! The Italians have more properly with its name entitled malignitie: for, it is a qualitie ever hurtfull, ever sottish.

Peter Holbrook teaches English at the University of Queensland.

Quotations from Housman are from the wonderful edition by Archie Burnett (Oxford, 1997).

John Dale

On Smoking

John Dale's *Huckstepp: A Dangerous Life* was published in 2000 by Allen and Unwin. He teaches in the Faculty of Humanities at UTS.

My uncle died at the weekend. He had emphysema and pulmonary oedema and for the last three years had been kept alive by an oxygen cylinder which stood in the corner of his bedroom. He was sixty four. Although I had seen him rarely since I moved to Sydney, I remember him as a good-humoured man who loved cricket and tennis, and wore sports shirts and navy blazers. In every photograph I've seen of him he is tanned with a cigarette burning between his fingers.

When I was eleven he flew down to Hobart to star in an advertisement shot at one of the newer hotels overlooking the river. For years after, whenever that ad appeared on television, my sisters and I would run in to watch Uncle Arch on the small screen. We saw him chatting to a younger woman with shiny lipstick and a headful of gorgeous hair. Although we must have seen that ad a dozen times, I don't recall my uncle ever talking, only the orchestra music playing, while he flips open a pack of Benson and Hedges, peels off the silver foil, and the woman's long manicured fingers reach over the cocktails to ease out a cigarette. The woman slides it between her shiny red lips, a waiter appears alongside and with a click of his lighter fires both their cigarettes. My uncle and this woman inhale deeply, smiling at each other with the satisfaction of shared pleasure.

It was simple but effective advertising I guess, for both my sisters and I took up smoking early. I started on Marlboros at thirteen and then moved up to Viscounts at fourteen. For a while I tried Courtleighs. I bought an imitation silver cigarette case from Coles and used to keep my ration in it until I lost the case at football practice. In my last year of high school I began smoking a pipe at the weekends and, though it seems hard to believe now, none of the other boys found the sight of a fifteen-year-old puffing away on a clay pipe strange. It was only when my tongue developed blisters from the cracked stem that I gave the pipe away to a younger kid down the road and went back to buying cigarettes or begging them from relatives. All my friends smoked and there was a serious edge to our habit as if this were a secret duty imposed on us by the adult world.

When I moved to Sydney to live I dropped in to visit my uncle one time. He was out the front of his unit mowing his lawn and the smell of cut grass hung in the air. For some reason he didn't invite me indoors; he had no children and a much younger wife, and I was driving an old yellow Holden with a mattress in the back. We leaned our elbows on his low wooden fence and talked a little and, as I was about to leave, my uncle, happy that his only nephew had come to visit, went inside and came out with a carton of Benson and Hedges. He tore open that carton and pressed two packs of cigarettes into my hands and said how great it was to see me, and if I phoned in advance next time, maybe we could do something.

My father flew up for the funeral on Monday. I found him standing at the carousel waiting for his piece of luggage, a curl of blue smoke drifting over his right shoulder. In the car I said to him, 'I thought you'd given up smoking.'

'I have,' he said.

'Didn't I see you smoking back at the terminal?

'Not me, you didn't.' My father gave his head a firm shake. 'I haven't touched a cigarette in years.'

I wasn't sure now if I had actually seen the cigarette in his hand or just imagined it. We drove to the crematorium in silence, while

I glanced over at him from time to time as if I might catch him out. When I first quit cigarettes ten years ago the first thing I re-discovered was the power of smell. I could detect cigarette smoke in my father's sweat and in his hair and clothes. Even in the toilet after he'd used it. At the crematorium my father placed a framed photograph of his brother in police uniform on top of the sealed coffin. Orchestra music started playing and the coffin disappeared through a curtain. Standing in the grey light afterwards, I watched my father comfort his brother's wife. She called me over and took off her sun-glasses and looked me up and down. She told me how pleased she was to see me, that my uncle used to talk about me sometimes, tell her I was a lot like him. She gave my arm a squeeze and I went and stood over with the line of great aunts and distant cousins underneath the flowering bottle brushes.

The undertaker, a large man dressed in black, with shiny oiled hair parted down the middle, took out a pack from his inside pocket, placed a cigarette in the corner of his mouth and lit it urgently. I watched the muscles on his face relax as he stared off down the road. He took two quick drags, dropped the cigarette half-finished onto the path and crushed it out with the heel of his boot. I went over and asked if he had a spare cigarette. He looked at me guiltily, as if I'd caught him out.

'I've given up,' I explained.

He whipped out his pack. It was red and white and I caught the words WARNING SMOKING CAUSES before he palmed it back into his pocket. He handed me a single cigarette. 'Spose you need a light?' But I shook my head, told him I'd smoke it later. I went back and stood under the bottle brushes with the thin cylinder of paper and tobacco enclosed in my hand. I looked around and when no-one was watching I brought that cigarette up to my mouth, pushed the filter in between my lips, let it hang there. Staring down at a bend in the road, I realised what I missed most about smoking – it wasn't the kick as your lungs filled with nicotine, or the wisps of blue smoke trailing after your fingers, or even the taste – it was the way you could stand and stare at a bush, a rock, or nothing at all, and get lost in the moment. That never happens to me now. A light rain was falling, the tall trees were heavy against the sky and mourners began moving towards their cars.

I watched them go. I took the unlit cigarette from my mouth, placed it in my shirt pocket and walked across the gravel to the emptied car park. I felt a sense of loss that both my uncle and my days of smoking were gone. My father was waiting by the passenger's door, impatient, checking his watch. 'Thought you'd given up,' he said.

'I have.'

'Didn't I see you smoking over by those trees?'

'Not me, you didn't.' And I climbed into the car beside him.

John Foulcher
Diary Notes

Last night I set up camp
beside an ocean
I've never seen. Waves break here

without habit. Sometimes
there's a rhythm that's almost
human, a sense of dance.

Then it's the punch,
the muscle of currents. As I listen
to that thumping, my body

shakes, the tent shivers,
but the waves are all noise,
I'm not afraid. Sometimes, though,

everything stops, the sea
tucks into the sand like a neat
wooden joint. Then, I lie awake

and pray for the tides
to crank into action, but it's
lathed out there. Once I left

the tent, pulled tight about me
the hessian air.
The moon was a sigh

on my hand. My father
said that silence was reason,
there was power in it. Once,

I think, he camped here.
Yesterday the forest howled,
a storm of vines and branches

broke about me,
I saw no living thing.
The darkness was meat

salted with grains of light.
A bird coughed up a cry
that was old. My father

said there was no way back,
that the soft world died
when you left it.

It will be dawn soon,
I must stop writing this.
I pray for a word

to keep me from drowning
when I take the first step
onto that bound sea.

The sun's clear vowel
shocks the horizon.
This is the eighth day.

John Foulcher's poetry collections include *The Honeymoon Snaps*
(Harper/Collins 1996) and *Convertible* (Indigo 2000).

Peter Boyle

The hours are long before daybreak

Do the fish in their tank sleep at night,

their faces lulled by darkness,

the soft curl of water

closing all their fears?

It is difficult in a long night

of wakefulness and pain

to understand the magnificent stem of the appletree

blossoming steadily into light.

Even a little warmth lapping at my feet

puddles slowly upwards

to infiltrate numb hands, my throat gagging on memory.

There are no ways to say these things.

Where it hurts I can't even show

since it lies outside my body

but passes endlessly through my genitals and wrists.

Someone is arriving now on the ledge of a neighbouring building:

three birds who have brought the seeds of appletree

to chip at and discuss,

glancing with an almost maternal mindfulness

towards the window where I sit.

Their blessing is a wafer I will take and break in half –

the small mouths of the fish beginning slowly to open.

Windows rattle on a cloudless night

There is a city called 'Kite'. It dreams for itself a thin vanishing. Secretly by night it folds up its expanses, deserted streets, old archways, shuttered buildings and becomes a pale hand open to the wind of the stars. Made of stone condensed into air, the temple it offers us is all transparency.

Lives that narrow from oceans to measured streets, from wide boulevards to manageable rooms with small square windows and finally a voice in a room wheedling and apologising. Already the cicadas shake their rattle of heat and death. What is under the earth so longs to join the air.

The ship that sails out beyond the limits trails the last of the land bobbing at its shoulder. We shall not altogether go under.

Far over me, in the space of dreams, this city gliding resistance.

Peter Boyle's third collection of poems, *What the Painter Saw in Our Faces,* is to be published by Five Islands Press in 2001.

Marion Campbell

Goodness Itself

Marion Campbell
teaches creative writing
at the University of
Melbourne. Her most
recent novel is *Prowler*
(Fremantle Arts Centre
Press, 1999).

Diane's mum, Nancy, knew how to size people up. Like one of those TV Commanders she'd strafe over your life as if it was some little country to be annexed, and back in her headquarters, she'd spread out the map and plant her flags. So Vanessa's mum was Brick Veneer; Brenda's mum was Chenille in Rollers; and Allan's dad, Two Bob Short of a Full Quid. This was followed by a long pause, where you were meant to draw conclusions. And Esther's mum, Olive, was Goodness Itself. Each time Nancy said Goodness Itself, Diane saw Olive's benign bow-lipped smile and big brown eyes and knew that Goodness was a sweet dumb beast, mild-eyed, laboriously cropping the grass.

Nancy said she was glad that Diane seemed to like to go *there*; it would help her *appreciate* her own *privileged* upbringing. The family lived on a *Modest Income*. Of course it was *possible* that Goodness had chosen that maroon and beige vinyl lounge suite but it was probably a matter of budget. Goodness had *no boundaries*. Goodness was *blindly devoted*; Goodness let herself be *walked all over* by others; Goodness always came away from the P and C meetings finding that she'd become the fund-raiser, the secretary, the fete coordinator. Anyhow, there it was, permanently flying over Olive, a flag that said: *Goodness Itself.*

Goodness Itself was everywhere in Olive's house. Diane saw it aligning the few black hairs on Olive's shins under her silk stockings, in the pastel angora twin-sets she wore, in her big, round, clip-on earrings, in the perm she'd have every few months, in the white roots which pushed the reddish tint away from the crown. Goodness was there in the wide pathway of her sparsely sown eyebrows, in the big, honest statement of her bumpy nose. Diane tasted Goodness Itself in the lime cordial Olive served Esther and her in twin anodised aluminium glasses along with scones, jam and cream, on TV trays with little folding legs. Goodness Itself waited upon them, never making comment about More Useful Things the girls might be doing when they sprawled side by side on the Axminster carpet watching *Gunsmoke* or 77 *Sunset Strip*. Goodness itself never said a thing about the rusting car bodies up on bricks in the back yard of her Manning house.

'One of those basic two-bedroom plus sleep-out War Service places, adequate, I suppose,' Nancy said of Olive's house. 'Obviously neither is very interested in the garden. Well, to say 'garden' is to dignify it; it's an unkempt yard, littered with car bodies, Poor Soul. Her husband's one of them, a tinkerer who never finishes a job.'

Tinker, tailor, poor man, thief. At least tinker was at the top of the list. But tinkerer?

Diane saw Goodness Itself skirting those car bodies and pushing backwards and forwards with the hand mower, a haze of green clippings tossed by the spiralling blade, through the onion grass, the clover, and the long hairy couch between the Apple Blossom Hibiscus and the Oleander. Esther's dad was doing two jobs back then, one as a salesman, Esther said, and another as a night watchman. So you couldn't blame him. Still, there was a sort of sadness that tightened her throat when Goodness Itself tried every time to correct the lean of the metal letter box, and sing as she looked in, 'Oh dear, nobody loves me,' and smile widely with her cupid's bow in bright red lipstick stretching under her big, bumpy and slightly hooked Goodness Itself nose.

Esther, Daughter of Goodness, kept her distance, like she could catch something from her mother. Esther would look daggers at Diane if she said so much as thank you, like it was breaking the rules. Esther changed the rules so quickly; it was hard to keep on the right side of her. Diane's mum said Esther had developed a *sly look* lately, *like an ermine*. It looked like *trouble down the track*.

Esther's big brother, Brian, was something else again, with his snowy blond crew cut. He moved without words mostly; he had pictures, though. He drew in lead or the faintest coloured pencil battleships with planes he said were Lancasters bombing them. The exploding bombs festooned the sky like crazy, just under the bellies of the planes. He drew all this like it was the work of fairies, delicately. Diane couldn't even remember asking him, but there she was in his shorts, climbing from the rusty chassis of the Renault, onto the branches of the weeping peppermint. She liked the rippled elastic and the way the pockets made room for her fists, which was the form she thought her hands should take. Whistling, with her fists in those pockets, she was inside the riddle of the quiet boy who made the sky festive with bombs, who made the sea laugh with torpedoes.

Down at Rockingham, where Wally and Olive rented a beach cottage, the kids were allowed to go buy fish and chips for tea almost every night. They'd spread the paper out on the jetty, slurping in turns from a shared bottle of Coke, and throwing chips to sea gulls. Diane wanted thighs hard like the Rockers who hung out at the Dodgem Cars, sheathed in tight, black jeans; she wanted one of those insolently hunched torsos in black T-shirts or leather jackets; she wanted sideburns with greasy, messily crested hair; she wanted to kick into the sand with her black suede desert boots. She wanted to dangle a cigarette from her lower lip and look at the world through narrowed eyes. Maybe Esther would look back at her then.

Brian and his mates, who reckoned they were Teds, but didn't have the long jackets or the motor scooters to go with their stovepipe pants, would ram the girls in the Dodgem Cars. Diane could smell their sweat as they came close and they'd play the squealing girls act, spinning the steering wheel, roaring and grimacing with the jolting and thudding, turning up their faces to watch the electric conductors shower sparks as they trailed the mesh above. The boys would see Diane's swollen nipples tremble. Esther was already in a trainer bra, not that she needed it; she'd just pestered Goodness Itself, who gave in quickly, like she was relieved that Esther would ask anything of her. They both wore pastel Bermuda shorts and little striped midriff cotton tops that showed their belly buttons. Their leather sandals had a loop for the big toe and strap which criss-crossed, Roman-style, at the ankles. Their shoulders were like the topographical maps in their Jacaranda Atlases, the deeply tanned, withered skin giving way to tender pink as they peeled it. This in turn they re-plastered with coconut oil and then re-burnt. Olive said she didn't like the look of the sprinkling of black moles that had appeared on Esther's shoulders and around her chin but Esther said, 'Oh, lay off Mum,' and that was that.

With the green sky fading as the fun fair lights came on, the sea-salt tightening their skin, their blood still pulsing from the sun, they barely needed to talk, and Esther seemed calmer. She said she dreaded going back to Manning now He had given up his security job: He'd be snooping around her all the time. When she spoke like this, of Him, Diane felt she'd missed something in Wally's flat-cheeked face, in his thin, straight moustache and his slatted green eyes. All Nancy had to say about Wally, apart from the Tinkerer bit, was that he was Rather Weak; so that his flag fluttered above him blank and apologetic.

Right now it was just her and Esther walking along the dirty dimpled sand south of the big jetty with the Rolling Stones' cover of 'Under the Boardwalk' blaring from the fun fair. Esther was biting her lips. She had put on her I'm-Not-Home look. Diane's hand sort of moved up and out and hovered near Esther's shoulder but she called it back. She knew she'd be shrugged off like Wally. She liked Esther's lashes stiff with mascara globules and the wide arcs of her plucked eyebrows. She wished she had the guts to apply charcoal eyeliner like Esther to get the Smouldering Look. Wally would say, 'Walk into a door or somethink?' Or, 'You want to make out your ol' man's been beating you up, Bubs?' Esther's forehead was high and rounded but her long cheeks were thin, almost flat, like his. Her lips weren't full either, but she picked out a shallow Goodness Itself bow with the Moonstruck lipstick, a sort of opalescent beige.

They stopped at an up-ended rowing boat, loosely tethered to a metal pole. Eyeing one another they turned over the hull: there were the oars, sweetly sleeping, just waiting for them. They unbuckled their sandals and tossed them in, untied the rope and dragged the boat down to the water, all the time locking their eyes, silently laughing, thrilled with their luck and with their daring. Diane had passed some sort of test for Esther: she'd been admitted to a new place. All she needed now was to slide into that quickly lapping water, where the broken oval of the Ferris Wheel turned. It was an agitated lapping, sort of urgent. With the oars in the rowlocks, Esther was ready and laughing, her teeth flashing blue-white, like Ephrim Zimbalist Jnr's. She looked like she'd done this lots of times. Diane splashed through the shallows, pushing, and as she leapt in, they shot forward. Now it was the Little Red Rooster's moan coming across the water, *too laeeeete to crow the dawn.*

Mick Jagger's voice ballooned and stretched, broke and faded, then floated out to them again as the beach shrank to a shimmering line and the Ferris Wheel lights blurrily turned through the water. Diane wanted just this, the fullness of it, all of it, the salt and vinegar still on her lips, the sun in her blood, the burn of her skin, the air pulling warm and soft like a dressing on a wound, Esther's smile, the water gathering the dark, and the Little Red Rooster coming out on the prowl.

Further out there were yachts and launches, laughter and voices, rocking cabin and fairy lights in the inkiness. There was a slight thud and Diane saw that they'd nosed up close to the side of a big white launch. It was called Blue Lagoon. A tall man was at the stern.

'Hi,' he said, with a sort of question mark. *Hi?* His face leaned down, shadowy, inside a halo of whitish hair.

'Hi,' Esther said.

'Why don't you girls come on up and join me?' Look, there's a rope. Tie your dinghy up at the ladder and come on board. Like champagne? Pink champagne?'

Already Esther had laid down the oars and was clambering up.

'C'mon, Di, don't be a pill,' Esther's look urged Diane over her shoulder. Either way it was too late: Esther was climbing up to this stranger but so was she hauling herself up the metal ladder, and now, her arms trembling and her calf muscles heavy, she was nearly at the top. If anything happened, they could always dive over-board. The thing was to stay on the deck, not to climb down into the cabin, like Esther was already doing.

'Hugh,' he said.

'I'm Esther and that's Di.'

'Esther. Di. Drink?' He was using his thumbs to ease the cork out of a bottle of pink Champagne.

'Why not?' Again, Esther's eyes challenged Diane.

'You girls on holidays? Still at school? I bet... Let me see. You've just... done your Junior?'

He turned on a transistor, a big one, in a fitted leather jacket with windows for the dial and portholes for the controls. It was Dusty Springfield's 'I Only Want To Be With You'. He pulled out segment after segment of the telescoped aerial.

'Nup. Not yet. In a year but. I'm at Kent Street; she's at Mod. She's the brainy one.'

'Are not.'

'Are so.'

'Are not.'

'Oh, shut up. Who bloody well cares.'

Diane looked down at her polished knees and freshly shaven brown calves. She blinked; it was like the words trickled in acid at the back of her throat. She felt like one of those sailors in the Middle Ages, *perilously* close to the rim of the known world. No one said *perilously*. Hugh sank back on the red-studded upholstery, beckoning them over to join him. His open palm with the fingers slightly curled was meant to include Diane but she knew it didn't really.

'Your friend doesn't have much to say. Cheezel, Di?'

She hooked one on her finger. He wasn't a teenager. Maybe he was in his twenties. His hair was ash-blond. His face was a bit like a spade: long jaw, long chin. His eyes were dark for a blond. You couldn't tell their colour. His hands were slightly reddish, like burnt by a chemical or something. When he laughed, he showed a gold filling. His shorts were shorter than Bermudas, maybe to show off the rope-like muscles in those long thighs. The hairs on them made a mesh of little white wires when he approached the bench-side lamp. Esther lurched, almost spilling her drink. Diane's cheeks felt scorched. Esther had sunk back, thrusting her hips forwards, her face turned towards Hugh. He was inching closer to Esther, leaving Diane to drift away into the shadows. Like one of those satellites, she had strayed from orbit. Like a lost bloody Sputnik, she didn't show up on their screens.

'C'mon, Di, don't be so...lighten up.'

Diane took a slug of her drink. It had a burning sweetness. It wasn't even cold. How could Esther pretend she liked it? Now the two of them were up. *Esther and Hugh*, she said to herself, *are smooching*.

It was Gene Pitney: 'And then I kissed her, caressed her...'

'Oh that's awful, Diane. What on earth have you got on?' Diane's mum had said.

'It's not. It's Gene Pitney. He's got three octaves.'

'Octaves or not, it's awful.'

Hugh had his hand between Esther's shoulder blades now, somewhere near that little lacy trainer bra, steering her in their tight little dance. Gene Pitney's high voice worked at Diane's stomach in little hiccuppy scoops. She was going to throw up.

How did it happen? She'd strayed from her orbit and there she was climbing back up onto the deck. Now she was easing down the metal ladder on the stern, unhitching the rope from the rowing boat, dipping the oars and slipping away. Why was her heart wildly banging like this? What had Esther done to her? She'd only told her to, what was it – *loosen up*? *Lighten up*? What was wrong with Esther calling her *she*? No one would see that as hurtful. You could hardly say, 'And do you know what she did then? She called me *she*,' could you? Still to free her throat, to let her heart bang out into the gorgeous summer night she wanted to lie down in that rowboat and howl. She tried to get the oars into a rhythm but the boat turned round and knocked the launch again. There was this cold inside her now, despite the softness of the seaweedy air, and she realised her teeth were chattering and that her shivering was all she could hear: VR-VR-VR-VR, no Hugh, no Esther, no Gene Pitney. What if they tried to stop her, but then, why didn't they?

As the space opened up again and she saw she was pulling away strongly, it came to her clearly. Esther was alone with that man; she had left her alone with that man. Who knows what he might do to her? He might be a Maniac; her mother talked about *Maniacs*. They had axes or guns, which they raised or pointed on the other side of the plate glass. They could get you when you were eating toast on a lounge, baby-sitting, about to draw the curtains and turn on the TV. Esther would either have to beg his mercy or swim ashore. It was a couple of hundred yards from that launch. Diane thought of his red hands. What if the headline in the Daily News went: TEENAGER MEETS DEATH IN THE BLUE LAGOON? Was Esther strong enough to swim that far? Of course she was. And she'd been purring; she had her eyes half-closed like Ava Gardner, as she sipped that drink. So what'd she expect her to do? Olive and Wally. Diane would have to tell them that she had lost Esther somewhere after the Dodgem Cars. But then, Brian and his mates saw them there together. *They looked happy then*, they would say.

Now, as she was trying to drag the boat up the beach, she saw their sandals, in the hull, looking like evidence, with a pool of water swishing over them. Should she leave them there, turn the boat over as they'd found it or leave it, hull upright, so They could see them? Should she leave Esther's sandals stranded in the middle of the beach? That would look terrible, like she was kidnapped, dead. Should she row back to the launch, tie up the dinghy and swim ashore? Row back, yell out to Esther to give her another chance? Then she saw it clearly: she'd run back to the beach cottage to *Get Help*. She was *rescuing* Esther; of course she was. But how would she explain it to Goodness Itself? It was like a million tiny torpedoes were dimpling the water between her and The Blue Lagoon. Now even her running was like treading water; it was the dream where your struggle to move sets like lead and the terror banks up in a tidal wave behind you.

The sand was wet and heavy and bits of seaweed were catching between her toes and the four flapping sandals were lashing her thigh with their wet leather and buckles as she ran. She'd park Esther's sandals at the back door; that's what she'd do. Then they wouldn't freak out at the sight of her, dangling from her hands all that remained of their daughter. Near the Fun Fair, in front of a motel, a girl was bouncing high on a trampoline, her hair flapping like bats' wings around her face, her wrap-around mini-skirt blossoming at her hips. The rockers were standing around going Whoah! If only she could be in that story, suspended in the land breeze, with the rockers going Whoah! The houses looked the same to her and she hated the extravagance of the huge plots and the wide, wide streets; it was all designed to freeze her forever in this trying-to-get-there. She hated the smug look of the houses fronting the street blind, with their verandahs turned into sleep-outs, clad in asbestos and fitted with louvres, their front yards as blank as Esther's in Manning, except for a long apron of couch grass, and maybe a couple of cactuses, sometimes a tea tree hedge. Diane felt wetness between her toes; she must have stubbed them against the rough, warm bitumen, in this forever-not-getting-there. She would tell Goodness Itself the truth. What did Esther expect?

Olive was reading in the kitchen in her floral lawn nightie. She was glowing in her Goodness, in her not-knowing that Diane had left Esther behind. She must have heard Diane's breathing; she looked up; it was too late. Diane could hear every grain of sand rasp under foot on the lino, feel the blood stick. She had done her Holy Communion; she knew how to confess.

'Hello, sweetie. Have a nice time? But you're puffed out! What's the matter?' Olive put her book down, cover upwards. It was called *Tobacco Road*. She took off her blue and silver-rimmed glasses, shaped like curled paisley leaves. She rose, blinking, to read closely in Diane's face. Diane wanted to throw herself into her arms and sob like a baby.

'What is it, darling? Where's Esther? What's up?

'We...'

'Oh!'

Clear of make-up, without the glasses, Olive's face looked naked and crumpled. Her eyes were big with alarm; her beige lips pressed together and then hung apart, as if forgotten.

'We borrowed a rowboat. Esther's with a man on a launch.'

'Esther's with a man on a launch. But how did this happen?'

'He asked us on board. He's called Hugh. Esther was dancing with him. I rowed back ashore. I thought I'd better tell...'

'But. Oh Goodness! You left her there! We'll wake up Wally and call the police. That's what we'll do.'

'Oh, can't we just go there and get her? We can borrow that rowboat again. Esther'll never forgive...'

'I don't know how...Even if you two were silly enough to get on his boat, I'm surprised that you rowed away, leaving her with a stranger, without the...without any way of getting back!'

This sounded more like Esther's mum. It was the word *Surprise*, like an alternative to *Disappointment*, which was Nancy's favourite. Surprise was opening up a great distance between Diane and Goodness Itself. She saw that she was definitely, irreversibly, adrift.

'In the car, quick,' Wally said, his look at Diane murderous. Sliding onto the rear bench seat of the E.H. Holden, Diane saw that she was now done for, dead, a corpse, no longer adrift, but sinking.

'What about Brian?' Olive was saying.

'What about him?'

'You think he'll be okay?'

'Of course he'll be okay. He's a sixteen-year-old boy, for Pete's sake. Bubs might be being raped at this very moment and you're worried about your great big boy.'

Wally, in his dressing gown and striped pyjamas opened the phone booth door.

'The cops said to meet them at the jetty. They'll take us out there in their launch.'

The headlights tilted towards the peppermints next to the jetty and picked up a figure running: hair streaming, long legs moving like a slow machine. It was Esther, her clothes plastered to her skin, her hair stringy, dripping.

Olive thrust open the car door as Wally tooted. Goodness Itself had thought to bring a large beach towel, equipped with mermaid, shells, anemone, and coral waving wicked fingers like rubber gloves.

'Oh, sweetheart!'

'I'll speak to the cops,' Wally said.

In the back seat Esther was cocooned in the towel. She was look-ing into the night, her back refusing Diane.

'Sorry!' Diane tried, 'I was worried what might...'

'Worried!'

'I thought...'

'Oh, shut up!' Her whisper was fierce.

Diane's ribs pressed in on her lungs.

'The thing is, you're safe now, darling. Diane thought she was doing the best thing, I'm sure,' Goodness Itself said.

Later, from the top bunk, Diane tried again as Esther slid on her shortie pyjamas, in the shadows. She didn't want Diane's eyes on her; that was clear.

'I'm *really, really sorry!*'

'Arrgh. Don't say anything. I know why you did it. You were jealous, jealous. And you're a suck. You give me the creeps. I'm really really sorry! I bet you're dying to know what we did. Well, I'm not going to tell you. You know what? I think you're bent. I reckon you really are. You with your *really really sorry* can go to hell, for all I care.'

Diane could feel it already as she turned her sunburnt body between the sandy, sea-weedy sheets. Behind her lids the quiet furnace persisted and she glimpsed in a visual stutter the face of Goodness Itself, cow-brown eyes staring and cupid's bow unsmiling, before the flames engulfed it.

BELOVED
LOST
DOG

SNUFF

PLEASE CALL IF SEEN:
62627196
62064058

Dorothy Johnston

A Script With No Words

Dorothy Johnston has published five novels, including *One for the Master,* which was shortlisted for the 1998 Miles Franklin Award, and *The Trojan Dog* (Wakefield Press 2000).

Several years ago, a group of Canberra sex-workers applied to the Australia Council and were granted $6,280 to write a film script. The organization WISE (Workers In Sex Employment) was involved. A local writer ran some workshops, characters were developed, a plot outlined. But the project caused a stir, and resulted in a good deal of bad publicity, most of which used the argument that funding prostitutes to write a film script was a waste of public money.

At the height of the fuss, the *Canberra Times* ran a front-page article, plus a cartoon showing a bearded man with glasses reading a script.

'There's a problem with the dialogue,' the man says. A curly-haired blonde woman wearing a low-cut blouse replies, 'There isn't any.' 'That's the problem,' says the man.

Prostitution was decriminalized in the ACT in 1992. I am researching the subject because I plan to set my new book in a Canberra brothel. My first novel, *Tunnel Vision*, published sixteen years ago, is about a Melbourne massage parlour. Even though it's over twenty years since I worked in a parlour myself, and that was only for about a year, since returning to the subject I've begun to feel absurdly possessive about it – that it belongs to me and I to it.

The idea of making a lot of money quickly, to finance writing fulltime for six, nine months, longer if I was lucky, was what took me to the Melbourne parlour. It was a selfish motive. I stayed for what was probably another selfish motive. I discovered that I knew how to behave. I knew what was expected of me. *I could do it.*

I finish reading the *Canberra Times* article and study the cartoon. It relies on the idea that the female prostitute takes part in a performance without words, that hers is a part with no lines. It assumes an intellectual and imaginative emptiness – that the prostitute's intellect and imagination are vestigial and redundant, in much the same way as they are assumed to be for a worker on an assembly line, in a factory or mill. It reminds me how all manner of absences – verbal, psychological, emotional, the willed absence of physical sensation – can be adopted by prostitutes as survival strategies. There is the withdrawal into numbness, withdrawal of the body and the mind into an imaginary protected place.

Yet I recall, as well, how words were fundamental to what was being bought and sold. Words were rarely adequate, often comically misjudged, transparently fallacious, or wide of the mark. In the old illegal days, prostitutes and their customers developed coded dialogues of need, desire, negotiation. They were scripts capable of endless repetition, of variation on a theme. After business had been discussed, there were conversations. I never had a client who did not want to talk, and, more importantly, did not want me to talk to him, felt short-changed if I refused.

A man came to the door of the Melbourne house one afternoon. He was tallish, friendly-looking, with curly dull red hair.

I showed him into the front room and shut the door.

'My name's Alan,' he said. 'I like to start with a soft massage on the legs and back, working up to a stronger muscle massage. Then I like a little slapping on the legs and buttocks. Then I like my pubic hair pulled and a little pain around the pubic area – '

He went on, giving a speech it was obvious he had given many times before. He spoke pleasantly and evenly. When he'd finished, I replied in the same tone, 'I don't do bondage. None of the girls here does bondage.' And he left.

The most important code, which I never got to with the red-haired man, set out each of the services we *did* provide, together with its price. This is how I wrote about price codes in the early 1980s, for a book called *So Much Hard Work,* an Australian collection of writings about prostitution.

'For $50 the client naturally gets more than for $30. But the agreement, while broadly determined by the sum of money, is still a matter of individual determination. Where I worked, a G-string massage was worth $28 and a nude $38. Both of these included hand relief, though that was never stated. A "massage complet" (French pronunciation), meant genital sex and was worth $50. The client, having paid his $28, would try to feel you up under the G-string. If you let him, you were cheating yourself of $10. The client would try to get on top of you when he'd only paid for hand relief. It was your job then to persuade him to pay for the "extras" before you went any further.'

A successful negotiation, from the prostitute's point of view, required of the client a sense of fair play, and of herself a degree of deter-mination and an ability to speak up. The most successful were conducted without explanations, which could be dangerous. The first-time customer asking what was meant by 'G-string massage' might be a policeman. So it followed that negotiations left a lot of gaps. After a price had been agreed on, two strangers found themselves alone in a room with a massage table, with nothing, and at the same time suddenly everything, to be worked out.

There is the frailty of language as a bridge, the foolhardiness of speech that both makes and breaks a spell. When I think about the speech I made, often five, six times a day, a speech beginning 'For twenty-eight dollars you can get a G-string massage,' I recall my fear of getting busted, that moment of silence, with any first-timer, after my speech ended, the moment which, once passed, might reveal the new customer's identity. There is a nervous silence which words can never fill. There is the sound of the shower running, the inspection which will follow, that step forward.

I have forgotten the demands of architecture. That old house. No ensuites. Clients had to share a bathroom. It seems preposterous now. I recall waiting in one of the rooms with my client for the sound of running water to finish, the step in the corridor, creaking floorboard, till the coast was clear. They did not like passing each other in the corridor, but they shared the bathroom.

The coast clears. My client takes his turn in the shower. This hiatus, these few minutes, are the worst for me. When he returns, I will inspect his penis. 'Complete massage,' until then words that I could hide behind, won't be that any longer. Though they are not supposed to, cops have been known to go through with the service and then bust the girl. They have been known to return a second, third, or fourth time and then bust the girl.

There are many stories of clients who rip their condoms off and ejaculate immediately without them. This has not happened to me yet. I fear it more than I fear getting busted.

There is the layout of a suburban house, its familiarity, then what is made of it. The familiarity is that of a certain type of Australian weatherboard, three bedrooms, verandahs front and back. When I walk up to the parlour on the first day, it reminds me of a house I lived in as a small child. The smell of the front verandah is the same, a mixture of dust, peeling paintwork, rotting upholstery.

The backyard has a rectangle of mowed lawn, a Hills Hoist, concrete paths. There is a small hallway, a straight corridor from front door to back, a bathroom in need of renovation, a kitchen.

What were designed as bedrooms are not called bedrooms because there are no beds in them. They are called 'the rooms', and, when distinctions are necessary, the front, second, and side room. The front room, once the house's master bedroom, faces the street, the second, which does too, used to be the living-room. The side room overlooks a path and the house next door. Venetian blinds and curtains are always drawn. When we open at eleven in the morning, I go around opening the windows, for which I suffer, and am deaf to, daily reprimands.

The front room has an extra cupboard. Each room is lit by a low wattage lamp on a small side table, which also hold towels, tissues, talcum powder, baby oil and condoms. There is a radio which is supposed to be left on.

At the centre of each room stands the massage table, covered with a white sheet, long enough for a man of six and a half feet to stretch his legs out comfortably, but not nearly wide enough for its dual purpose. It is the right height for a massage, that is, high enough to save the masseuse from having to bend over too far and strain her back while squeezing recalcitrant thigh muscles. I much prefer using baby oil to talc, though I hate the smell of both. I am becoming quite a competent masseuse, but it is difficult to regard the tables as anything other than a joke against the kinds of masseuse we are required to be – a joke that exacts its daily quota of bruised knees.

Our backs are sore from being pressed into the wood. We have experimented with foam padding, extra towels. Our manageress has a blind spot here, as she has in other areas which concern our comfort. There are standing positions. There is the floor. By early evening, the floor begins to look like the best option. The preliminary massage is not an option. It has to be performed no matter what. The massage is a last breathing space during which a policeman might declare himself.

The radio is a background noise meant to replace the need for conversation, or the awkwardness of silence. I have many arguments with the manageress over whether or not I am allowed to turn it off. One of my first published stories, 'The Man Who Liked To Come With

The News', is set during the 1975 constitutional crisis, when even commercial stations ran news broadcasts every ten minutes. The news is harder to shut out than music.

The kitchen sings with light. This is because the venetian blinds have been removed, curtains tied back and windows cleaned. They are left open if the day or evening is fine. No client is allowed in the kitchen.

As with other commercial transactions, there is a gap between advertisement and product, dream and commercial limitation, the ideal and its substitutes, which are acceptable, though not entirely. Consumer satisfaction always contains within it the underlying promise of consumer dissatisfaction, a reason to keep on buying. After I have been working for a few months, I begin to suspect that, from the client's point of view, the perfect orgasm is both an unapproachable ideal, and an essential part of a business-like approach which, in some way I do not yet understand, seems tailored to correspond to mine. Customers avoid expressing general disappointment, which would mean admitting they have wasted their money, yet retain an edge of disappointment as part of their motivation for a return visit, when they will request another girl. For the girls, for us, variety is built into the system. We can hide behind the automatic nature of it, should we wish to. Should we wish to, and within limits, we can pick and choose.

There are young men whose mates have paid for them to visit a parlour. I recall one in particular, with long fine blonde hair, a surfer's muscles. He was about to get married. I was not at all physically attracted to him. It was clear that he was not attracted to me either, but there we were. His mates were waiting in the car outside. I knew the other two girls working at the time were busy. In any case, he didn't ask to see them. He was wound up tight by his own daring, his friends' generosity, their expectations. I already guessed that his re-living of the experience, the post-mortem that would take place in the waiting car very shortly, would be nine-tenths invention.

He was clean, quick, efficient, for which I was, as always, grateful. What made it bearable for both of us was the easy, matter-of-fact way he talked, about himself and his engagement, his friends, what they were like, their tastes in women, giving me to understand, with a tact which was mutual, concise, that it was *them* he did not wish to disappoint, their imaginations he would use as a model when he made up his account of a satisfyingly voluptuous encounter in a few minutes' time.

I recall conversations with clients as *the first and only conversations there will ever be.* I tell lies, and embarrass this and that one by putting on my educated voice. I am deeply bored, by them and myself. I remember strange eruptions of the ordinary, the ordinarily professional, such as the doctor, a man in his sixties, who discovered that one of my legs was shorter than the other, and proceeded to examine them, and explain the consequences for the curvature of my spine. The question did not arise: was he really a doctor? What was he really?

I think about passivity and openness, and try to fit them into a framework that might help. I read Kevin Hart in conversation with Robert Adamson in *HEAT* 4. Kevin Hart says that what interests him is 'when experience is understood as a risk, an openness which is ungrounded and insufficient to itself...an exposure of the self, a moment when you give up, when you let yourself as a personality be exposed to an anonymity that is, I would say, within yourself, at the base of the "I".'

There is something here for me, especially the notion of exposure to anonymity. But the problem with it is that the kind of passivity the poets are discussing doesn't correlate with sexual passivity, much less with willed absence of feeling as a survival strategy in a brothel. Yet it suddenly seems clear to me that there is a link between passivity which has an artistic aim, and the sexual passivity of the prostitute. The link is the contradiction both contain, whereby passivity, in the sense of *allowing oneself to be acted on,* is a necessary pre-condition, yet never more necessary than when it is about to change.

Passivity contains its own capacities, in the face of experience, art, knowledge – which comes first? – in the exposure to, the allowance of absurdity, the knowledge that hovers within and around the absurdity of selling sex. There is something about the absurd, about exposure to it, that is irreducible.

A necessary pre-condition first of all for art. Art, literature, is what I wish to put first, but the production of it I am starting to think of as primarily physical – a physical openness and waiting, which is indistinguishable from imaginative openness, which leads to the making of fiction.

There is the slide from passivity to physical cruelty. Genet understands how dramatic, plumed and brightly coloured it can be. But I don't want to get side-tracked by Genet, and anyway when I pick up *Our Lady Of The Flowers*, once a favourite, I can't get past page five.

Before and after the rooms, there are false names. There are the meanings that gather around, pay their own kind of respect to, a *nom de guerre*. I talk to 'Eve' in the kitchen. I refuse a false name and write 'Dorothy' in the booking diary, say my name in the rooms by way of introduction. I have this pair of soft leather shoes with a strap across the instep that I enjoy wearing. Eve calls them my Dorothy shoes. I laugh and click my heels together, but don't fly back to Kansas.

I love the way Eve buys treats at the delicatessen for our lunches, and different kinds of teas. I am beginning to understand the importance of the kitchen.

Instead of assuming the willed absence of feeling as necessary, why not posit, as a place to start from, a bewildering multiplicity of sensations, responses, scenes and dialogues? No single one will have any more inherent survival value than another. Passivity will be one kind of capability. Anonymity will be one possible stance among a range of stances, neither more nor less theatrical than others. Will art then have to take its place *alongside these others,* no more privileged than the rest?

One of my clients was an aspiring artist, who used to bring along his paintings to show me. They were landscapes mostly. He'd line them up along the wall, opposite the massage table with its white sheet, under one of the windows which, as soon as the doorbell rang, I had to run around and close. When I left the parlour, he gave me as a goodbye present his painting of the Box Hill Brickworks. It was a huge, gloomy canvas, all browns and greys, and to this day the most depressing painting I have ever seen. I didn't know what to do with it. I left it in my flat in St Kilda, behind the wardrobe, when I moved away.

I go to see one of the founding members of WISE, the organisation which received funding for the film script. She tells me a story about a parlour where she used to work, about a man who died on the job. The girls dressed him in his suit and sat him in a chair at the reception desk before calling the police. She says they did this to spare the feelings of his family, so it could be said he died while discussing the services, before availing himself of any of them. Who were they pretending for? Not the police. And not the family, although this was their stated aim. What family member could be comforted by such a lie, in such a situation? I think it most likely that they were pretending as a gesture of good-will, and for each other.

I write an opening paragraph for my new novel.

'Eden Carmichael, Independent MLA for Monaro North, was found dead on a hot Tuesday afternoon in January. He was lying across a double bed at Canberra's best known brothel. The bed's covers had been pulled off and lay on the floor. He was wearing a blue and white flowered silk dress and a blonde wig.'

I think of the corset in the cupboard in the front room of the Melbourne house, how it's shared by successive clients, how they know this and don't seem to mind. The corset is white, a replica of the old-fashioned type with drawstrings. The cups are boned white lace. I remember opening the cupboard door and staring at the corset, how it stared back at me. When I put it away, I put it right at the back of the cupboard, underneath the towels and sheets. I think of the cover of my edition of *The Female Eunuch.* I wash the corset carefully in a hand basin in the laundry and hang it on the line at the back of the house. We don't wash the sheets and towels ourselves. That would take forever. The amenities of the house, in the laundry and kitchen, are very basic, but I like it that way. I like unpacking the freshly delivered laundry. I think about the fact that the men don't mind sharing the corset, and whether they dress up at home, and in what. I think about how this seems part of their business-like approach.

I decide that the blonde wig in my novel, the one Carmichael is found dead in, will not belong to him, but will remain at the brothel. He will take his dress home, however, and will wash it himself between visits. The wig contains a clue to Carmichael's death, but I don't know yet what it will be.

I think about individuality, and how it appears and disappears through the deadpan requests of the men I service, in the ways they ask for this or that, in the detail that I keep returning to – so it must have something more to tell me – that those who fancied a bit of female underwear didn't mind sharing the corset – in the practicality of a client

I can suddenly remember very clearly, who never stayed longer than twenty minutes, who visited in his lunch-hour every second Friday, who could never take his shoes off because when he got excited his feet swelled up and he couldn't get them back on again. After he'd ejaculated, he lay flat on the massage table without saying anything, and his feet looked enormous.

In the evenings, I play the piano and read a book on the Knossos labyrinth. I cannot read fiction. This has never happened to me before, though it has happened to several of my friends. I practice a Schubert impromptu with five flats. It is too hard for me. I have only recently started playing the piano again. I long for that understanding of the fingers, once part of a despised discipline. Occasionally I can feel it coming back. Nothing matters except that the notes should sound together as they are meant to.

In the 1970s, St Kilda was becoming gentrified. I was living in a flat in Eildon Road. The brick fence at the front of the flats was warm to the touch when I came home after a day's work. I would sometimes stop and chat to the street workers. Once I had a long talk to a woman, while both of us sat on the brick fence, but talking for any length of time was unusual. Something else was unusual too, a meeting at the St Kilda Town Hall that took place towards the end of 1978.

A residents group called Westaction was campaigning vigorously to get rid of street prostitution. Their tactics included throwing stones and buckets of water. Property values were one worry, but some Westaction members had a comprehensive view of how the suburb should be changed. One woman told me, 'I don't believe we should have the theatres, the artistic or entertainment element, where we have children to bring up.'

The title of the meeting was 'The St Kilda Public Forum on Residential Amenity'. A letter of invitation lists the speakers as a Westaction representative, the Commissioner of Police, a St Kilda Council representative, and a State Government representative. Eight hundred people turned up to the Town Hall. In my chapter for *So Much Hard Work,* I described it as a rowdy meeting.

'Tempers were high. A small group of women calling themselves the Prostitutes' Action Group appeared. Despite a lot of protests, they were allowed a speaker at the last minute. I was there with them.

I think our unexpected presence — people realised suddenly that Westaction wasn't going to have things all its own way — was probably the cause of many people losing their tempers.'

What I remember best is fear for the street workers who got up and said St Kilda was their suburb too.

Our clients received the answer 'no' to most questions which began, 'Do you do?' or, 'Have you got?' We were plain and simple, offering only basic services. We did not do bondage, work with dogs or whips. We did not wear black suspender belts, or dress up as school-girls. We had no theme rooms with silk wall hangings, or spa baths in the Roman style. The word bordello comes to mind by way of contrast with our small shabby house, a house that was replicated, with minor differences, all over Melbourne.

It is Ed Carmichael who continues to take me back there, now I have imagined him. I do not know much about Carmichael's past. At night, when I am tired, it depresses me that the Melbourne parlour will not yield the facts I need, will not tell me how or why he died. Though it *has* told me that he takes his flowered dress home to wash. I see him standing at the bathroom basin in his flat. He does not use the building's communal laundry.

In spite of all those times doing up the corset, pulling it tight, I know almost nothing about men dressing up in women's clothes. Carmichael crosses and re-crosses borders largely mysterious to me, yet I have no doubt at all that he must travel in this way, or that he dies on one of his habitual crossings.

In the dim light from the lamp in the front room, the cheap white lace of the corset stands out, at one with the white sheet covering the massage table. It stands out also against the client's black and grey chest hair, shiny from the shower. I pass my fingers over the lace. No matter how many times it's washed, it never feels soft. I smell damp hair, talcum powder, anxiety. I do not look down and neither does he. He has put on our bit of female underwear (the only one on offer) as a last resort, after other inducements have been tried, and failed. Impotence is stubborn. The client knows he has not sought, or arrived at, the right place for a cure, yet there is something stubborn in him that goes on hoping for, expecting it. He lies down and I take hold of him with my fingers of a competent masseuse, though we both know it will not be any good. Though he has paid to fuck me, he will not. Today will be like the other days. He will leave and I will hope, fervently, that he will not return.

There is something stubborn in me too, and young and arrogant, that refuses to participate in a failure of this kind. I barely speak. I refuse to dress up myself, in any costume, let alone this one, but it is a blanket refusal, it applies to all my customers. I push with both hands against the kind of complicity that would have me play the role of therapist.

What bothers me about the notion of play, in the way it's often talked about, is the assumption that all forms of play are benign, that anyone can learn how to perform with anyone else, and with words, but more importantly, can get away with doing so.

At the same time, there is *this other thing* – the mood of sexual readiness. There is no code for it, no true words, perhaps not even slighting or embarrassed ones. The doorbell rings and what are we – Pavlov's dogs? It seems that yes we are, but in spite of everything it seems also that there's a stubbornness, an energy for renewal in this too.

It is the one taboo, our physical arousal, the existence or extent of it. Should I assume that Eve and the other girls have never felt, or have overcome it? We joke about the size of clients' dicks. We talk a lot about getting busted, and how to avoid it. Our manageress boasts that her regular payments to the police ensure we won't be. Regular payments have been known to fail. Cops can be recognized by the look in their eye, blue eyes of a certain tint, moustaches of a certain jaunty angle. If you suspect one, keep him talking till he gives himself away. You can't be busted for talking about the price of a complete massage.

We keep the money in the stove. The police, were they to raid us, would find it within thirty seconds. We don't pretend it's safe there, but somehow, when we discuss alternatives, none seems more attractive. I like opening the oven door and looking at the money. We tell combat stories. I tell the story of the shoes and swollen feet, aware of a small prickle of betrayal, because I like the swollen-foot man. He's a regular and no trouble.

Physical arousal is fugitive and unexpected, inside the rooms as elsewhere. Yet for the time I spend working in that house, I trust that

I will eventually find the code for it, or no longer need one. It is the case that words reveal nothing of the mood of waiting for the doorbell. Waiting belongs to raised hair along the forearms, to nose and eyes and skin. Words can be retained for their uselessness, as well as for any other reason.

Something else occurs to me. If I've been thinking of conversation as a bridge between strangers who catapult themselves into sex paid for by the half-hour, then the plainer I make their conversations, the better it will be. I will make my characters speak very plainly to one another. Their inferences and allusions will be couched in the simplest words, as though this itself, if tested, tried, tested once again, might become a form of trust. Carmichael, with his politician's education, will not be an exception.

I think about practising the piano when the house is quiet. At dusk, I take the dogs for a walk. Later on, I write this bit of the novel.

'A cloud rolled its huge golden underbelly over Lyneham oval. The green beneath it was the trees' hosed summer exuberance, shading into grey as colour dissolved, an expectant darkness waiting for the large one.

'Gold grew, spreading through the cloud. It touched the spears of poplars that lined Sullivan's Creek, vertical to its high horizontal. This last light was massy, indiscriminate and yet precise. I thought of the divisions within and through my city, on highways, roads, cracks in Civic footpaths that were familiar, nondescript, repeated as often as the scene in front of me was repeated, glowing and then gone.

'To play is always to risk ridicule and censure, even the games that others ask for, even sex – to play is to risk running too fast, not fast enough, stumbling, tripping over your big feet, tripping another – oops, and sorry not enough. To play is to let the wind under your skirt at the wrong moment, that skittish wind that follows sunset and leaves before true dark. Or your trousers, held together by a piece of string. Or your blue dress, gorgeous in the last light, and the yellow soft enhancement of your wig.'

Kate Camp
Sign of salute

Always give a word or a sign of salute when meeting or passing a friend,
even a stranger, when in a lonely place.
CHIEF TECUMSEH, SHAWNEE NATION (1768?–1813)

People go to South America:
they can't be got back from there.

They are train robbers
and those whose identities can never

be known. Sisters too
looking to walk the steep

dizzying paths
of the Inca trail.

You never let a furry animal bite
or lick you in South America

and you carry
at all times

a photograph
of your imaginary husband.

You never admit you know
what cocaine is.

When people spill mustard on you
you don't pay any

attention
but just keep going

with your wits
about you.

How are you getting there?
The book asks in Spanish.

By Car? By Credit Card?
By Chance?

She is a mouse
with a giant hat

under desert stars
Ariba, Ariba she says

and it means
upstairs, upstairs.

Days without mail

My neighbour's new piano
is played upon with the greatest care.

I learned the truth at seventeen
that love was meant for beauty queens

she plays and the theme
of Hill Street Blues.

Every evening the man brings home his trailer
of vegetables. He bruises them rushing over the kerb.

In the house across the way a mirror waits
glowing and alone for all the lighted day.

Out on the street all sorts of people are giving way.
You can see from here the single green light

while it lasts and the door of the fish shop
opening and closing with a ring.

There is a huge white shine over the hill
as if the moon might rise there suddenly

and give fright to pelicans tucked up
for the night, to the sleeping lions

in their home of limited dimension.
It is the hockey stadium, Mt Albert

a beauty worthy of worship
never found quite how you expect it.

Just been kissed

Light shines.
They open me up.

I am a watch.
They gaze at my workings

with jewellers eyes
with special eyes

they love me.

They love me with their needles and clamps.
They love me with their vinyl and tiny pillows.
They love me with their screws and little mirrors.
They love me with water and air
with their porcelain
with their precious metals.
They love me with their strong, taut hands
using my face for purchase.

This is flavoured of pineapple they say
as they shoot it into me.

And when the ladies have finished with me
and their conversation of boys and school
trips to Copenhagen is neatly packed away
and all the instruments that need to go

into the autoclave have gone to that chamber
of steam and all the debris is whirlpooled
down I am set free in the streets
victim and champion
red and rubbed lips softer than anything else
and I can't help can't help but touch them
as if to feel and I can't feel as if to feel
where I have
just
been
kissed.

Kate Camp is a Wellington poet whose second collection, *Realia*, will be published by Victoria University Press in July. Her first, *Unfamiliar Legends of the Stars,* won the 1999 Montana NZ Best First Book Awards.

Michael Farrell
late change

& now im a duck with a green
front hang eric clapton
what a change of heart & that's how i start
forbidding my soldiers to
eat chicken dinners & writing
novels on jungle villages
at eleven thirty approx
delayed by radiology
& rat races freezing my bum off
forking out money for foxtails
& new bill brushes talking to
rushed filmmakers in the pouring
i want separate toes they call
it elective i go up the
bank past overgrown cats & roses
scared by organs en masse i try
a crash course in spanish drama
i need earplugs & sedatives

red cues

any poem can be a diminishing thing
taken from the sea & standing in for you &
a remedy we eat what they eat but thats not
reality the spoon falls in the phone rings im
fast im not that fast the money in the bank falls
out while I meant to write you into my life black
& white americans say julies a sunset
marxist i take a camera from my pigmy
boyfriend feel his arrows of love a near cliche

flea

it falls a red & gold tribute from its circus
this is the season of the existentialist
icon you fashion what i need a dress of fleas
they dont wear out keep the goats going when theyd rat
on life die in labour in the snow without ants
without entertainments thats rich you climb up to
a flea hive like its laden with honey for goats
while your few supporters stand idly scratching through
the wool & the snow & we marry another
transgression i turned insect took it from your book

comet

it has ways un deux trois quatre
& like space it can be shocking
when it seems to twirl itself &
make anyone in front look bad
it can be pacifying like
gaol years writing letters to
younger loves who don't know what they
should do with it noone told me
thered be a man to meet me just
identify myself i was
prepared for action but not for
unreliable emotion
the type with the lip could he be
the messiah for once could he
go back in time & meet helen
hunt count them out of underground
shame let them meet the wave as it
comes as the milk of the tail like
the high boot of southern europe
fall on their one two three four feet
its his best death its her last truth

Michael Farrell's first collection, *living at the z*, was published by Vagabond Press in 2000.

Gig Ryan

'Evil has no witnesses'

On Pramoedya Ananta Toer

'It is those who have been most oppressed who can best understand the meaning of humanitarianism. Those who have had their rights usurped know best the meaning of self-respect.'
The Mute's Soliloquy

Indonesian writer Pramoedya Ananta Toer (b.1925) has the distinction of being banned and gaoled by three governments: the Dutch colonial Government in the 1940s, Soekarno's 'Guided Democracy' Government in 1960, and Soeharto's 'New Order' Government from 1965–1979. A prolific writer, Pramoedya has published over thirty books and has been translated into at least twenty four languages. His work is political in that it is impelled by a Socratic questioning of any existing social order. As every adjective is to the reader an interpretation but to the writer simply accuracy, so all art is political – a writer's politics are revealed whether the writer wishes it or not. Unlike the self-discoveries of many contemporary writers, Pramoedya looks at the 'big picture', the mechanisms by which society functions, and the 'traditions' that serve to maintain hierarchy. His novels and short stories are set in tumultuous nineteenth- and twentieth-century Indonesia: his early stories are of traditional and contemporary life; the acclaimed *Buru Quartet* is set at a time when Indonesia was still a Dutch colony and covers the years 1898–1920; and his most recent work is a collection of unsent letters to his children, written during his imprisonment in the 1960s and 1970s. Pramoedya, like all writers, records and remakes history, and just as all art contains an implicit criticism of former art, so Pramoedya's historical novels contain an implicit criticism of official versions of history. Those seeking to understand so-called 'Asian values' need not look far. Pramoedya's short novel *The Girl from the Coast* is based on the writer's maternal grandmother. A village girl, she is sent at the age of fourteen to be a 'practice wife' for a nobleman, as was the custom. After she gives birth to their daughter, the nobleman throws her out, but keeps the daughter. This story is updated in the *Buru Quartet* where both Nyai Ontosorah and later her niece are sold to Dutch managers.

Pramoedya's early short stories are jagged, vivid and wide-ranging with an uncommonly perceptive grasp of family interaction and a panoramic cast of characters: prostitutes, beggars, thieves, soldiers, aspiring writers. 'The Vanquished' revolves around one family in the village of Blora where Pramoedya was born, and is set just after the Japanese occupation, during which over four million Javanese farmers died as forced labourers and 'cannon fodder'. The eldest girl, now a

Red, is told by her younger siblings that their father has been taken by other Reds, probably to be killed – 'They were like nails stuck firmly into a board. Only their eyes moved. Desperately. And despite themselves mutual suspicion ran wild among them.' The brother they thought had died fighting for the Republic returns to Blora having in fact joined the Dutch Army, and consequently the family house is set alight – presumably by the Reds – leaving the children homeless as well as orphaned.

Unimportant Blora was now quiet. Each day goods from overseas flooded into it. Every day the Dutch caught someone and made him a prisoner, an employee or a corpse – just as the Japanese, the Reds, the Siliwangi (a division of the Republican Army) and the Republic had done...While the government lived proudly in a castle in the sky somewhere above our small unimportant town, Sri and her family lived in a cardboard shack.

'No Night Market' takes us inside the head of a restless dissatisfied individual whose tone is similar to that of some Dostoievsky characters:

I was sad. Democracy is a beautiful system. You can be the President...You can have the same rights as everyone else...But if you haven't got any money you can go to hell. In a democratic country you can buy whatever you like. Unless you haven't got any money, in which case you can just look at whatever you want. That too is a sort of victory for democracy.

The Fugitive, Pramoedya's first novel, is set around the time of Soekarno and Hatta's audacious declaration of the Republic on 17 August 1945. Pramoedya's images are immediately jolting:

One of the beggars was still quite young. Like the others, his ribs and chest bones protruded like a xylophone...When the beggar-guests were swept away from the shelter, they formed a choir, a roaring wilted choir, which was of no interest to anyone.

The Fugitive echoes the traditional Javanese wayang shadow plays that are based on stories from the Mahabarata with Hardo, the fugitive of the title, as the Arjuna figure. Having lived for months in a cave hiding from the Japanese, Hardo reappears as a barely recognisable and enigmatic figure. He argues with his father-in-law who then betrays him to the Japanese. Between these two there is an 'inconclusive battle' which Hardo more or less wins, at least morally. Like James Joyce's *Ulysses*, *The Fugitive* uses traditional culture to legitimise and highlight contemporary life and, as in other stories of Pramoedya's, there is an ambiguous father-son relationship. 'I don't like patriarchs, no matter who they are.'[1]

Pramoedya's own father was a schoolteacher, activist, composer and writer, involved in the Boedi Oetomo, a Javanese nationalist organisation. As a consequence, the house he grew up in was crowded with activity, discussion, Javanese literature and nationalist songs – some composed by his father, who also constructed the name Pramoedya from a phrase meaning 'first on the battlefield'.[2] Pramoedya admired his father's public life but became increasingly critical of his private life. When Pramoedya's intelligent and tirelessly encouraging mother died of TB at the age of thirty four, his father turned even more to gambling, and left him, aged seventeen, to take charge of his eight younger brothers and sisters. Pramoedya then moved to Jakarta to seek work. From 1947–1949 he was gaoled under the Dutch – who had returned to power after the Japanese occupation – for possession of anti-Dutch pamphlets, and wrote *The Fugitive* while in prison. In the early 'Stories from Blora' one of the characters defines Pramoedya's own position: 'We writers are...a resistance force, an unofficial opposition'.[3] Literature is memory, and for Pramoedya in Indonesia the most trustworthy record of events.

In the 1950s and 60s Pramoedya lectured and edited, travelled to The Netherlands, India, Russia, China, and translated many Russian novelists including Tolstoy, Dostoievsky and Gorky. In 1960, under President Soekarno, Pramoedya's history of the Chinese in Indonesia, *Hoa kiau di Indonesia*, was seen as too sympathetic, and was banned. Again Pramoedya was jailed for nine months. In 1965, when possibly one million Indonesians were killed, in retaliation for the so-called attempted Communist coup, Pramoedya, by then a well-established and respected writer, was arrested by the military who had in effect seized power under General Soeharto. He had been prominent in Lekra, the cultural organisation that was, like many organisations, connected to the influential Communist Party, the PKI, which at this time was the largest Communist party in a non-Communist country in the world. But he had not been a member of the PKI. He was imprisoned without trial. His house, library and papers were burnt. At the time of his arrest, he was editing some stories by President Soekarno, and working on a history of the early Nationalist awakening in Indonesia. He was eventually sent to remote Buru Island, along with fourteen thousand other 'political' prisoners, where he remained until 1979. Not allowed writing materials for years, he composed the *Buru Quartet* in his head, reciting pieces to the other prisoners each morning to ensure his historical research would not be lost. The first two volumes of the *Quartet* were published in Indonesia in 1980 and – to the Government's embarrassment – quickly became best-sellers. In May 1981, the Soeharto Government banned all his work, including an anthology of Malay fiction, on the grounds that it subtly propagated Marxist-Leninism. He was put under house arrest, and has only been free to travel outside Jakarta since Soeharto's overthrow in 1998. Far from silencing Pramoedya, his years in detention sharpened his quest for a just, democratic society and emphasised to him the importance of recording history. In the Dutch documentary *The Great Post Road* Pramoedya says openly, 'Soeharto is a murderer'; and in another interview he has summarised his position – 'I am only in favour of justice and truth…If that is what you call a communist, OK, I am a communist'.[4]

The *Buru Quartet* was originally inspired by the life of Tirto Adi Suryo, publisher and editor of the first Native-owned daily paper and co-founder of the first modern political organisation, as Australian translator Max Lane writes in his excellent introduction to the third volume, *Footsteps*. Pramoedya had previously published a non-fiction account of Tirto Adi Suryo's life as well as an anthology of his journalism and fiction. *This Earth of Mankind*, the *Quartet*'s first volume, begins in 1898 in the multi-racial seaport of Surabaya. Minke the eighteen-year-old narrator is honoured to be the only Native at an elite Dutch Boys' School and is inspired by the French Revolution's ideals of Liberty, Equality, Fraternity. He is infatuated with European culture and disparages the caste system of his Javanese family – he must crawl on his knees to his father, a *Bupati* (Regent), and must use the correct form of address when speaking to him in High Javanese. When Minke prepares for his father's inauguration as *Bupati*, an Italian dresses him in clothes designed by Europeans in the 1600s for the Native aristocracy. Dress, like language, specifies race and class and caste, but these traditions of formal attire had in fact been installed by the European rulers to further maintain hierarchy and class division among the colonised population. Minke's Eurasian schoolfriend Robert Mellema introduces him to his family – his sister Annelies, and his mother Nyai (literally, concubine) Ontosorah who was sold as a young girl to Herman Mellema, Robert's Dutch landowner father. Nyai Ontosorah, educated by the once-kindly Herman Mellema, now astutely runs his profitable business and is an imposing and informative figure to the 'question factory' Minke. He begins to write stories based on Nyai's experiences, and his writings are published, unusually, in a Dutch newspaper. But as his writings begin also to record Dutch corruption, his work is censored by the editor to protect the paper's owners, the Sugar Companies.

Minke marries Nyai's daughter Annelies and before the wedding his mother reminds him of his inheritance:

You yourself are a descendant of the knights of Java, the founders and destroyers of kingdoms. You are a knight…and the five attributes of the Javanese knight are: house (trust), woman (life), horse (advancement)… The fourth, the bird, is a symbol of beauty, of distraction, of everything that has no connection with simple physical survival, of only the satisfaction of one's soul. Without this people are only a lump of soulless stone. And the fifth, the keris (knife)…a symbol of vigilance…Without the keris, the others will vanish.

When Herman Mellema's legitimate Dutch wife and son decide to claim the famously beautiful Annelies as their own, Minke learns of his and Nyai's powerlessness under Dutch law. Nyai is not recognised legally as Annelies' mother, nor is Annelies' marriage to Minke recognised. 'I know them, those Europeans, cold, hard like a wall. Their words are expensive…I understood at that moment, we would be defeated and that our only duty now was to fight back...like the Acehnese in their fight against the Dutch.' The Mellema family wins, but the fact that a Native concubine and the educated Minke can dare to challenge the Dutch creates a sensational court case.

In the second volume, *Child of All Nations*, Annelies, already sickly, dies in The Netherlands. To distract the bereaved Minke, his more politicised friends take him to the country in the hope that he might record first-hand the daily exploitation of the villagers and plantation workers. His idealisation of European justice is further eroded and he begins to integrate European with Native knowledge:

The old people teach us through their legends that there is a god called Batara Kala. They say it is he who makes all things move further and further from their starting point, unable to resist, towards some unknown final destination...People say that before mankind stands only distance. And its limit is the horizon. Once the distance has been crossed, the horizon moves away again...No one can return to his starting point. Maybe this mighty god is the one whom the Dutch call 'the teeth of time'.

This volume ends with the visit of Herman Mellema's Dutch son, who can legitimately claim the business Nyai has so successfully built up. Again Minke and Nyai face defeat against Dutch authority, 'we fought back...even though only with our mouths.'

In the third volume, *Footsteps*, 'Minke goes beyond simply wanting to understand the world to wanting to change it', as Max Lane writes, invoking Marx.[5] Minke leaves Surabaya and the over-powering Nyai to study medicine in Betawi (now Jakarta).

I could not find what I was looking for. The first-class compartment contained mostly Eurasians, with their dried-up skin and arrogant posing. Next to me sat an old Eurasian grandmother scratching her hair – probably forgotten to comb out the lice. Opposite sat a thin middle-aged man with a moustache as big as his arm.

Minke comes to see that his role as writer and journalist must be as a disseminator of knowledge. Inspired by the work of local Chinese activists and 'the girl from Jepara' (Kartini, 1879–1904, one of Indonesia's national heroes who set up the first school for Native girls), Minke starts his own organisation, the Sarekat, and a newspaper, *Medan*, in which he can record uncensored the corruption he has witnessed and also explain legal rights to the Native population.[6] The constant mention of the different languages spoken, often within one conversation, shows how unwieldy and secretive the Dutch East Indies had become – characters speak in Dutch, English, High and Low Javanese, Menadonese, Sundanese, as well as Arabic and Chinese, Educated and Common Malay. Minke, by now disillusioned with European culture, decides his newspaper must be written in Common Malay to reach the large unrepresented majority, but other organisations debate his choice: 'They wanted the kind of Malay they had learnt at school. They wanted a language that knew where heaven and earth was, not a bazaar language that floated about without roots, disoriented.'

The turn of the century bursts with ideas – women's emancipation, freedom of the press, rejection of the patriarchal feudal caste system. The Philippines rise up, the Japanese become a world power, Chinese and Russian revolutionary fervour ring in the air. Political, nationalist and ethnic organisations flourish: Arabic, Islamic, Javanese, Chinese. Soon Minke's unprecedented position as an educated Native and as leader of the three hundred thousand strong Sarekat allows him to meet the Indies Governor-General.

All eyes were focused on the General, famed for his conquest of Aceh. I had been observing him closely. I wanted to get a feel for how a killer talked and behaved…His movements and the way he spoke were enough to make one feel confident in predicting that more wars would be breaking out everywhere. More Natives, armed with bows and arrows and spears…would die in their hundreds on the orders of this man. For the sake of the unity of the colony, for the security of big capital in the Indies…
  'And they are the source of strife,' van Heutsz stated firmly.
  'Perhaps they think we are the source of strife, General.'
  Van Heutsz laughed and nodded vigorously. He seemed to be enjoying the debate. Then: 'That's why we make, buy and use guns.'

And whoever does not make them, buy them and use them... now
I understood – they became targets and victims.

Minke marries Mei, a Chinese revolutionary activist. During
this time 'the girl from Jepara' is forced into marriage – 'She suffered
no less than any other woman who lived under the yoke of a man's rule'
– but her example spurs Minke forward. He struggles to free himself
from the effects of patriarchy and his aristocratic inheritance – for
example, when at first a peasant speaks to him without using formal
deferential address, he feels he must suppress a sneer. Nevertheless he
describes his wife as doll-like. Minke is surprised when his fellow
students visit concubines – 'If a woman prostitutes herself, she is
considered evil and is given no chance to become decent again. But if
a man goes to a prostitute no-one objects and he is still free; he can even
boast of it in public.' And elsewhere – 'Mother said such women were
basically prostitutes. And perhaps men such as these were also prostitutes.'[7] Indonesia has a long history of women activists and warriors.
Minke and his friends speak admiringly of the women fighters of Aceh
and Bali. In the first volume of the *Quartet* when a more naïve Minke
examines a painting by his disaffected French friend Jean Marais, he is
astonished to learn that the murderous Dutch soldier depicted in the
painting is Marais himself, but even more astonished to learn that the
Acehnese fighter he is depicted as being about to kill is not only a
woman but also later the mother of Marais' much-loved daughter.

Minke sees himself as being like Romulus and Remus, suckling
on knowledge gained from his Dutch education and from the Dutch
radicals he befriends. As founder of the Sarekat organisation he travels
the country visiting his branches:

On every tour there was always somebody...who proposed that I marry their
prettiest daughter...so that I might leave my seed amongst their
family...This wrong view about blood and ancestry has such strong roots in
the literature of Java. The Mahabarata and Bharatayuddha provided nothing
to grab hold of for those who wanted to enter the modern era...This people
waited for the Gong, the Messiah, the Mahdi, the Just King. And he whom
they awaited never came...We were aiming for a democratic society where

nobody stood above another. There were no special people, who stood closer or were the special beloved of the gods or God.

As in the historical novels of Eliot, Dickens, Tolstoy and Henry Handel Richardson, we learn much in passing – that the average Native life expectancy at this time was twenty five years, for example. Pramoedya's *Quartet* also contains stories within stories, letters, and addresses within the narrator's mind to various characters.

In the final volume, *House of Glass*, we review Minke's political awakening through the eyes of the figure sent to track him – now the narrator is Police Commissioner Pangemanann, employed by the Dutch to suppress Native revolt. We know Minke has met his nemesis when Pangemanann enters his office late in the third volume, *Footsteps*. Pangemanann ominously comes in the guise of a writer with a manuscript to offer.

[Pangemanann] suddenly turned the conversation: 'It seems you are really determined.'

'There is nothing to be afraid of, is there? What is it that we should be afraid of?'

'He-he-he, no. I mean it seems that you are very determined and committed in carrying out your work. Committed people must be respected. That is why I respect you.'

'And where do you see this determination in me?'

'In your attitude.'

'It appears that you seem to see some danger ahead of me. Or perhaps it is you yourself that are the danger to me?' I joked.

He let out a rather indecent laugh...

'I like the way you talk. Bold. Sharp. No mincing words or suchlike.'

'You are a true man of letters,' I said, praising him, 'taking so much notice of every word spoken and how it is spoken.'

'Yes, it is a hobby of mine.'

Pangemanann, a guilt-ridden Catholic Native who has studied at the Sorbonne, is ordered – unlawfully – to 'get rid' of Minke. After several attempts, Minke is arrested and exiled to Ambon.

House of Glass begins in 1912. The narrator Pangemanann becomes enthralled by the 'notes' he must study – that is, the first three volumes of the *Quartet*. Pangemanann had begun his successful career as an honest policeman sincerely upholding the law, but his promotion ten years before was due to his suppression of a Native revolt: 'the truth was that I was losing my backbone, my principles, like a crawling worm, just like the criminals I used to arrest.'

As in Dostoievsky's *Crime and Punishment*, it is a stalking police-man and his prey who dominate this last volume: but Pramoedya shows instead how Pangemanann is stalked in turn by the justice of Minke's cause. The suppression of organisations results from Pange-manann's investigative reports, and though his orders conflict with his conscience, guilt has no effect on his official duties and exists in counterpoint to his active life, a life he now half despises – 'I left that cemetery of the past,' he says, referring to the State Archives Office. Pangemanann imagines the characters he is ordered to study kept as if in a house of glass on his desk. His respect for Minke is mixed with jealousy, and he also harbours ambitions for his own thorough and traitorous research – 'Yes, it is only proper that Pangemanann too be read by the world!' He addresses Minke in imagination:

You have to understand that during the three hundred years of Dutch rule in the Indies they built a pyramid of Native corpses, and that is their throne… You were too small in the scheme of things to challenge this power. You never saw the pyramid of your people's corpses that has been their throne. If you had seen it, you would have run, run without ever turning back.

Yet, like any reader of these volumes, Pangemanann too becomes con-vinced of the historical inevitability of the nationalist movement that he is paid to suppress, and therefore of the ultimate futility of his own work: 'Europe…now faced its own pupils who had more ambition than knowledge – the ambition to become a new nation… And these Natives were not armed with swords and spears, nor with patriotism, and not with religion either. Today their weapons were… speech and pen.'

When Minke returns from his five-year exile in Ambon, he is fundamentally unchanged – his asceticism and integrity are in jarring contrast to Pangemanann, whose last clutching-the-rosary-beads gestures drip with hypocrisy.

He [Minke] had lost only his freedom…I had lost everything: principles, wife and children, my honour…I would have to face him in all his greatness… he would be like a crab whose legs I have cut off… it would burst my insides because I would be meeting with all that is my opposite.

Minke believes in the democracy he has been taught at school, in which all human beings are treated equally – a democracy that exists nowhere in the world in 2001 – and Pramoedya's relentless irresistible logic, as expressed through Minke, is one of the chief magnets of his writing. In one crucial scene, Pangemanann accompanies Minke to the police station to persuade him to sign away his freedom of speech:

'You know what is in the statement?'
 'A promise not to become involved in politics or organising,' Minke hissed.
'Very beautiful. Just like in a palace comedy… So the idea is that only the Government can get involved in politics or organisations?'
 None of us expected such a sharp refusal or question as that. We were all dumbstruck.
 'Not allowed to get involved in politics or organisations,' Minke whispered to himself. Suddenly his lips were pulled back into a smile, and his voice struck out clearly: 'What do you gentlemen mean by politics? And by organisation? And what do you mean by "involved"?'
 We were all still dumbstruck.
 'Do you mean that I have to go and live by myself on top of a mountain? Everything is political! Everything needs organisation. Do you gentlemen think that the illiterate farmers who spend their lives hoeing the ground are not involved in politics?…Or do you mean by politics just those things which make the Government happy?… And who is it that can free themselves from involvement in organisation? As soon as you have more than two people together, you already have organisation… Or do you mean something else again by politics and organisation?'
 The three of us were still dumbstruck.
 'From the time of the Prophet until today', he lowered his voice, 'no

human being has ever been able to separate himself from the power of his fellow human being... Do you want me to sign my own death sentence without there ever having been any trial, just as I was sentenced to exile without any trial? Or is this ridiculous letter another part of the Governor-General's Extraordinary Powers? If so, let me see proof that such new regulations have been introduced. I want to see them.'

He knew we had lost our tongues, and he put out the cigar in his ashtray and smiled victoriously.

Pangemanann, the 'paid destroyer', insists on accompanying Minke on a tour of his former haunts, obsequiously displaying his knowledge of Minke's life and inserting comments like a travel-writer. Slowly Minke discovers that even his former home has been 'given' to Pangemanann who, when they arrive there, sadistically addresses him:

'You must be tired. You can use the guest room.'

I suddenly recalled the time I had visited here, but our positions as host and guest were reversed then. I quickly added: 'We have met before here in this house, haven't we? We are not new acquaintances, are we? It's just that our positions are different now.'

Minke swallowed, then: 'Thank you...With your permission, I shall be off.'

'Where do you want to go so late in the afternoon?'

He gave a nod of respect... and left.

I knew then that I had turned into a sadist... I felt no regret about what I had done. I had even felt honoured to be able to torment him like this... [it] made me feel even more important and powerful, and I felt even more disgusted with what I had become.

What Pramoedya reveals in this final startling volume is how colonial power necessarily corrupts even its obedient subjects, and that no matter what Pangemanann's inner thoughts are, it is his actions that historically define him. The *Quartet* finishes tragically for Minke, but as World War I ends the Dutch East Indies are in transition and the fight for the Republic of Indonesia has commenced. 'He had been destroyed but he had finished what he had begun. From that beginning he had multiplied himself into so many other people, spreading like fireflies throughout Java.'

Each volume of the *Buru Quartet* represents a new world. In *This Earth of Mankind* it is the world of learning, through both Minke's schooling and his place in Nyai Ontosorah's household. In *Child of All Nations*, after Annelies and later her brother die in The Netherlands, the seat of colonial power, Minke discovers the world in which most colonised Natives live. In *Footsteps* Minke carves out his role in the world of political action in Betawi. In *House of Glass* the bureaucratic world unfolds through the tortured Pangemanann, the instrument and pawn of Dutch colonialism. Each volume ends with a decisive clash between the Dutch colonial government and the Natives, and in each case Dutch colonialism wins. *This Earth of Mankind* concludes with the court case over custody of Annelies. *Child of All Nations* concludes with the visit of Herman Mellema's legitimate Dutch son, who legally claims the business that Nyai has built. *Footsteps* ends with the enforced closure of Medan and Minke's exile. *House of Glass* ends with Minke's death and Pangemanann bequeathing Minke's 'notes' – that is, the first three volumes – to Nyai Ontosorah.

The New Order government of President Soeharto may well have felt itself to be looking in a mirror in Pramoedya's *Buru Quartet*, though this was not Pramoedya's intention. No doubt when he was imprisoned, the urgency to record the historical period he had researched was immense. Nevertheless it is impossible not to draw parallels between the injustices of the early twentieth-century Dutch East Indies and the injustices of the late twentieth-century Republic of Indonesia. By publishing his *Quartet* as 'written on Buru Island', Pramoedya bluntly revealed to the Indonesian public that Buru was in fact used for political prisoners. The Government incidentally also ignored the rights of the indigenous Burunese population. As Pramoedya wrote in *The Mute's Soliloquy*: 'I became a soldier to fight for this country's freedom but since independence I've experienced a good deal more repression than freedom… It's a pity that the country I imagined became, in reality, a primitive and fascistic society ruled by militarism.'

Pramoedya's *Quartet*, like all his work, is finely attuned to exposing exploitation, inequality and injustice wherever they occur, and it is inevitable that readers will draw parallels with their own societies – the similarities between racism and sexism being one obvious example. In the apparently democratic West, where the predominant viewpoint is white, masculinist, and capitalist, one cannot truly express shock at Indonesia's colonial era – in Australia for example, the average Aboriginal life expectancy is still twenty years less than the non-indigenous majority's.

When I met Pramoedya, whose work I had admired for fifteen years, in Jakarta in March 1998, two months before the overthrow of Soeharto's thirty-two-year rule, he was as I had imagined: unassuming, nervous, fearless. He pushed the manuscript of his most recent work across to me. At the back of this heavy book of unsent letters from prison, he had resolutely listed all those political prisoners who had died during his time on Buru Island and their causes of death, in many cases 'shot dead'. This was a week when student leaders were disappearing, presumably murdered, and there were mass demonstrations daily against the Government. Pramoedya was still under house arrest and all his works were still banned, and my Indonesian translator – a family friend – was increasingly nervous. Yet this manuscript was the most explicit indictment yet of Soeharto's regime. Pramoedya is brave through logic: he knows that his history – so different to the Government version – is unquestionably factual. In *The Mute's Soliloquy*, the manuscript he had shown me, he finds that when he is officially presented with paper and pen after four years' imprisonment, he is unable to write.

Since 1950 writing had been, in all practical terms, my family's sole source of income. It was the only work I felt capable of doing. But in the four years of imprisonment since 1965, the only thing I had been allowed to write was my signature on official documents. In that period the thinking process, which serves as a prelude to writing, had in me been paralysed... Suddenly, focusing my attention was not nearly so easy as I had thought it would be. Then it dawned on me that I, like most of the other prisoners, had also lost my self-confidence...Further reduction of our food supplies made 'recuperation' much more difficult... Just to remember the name of one of my (eight) children might require a week's time.

Conditions on Buru were primitive, brutal and often sadistic –
at one stage eleven prisoners were shot for 'entertainment' – and many
prisoners starved or died from lack of medical treatment. It is
astounding that any survived, and no one who reads *The Mute's
Soliloquy* could be surprised by recent revelations of implicitly sanc-
tioned Indonesian atrocities.

Pramoedya's answers in the interrogations and interviews he
underwent show his unassailable logic and intelligence, and reveal
the blindness of his interrogators. 'The treatment that has been
shown to me has not been educational and will not contribute to the
development of a better society…What is the use of studying the
principles of freedom if one has no personal guarantee of freedom?'
The sessions are absurdist and self-satirising, as the prisoner
eloquently uses the language of the new Indonesia his interrogators
supposedly represent.

Prisoners who failed the screening process have all been noted down,
transformed into notes… found in sentences uttered by tourists about
Indonesia's high level of culture, its remarkable civilisation, and the
extreme friendliness and politeness of the Indonesian people. At some
future time there might be someone capable of writing about them
without his hand shaking uncontrollably or his notepaper becoming
wet with tears. But that person will not be me. In the world of the dead
there are so many souls whose presence I know nothing of. All I can do
here is try to make note of the souls whose names I do know… A few
of them managed to die on their own, without assistance from the
authorities.

Yet even in this deprivation he was able to observe the prisoners'
usurpation of the indigenous Burunese and to sympathise with their
dispossessed plight. He also observes how the Burunese women were
hired out as prostitutes by their own impoverished husbands, the
rights of these women being even less than those of actual prisoners.
Pramoedya's acute and scalding awareness of oppression and his
realisation that all oppression is linked, whether it be by race or sex
or class, is a constant theme in his work, but another theme is that

of the individual as an embodiment of history – his tragedy, his imprisonment, his history, are of course no more important and no more unjust than those of the other fourteen thousand political prisoners.

Journalist: What do you have to say about your ten years of detention?
Pramoedya: It has not been ten years; it's going on thirteen. I view this period of thirteen years as one consequence of the nation-building process.
Journalist: And your own feelings? Your personal feelings?
Pramoedya: They're not important. As an individual I am not important in this process.

Gig Ryan's poetry collections include *Pure and Applied* (Paper Bark Press, 1998), and *Heroic Money,* to be published in 2001 by Brandl & Schlesinger.

Reference is made in this essay to the following works by Pramoedya Ananta Toer: *The Mute's Soliloquy* (Hyperion Books, 1999); *The Girl from the Coast*, trans. Harry Aveling (Select Books, 1991); 'The Vanquished' and 'No Night Market', in *A Heap of Ashes*, trans. Harry Aveling (University of Queensland Press, 1975); *The Fugitive*, trans. Harry Aveling (Heinemann Educational Books, 1975); the *Buru Quartet: Awakenings* (*This Earth of Mankind* and *Child of all Nations*) trans. Max Lane (Penguin, 1990); *Footsteps*, trans. Max Lane (Penguin, 1990); *House of Glass*, trans. Max Lane (UQP, 1992); 'Stories from Blora', *From Surabaya to Armageddon*, trans. Harry Aveling (Heinemann, 1976); *Crossing The Border: Five Indonesian Short Stories by Danarto and Pramoedya Ananta Toer*, intro. and trans. Harry Aveling, Working Papers 38 (Centre of South East Asian Studies, Monash University); 'Encounter with the devils', *Index on Censorship*, 25, 6, (1996); *Tales From Djakarta*, South East Asian Program Publications (Cornell University, 1999).

Other sources include Anthony H. Johns, *Cultural Options and the Role of Tradition* (ANU, 1979), Chapter 6, 'Pramoedya Ananta Toer – The Writer as Outsider'; *The Great Post Road* (includes interview with Pramoedya Ananta Toer), Fortuna Films, Amsterdam, The Netherlands (broadcast on SBS in 1997 and 1999); Keith Foulcher, *Social Commitment in Literature and the Arts (The Indonesian 'Institute of People's Culture' 1950–1965)*, Centre of South East Asian Studies (Monash University, 1986); Tineke Hellwig, *In the Shadow of Change: Women in Indonesian Literature*, Centre for South East Asian Studies (University of California, 1994).

1 *Footsteps*, p.83
2 *The Mute's Soliloquy*, p.107
3 In *From Surabaya to Armageddon*, p.71
4 *The Age*, 20 January 1994.
5 *Footsteps*, Introduction, p.x.
6 Pramoedya also wrote a biography of Kartini, published in 1960.
7 'News from Kebajoran', in *Tales from Djakarta*, pp.33,36

Emma Lew
Light Tasks

I arrived in bits,

furious at Copenhagen.

The swans were stretching their necks and biting.

The donkeys stumbled badly on the descent.

How nice your compliments sounded –

it was as if the lights in the priory hall

had been turned on all at once.

The cabbage was marvellous.

Oh! If only I were dressed better!

You seemed a little wanton.

Thistledown, someone said.

And all were weeping, men with white beards.

The dog had perhaps been noble and faithful.

Thousands of pineapples came by steamer.

The policemen on the streets gave directions

in the most attentive fashion.

The church arches were splendid;

the pillars slender,

and when we were walking on the road

you wrote something in the sand with your foot.

My mind was like an angel sinking.

Among the ruins of four walls you showed me the sea –

how it and the starry sky were constructed.
It was ebbtide. I undressed.
How many hearses in the coming year?

The children herding cows were so beautiful.
One questioned me about the darkness.
Ships with all their sails, I said.
All the melodies of pain at every shift,
and then the endless moon, growing and growing.

Emma Lew's prize-winning first collection of poetry, *The Wild Reply,* was
published in 1997 by Black Pepper Press.

Eden Liddelow

I'm Not Just A Writer, I'm A Person

An Interview with Susan Sontag

Eden Liddelow is completing a book on twentieth-century fiction. Her most recent novel is *The Quarantine Station* (Acland, 1998).

Susan Sontag has always represented the avant-garde. Although primarily known as an essayist ('On Interpretation,' 'On Photography,' 'AIDS and its Metaphors') she began her career as a novelist with the very abstract and French-influenced *The Benefactor* in 1964. This was followed by *Death Kit* in 1967. Ironic, melancholy and hallucinatory, it pursues formal experiment within a black and often hilarious satire on the life of US corporate man.

Her third novel *The Volcano Lover* (1992) marked a change. It is a graphic and mostly realist account of a group of expatriates becoming caught up in the aftermath of the French Revolution in Naples. The volcano presides over a bloody collision of self and other on a scale that is both intimate and stupendous. *In America* (2000), by contrast, refuses pessimism or metaphors of upheaval in its story of migration from Poland in the nineteenth century.

The historic realism of both recent novels is challenged by two things: an ironic introduction by a modern narrator, and closure with the form Sontag has now made her own – the long monologue in summation of a life. Characters hitherto deeply involved with others now stand alone, delivering an apologia or plainly speaking difficult truths. In *Volcano Lover* we hear from Lord Nelson, his lover Emma Hamilton, and the young revolutionary Eleonora de Fonseca Pimentel – *after* their deaths. *In America* closes with the famous American actor Edward Booth. In these accounts, Sontag's famous irony seems to have met its match.

EL: In your novel *Death Kit* – which appeared in 1967 – you wrote about the hero Diddy: 'Diddy the Depressed. How hard it is to say anything just for itself. With the best will in the world you find you're saying it for someone.' As Eva Ziarek says, melancholy is an excess of alterity. But it is difficult to say things just for yourself. Is this tension the basis for the four monologues at the end of *Volcano Lover*, and the one at the end of *In America*? They're speaking directly to the camera, they've got a bit of distance.

SS: I wish I could be the first author to say all my books are anatomies of melancholy. But I feel that to be true. However there was a sea-change between the writer who wrote *Death Kit* and the writer who wrote *Volcano Lover* and *In America*.

When I conceived of *The Volcano Lover*, it was as if great doors had swung open. For the first time I could put into a book a lot of what I know and feel, and I have never felt like that before. I'd felt everything I wrote represented some corner of what I felt, and after all what every writer wants is to touch every word in the language – but I never had that *triumphant* feeling that I got from *Volcano Lover*. If I went back to who it was who wrote *Death Kit* – the writer – I wouldn't change that much as a person, but I feel I have changed as a writer. But then again a reader such as yourself will see continuities where I see discontinuities. Which allows me to feel I'm beginning again each time. It's a necessary illusion.

What I must have meant by the distinction between speaking for others and speaking for itself, yourself, was contained implicitly in an idea of greater truthfulness. Not a refusal of dialogue, but a sense that to speak for others is to speak less than truthfully – out of fear of the others and what they can do to you, out of consideration, compassion, overdeveloped empathy. If you could speak only for it or itself or yourself this would be a chance to say something more truthful. That feeling has abated in me as a writer – not in me as a person: I often feel when I speak to someone that I'm speaking less than truthfully because I'm shaping what I say – to be civil, to be kind, to communicate, to be liked. All sorts of things.

And if one didn't have the rebound into one's solitary self, one wouldn't know what thoughts were real. So for me as a person that's a reality. As a writer, I adore the feeling that I'm addressing others when I write. I'm not aware of 'the other' when I write. I used to answer so easily when someone asked me, 'For whom do you write?' I'd say, 'For literature,' or 'I write for people who like what I write,' or 'I don't write for anyone, I just try to do my best.' All these phrases came easily to me – and sincerely. Now I have a better way of explaining it. I take immense pleasure out of people's responses to what I write, which I had never allowed myself to feel. I didn't understand it.

Volcano Lover felt to me like a turning point in my life. About the four monologues: the characters were dead so they could tell the truth, they had nothing to lose. They could be totally honest. It's not just that they're not speaking to anybody – there's nothing they can do. It's over and it can't be changed. It's that now they can tell the truth – and the truth beneath the truth, it isn't that there's one truth. To take the emotionally simplest character – Mrs Cadogan – it's full of contradictions. She's a naïve woman, who has to speak of herself – 'My daughter, my daughter, my daughter.'

EL: You wrote in your essay of 1979, 'Under the Sign of Saturn,' that 'the saturnine temperament is an unforgiving relation to the self, which can never be taken for granted – it is a text that must be deciphered.' Then I heard an interview with you in 1982 in which you said that you'd given yourself up to the directness of emotions in opera – someone is up there on stage saying, as in the letter scene from *Eugene Onegin,* 'I cannot forgive you I die I love.' Is opera an escape from the unforgiving relation to the self?

SS: Yes. I think of opera as blessedly – and absurdly, often – direct. So yes. The hyperexpressiveness of it – I had immense pleasure from it and hadn't understood why. Until a production of *Eugene Onegin*. I want to say, 'doesn't one,' but I should say 'don't I' long to have some of that directness! There was an opera character in *Volcano Lover*; and then it became a private joke, so I have another Puccini character in *In America*. It begins in 1875; it's about a group of Poles who go to America but the most important person in this group is the most famous actress in Poland. Their fantasy is Brook Farm and artists' colonies and living like noble savages; and they settle in Southern California and she goes back on the stage and becomes the most famous actress in America, Polish accent and all. Anyway, early on in her return to the stage she goes to a mining town, on a tour, and then she meets Minnie, who's another Puccini character from *The Girl of the Golden West* — so I had my second character. And then, in this trilogy of novels that take place in the past, the third novel is about Japan. Madama Butterfly's son is a character in the novel! My Puccini trilogy — it's a private homage to opera, and to Puccini — who is not a first rate composer — no serious lover of music thinks he's one of the great composers, like Mozart — but it's a deliberate homage to the expressiveness, the rank expressiveness, the eloquence of opera.

EL: Still on the monologues; in a sense they're like group photos. You wrote once, 'Strictly speaking one never understands anything from a photo — only that which narrates can make us understand. It is a world which denies interconnectedness, continuity — but which confers on each moment the character of a mystery.' For me, for all that these monologues communicate and narrate directly, they are so mysterious, like photos. Primarily, of course, because we don't know where they are.

SS: Yes, well that's the stipulated fantasy — voices *de l'au-delà, de l'outre-tombe*. They're nowhere, they're just voices. No, I think it's precisely the opposite of the photograph. I found these monologues intensely moving to write. At the execution of Eleanora Pimentel I actually wept. I also cried at the end when Emma sends her daughter to get the priest. What most pleased me was when people said, 'I cried!' I'd say, 'Thank you so much, I cried too.' The monologue — that's the payoff, that's what all leads to. Someone can finally say,

'This is what I really feel, this is what I was in real life.' A whirlwind of emotion.

This new novel begins with a monologue and ends with a monologue. The Prologue both introduces the story and is a *parable* about fictional imagination – how you imagine something, how you construct your story, how you invent. Then there's some sort of authored 'I' who follows things in my life – obviously not identical, she's not clever, this person in the Prologue. It ends with one long monologue, about thirty five pages. He's a man who makes the most glancing appearance in the book; he has the final word. This idea of having the final word go to him – over the top emotionally, very emotionally violent and passionate, an account of someone who is *profoundly* unhappy – is a very different narrative method. There isn't an omniscient voice. It's a bit of a handicap. I like the omniscient voice, dancing around, making contemporary references. I gave that up, I renounced that. I'd like nothing better than to write the same book over again, with a different story! But – ! It's very hard to detach from that.

EL: Nadine Gordimer writes a lot about the writer's relation to society – the need to be left alone and at the same time have a vital connection with others. Do you feel this, and is it difficult if that connection leads to political commitment?

SS: I'm not sure I have political commitment but I certainly have moral commitments, which take me into situations which people define politically. I spent a good part of three years in Sarajevo in the time of siege, from 1993 to 1996, there half the time, going back and forth. I just felt it was my duty to do something, doing *that* as opposed to running to other horrible situations which one might be drawn to; bear witness, or to be helpful. That was very much an accident. In a certain sense I have a connection to the Balkans, though nothing in my life or background has to do with that – my son who is a writer had gone there to write a book about the war. Which he did, successfully. He said 'You should see this, you should come,' – so I got myself there. It was very difficult – getting credentials – and gruesome and dangerous. I didn't write about it, partly out of respect for my son – I didn't want to upstage him, he has written extensively about his involvement with Kosovo, Macedonia. That's what he does. What I did was personal. That takes up a lot of time. To tell you the truth, I'm a bit more interested in doing things politically – or what I would call moral actions – as a person, putting myself in a place where I can do something – as a human being, not as a famous writer.

The classic struggle: of course the writer is alone. It's voluntary house arrest. Cocteau said you can never be alone enough – his fantasy being some basement where people would leave the food outside the door.

I don't write when I travel – I can't. During the three years in and out of Sarajevo, the greatest sacrifice was that I couldn't write because I'd be back here for a month, going back there for a month or two, and I was so obsessed by what I'd experienced and seen. And when I was here I did a lot – making arrangements for refugees – so that didn't leave much out of the three years. What can I say? I'm not just a writer, I'm a person. As a human being I have to do things – I think more of my duties as a human being than as a writer – but as a writer of course I want only to be left alone. I'm never alone in the true sense because I have books. Thousands of books – a great swarm of dialogues with minds, most of whom are dead. I don't have strong relations with contemporary writers, with a few exceptions, one of whom is Nadine Gordimer.

EL: In one of her essays she paid tribute to you for your courage and honesty in admitting publicly that writers on the left had been insufficiently critical of the faults of socialist regimes. But she goes on to ask whether it is really inconceivable that socialism can ever be achieved without horror.

SS: That's too abstract for me. I actually think very concretely. I think it's very important to tell the truth. I try to tell the truth. That's always a sacred duty. And I'm not attached to the idea of self-expression, that is, that I am expressing myself. As a writer, as Marguerite Duras does, whom I knew a little. Her work is about herself and her own consciousness. I'm not at all drawn to that idea. I know I'm the medium of what I do – I draw on myself, I can't step over my feet. That's not the point. I'm not drawn to Duras's work, it doesn't mean much to me. I read French – I'm bilingual – the music is seductive sometimes, but sometimes it's too small a world. By which I don't mean you can't just write out of your own experience – that you can't have, so to speak, a small voice. There are wonderful writers with small voices – Jean Rhys is an example. I love her work. She's not a big, ambitious voice – but she is writing about more than herself even when she seems to be writing about herself. Whereas I feel Duras isn't; it's egocentric in a way I find unattractive.

EL: Have you read *La Douleur*? It does move outwards. Could I ask a few things about language? There are these sliced verbal forms, supines and gerunds. 'Diddy bored (now).' 'Diddy sitting in the compartment.' I'm wondering if it's a cinematic vision, that says 'CUT to…Diddy sitting in the compartment.' Your books are about seeing – the camera hijacks the fictional language.

SS: I'm sure I'm profoundly influenced by cinematic philosophy. I always find the first pages of a book incredibly difficult to write. I can spend six months on the first ten pages, but I can spend six weeks on the last fifty pages. By the end of the book you have your plan. And, when I think about that struggle to begin, I think of two things: I have to establish the lexicon for the book and I have to establish a kind of philosophy – how fast the book is going to go, what kind of energy it's going to have – and I think about those first notions – they're accentuated by the fact that I certainly have had more pleasure from movies than from books of fiction in the last thirty years. I'm an endless re-reader, but when I pull down a book for re-reading it's not often a book written now. What I've read the last couple of months just for pleasure – it's the heroic period: Henry James, Tolstoy, Balzac.

The last new book I read through from first word to last is not a novel in prose but in verse, Les Murray's *Fredy Neptune*. The last book I read from start to finish – new contemporary book. Otherwise – opera books – the heroic, the age of heroic narrative, which is the late eighteenth, nineteenth, the first third of the twentieth century. I love Les Murray's work – I introduced him recently in New York. On several occasions.

EL: I like listening to him talk almost as much as reading him – the gems he produces just in passing. I reach for my pen, I have to write them down.

SS: He's a dazzling writer, dazzling.

EL: Coming back to your language: there is a *zoom sentence*, where a switch from past to present tense – sometimes in mid-sentence – is like the action of the zoom lens of the camera at moments of change or particular tension. As Benjamin said – 'The need to bring things spatially and humanly nearer is almost an obsession today – the close-up.'

SS: It's not movies as such – it's very specific directors who've entered my bloodstream. That's exactly what it is, I've tried to explain it to myself, never successfully. It's the zoom.

EL: But what it does is influence space and time. Speed things up.

SS: That's an element of his idea of the close-up. I don't think my own concerns, much as I revere him, are mediated by Benjamin's ideas, but the concept is of course the great convention of the cinema – the cinema image as opposed to what still photography did before the invention of the cinema. I think that's an analogy rather than describing directly what I did but because I feel my limitation as a writer – I'm acutely aware of it and hope to live long enough to reduce this. I don't think I'm a great describer of the physical world, which is something I admire intensely among certain writers – Lawrence, Hardy, Tolstoy of course, other writers – but what I'm really good at is describing consciousness. And I wish I'd had more skills at the start. I'm working on it but I'm not good at describing spatial relationships.

EL: But we don't need any more descriptions of spatial relationships.

SS: I'll tell you a writer who has come to be a model for me – and as much as I always liked her I never thought of her as a model – and that's Virginia Woolf. There are things in *Mrs Dalloway* and the first part of *To the Lighthouse* which are so stupendously moving and concise and direct and crazy – Septimus says it all. Not just the character of Septimus but also some of the descriptions. I've always loved Woolf but I'd never got close to her.

EL: Something that seems to have an affinity with Woolf in your work and Nadine Gordimer's is male protagonists – the desire of the writer to be both genders.

SS: All three of us are very old-fashioned feminists! To me this is feminism, but a lot of people don't see it that way at all. I just sort of take it for granted. Henry James created some very important women. Talking about describing – one of the things I adore about Nadine Gordimer's fiction is her way of describing erotic situations.

EL: She's so good!

SS: She's the best. It's not sexy – it's really described. It sounds so prudish – I don't mean language shouldn't be vulgar, but she doesn't lean on vulgar language to carry the weight, rude words for sexual parts and acts. I just mean that a lot of writers nowadays think they're describing something sexy just if they use the ordinary words. It's never that; it's really sexy, what she does, and it's really described. Just talk about a man's bottom – I can't remember, it's like six words...

EL: 'His clean equine rump,' from *Burger's Daughter*.

SS: Exactly. Isn't it wonderful?

EL: It's Chabalier. In *The Conservationist*, there's page after page describing a woman on a plane and what a man's hand is doing to her under the blanket. It's delirious. Women's experience described by men. Written by a woman.

SS: I love to admire it when it's someone I care about. There's a moment in *The Late Bourgeois World* where she goes to tell her son that his father has been killed. He's called out of school, she embraces him, and she smells the sweat of a child entering puberty which has turned from something very sweet, that smell of perspiration that children have, to something more acrid, when the hormones kick in at around thirteen. Oh! When she embraces him, she knows he's no longer a child. You know how right that is, how truthful it is. That's indeed what life is like. It's that concreteness. You know what I mean, it's that concreteness.

EL: Just going back to the way your language *describes consciousness*, as you say. In *Death Kit* there is frequent use of the word 'now,' but in brackets, and I feel it's in brackets because the new perception is an illusion, it's an illusion that anything is going forward, that there's any real change.

SS: Because it isn't so, because the whole book is a hallucination. Can you understand — you are obviously one of my very best readers — understand what I have trouble understanding, why I waited so long to write another novel — and don't think I didn't start four novels, that I started, that I left — between *Death Kit* and *Volcano Lover*.

The point is to not to have industrial weight of productivity. The point is to write a couple of books that will be read fifty years from now, that's all I want. I mean think of — I don't know — Charlotte Bronte. *Jane Eyre* and *Villette*. That's all, that's the lot. I love *Jane Eyre*, too, I read it as a child, it's one of those formative books. The important thing is to write one or two or three books people will want to read. And I'd think, it's not good enough, not different enough, it's not big enough. And then when I got the idea — everyone says, how did you get the idea? — it just fell into my head (I think of ten stories a day). It's preposterous, a Polish actress who starts farming in Southern California in 1876, and then goes back on the stage — why did I know that I could do something with this? But I like stories about foreigners, I like the condition of being foreign. I get a lot out of feeling not eternal.

EL: Coming to New York from Europe I felt so much more foreign. I was very aware of Bernard Shaw's idea that the British and the Americans are divided by a common language.

SS: But New York is a big international city, it's like a big ship anchored off the coast of America. It's not like the rest of the country. If I couldn't live in Manhattan I wouldn't live in the United States. I like New York precisely because it's not America. It's a very peculiar ship – with everybody on it. The borough of Queens has one hundred and eighty seven different languages spoken by children in schools, the immigrants there are from more different countries than anywhere else on the planet. This doesn't mean one hundred and eighty seven different countries, it's actually many more, because Spanish is spoken in so many countries. And I remember once during a bombardment in Sarajevo, constant of course, huddling in a basement, a very clever guy – perfect English, worked in television – and he said to me 'What do you think of us? What do you make of us?' subtracting the war, which is of course absurd, one can't control every second of one's existence. I said to him that everyone was white and everyone was or was pretending to be heterosexual. He roared with laughter, 'I see what you mean.' Because the Balkans are among the last all-white areas in Europe. No-one ever emigrates from Africa or North Africa or anywhere else to go and live in Sarajevo and so it's one hundred per cent white and then of course being a very old-fashioned place everyone who's gay is totally in the closet. Being a smart guy he knew exactly what I meant.

Whereas here everyone's kind of surprising. Just yesterday I met Ben – my secretary – close to his apartment which is on the East Side, 2nd Avenue and 3rd St, and I was looking for an apartment for my Italian translator, who's an academic and spending a sabbatical year getting all my things translated – and every person seemed to me so odd, so eccentric, so *done up*, performing in different ways – appearance, tattoos, metal in the face, hair colouring, girth, clothes – a very striking experience.

You should spend a little more time here!

EL: I'd like to redefine the term 'saturnine' that you used for melancholy.

The 'saturnine' could be more adaptive than melancholy.

Julia Kristeva talks about the use of melancholy as an example for young people. 'The individual threatened by the new maladies of the soul seeks a meeting with an experience – of someone who has "made her journey to the end of the night, fully aware of having lost the self, and got it back in some form." The speech it draws from that experience is a new knowledge.' That *coming out of* melancholy – it's like Eleonora de Fonseca Pimentel in *Volcano Lover*. Her situation is terrible, she's going to her execution, but she is able to say 'Perhaps one day even this will be a joy to recall.'

SS: Isn't that the most extraordinary thing? Of course a great deal of the novel is totally invented, especially everyone's thoughts, but there *was* a real Eleanora and she *did* say that. That's why she's in the book. That somebody could say that – I had to inhabit that person and I've put into her a lot of myself. Just that! About to be executed, to undergo something so atrocious. It's so great, so – noble. That's the thing that's gone out of our consciousness and largely out of our art. This nobility.

EL: Classical?

SS: I don't know if it's classical – of course it has anti-republican associations from the word go but we don't have a better word for it. But it's the notion of being totally beyond oneself in the most generous way, that's what's great.

Just this morning I was reading the *New York Times* – Baudelaire said there's nothing more grotesque than to read the newspaper first thing when you wake up, having a daily diet of vulgarity and horror – but anyway, some article was saying that of course in the 90s greed was taken for granted. It's not that you actually have to say your primary intent is making money – it's absolutely taken for granted, and you're consequently insane if that isn't *your* primary intent. First of all it's not true. I know lots of people for whom it's not the main thing.

If you were to ask me in my long life what is the greatest single change I've seen, I'd say it's the death of high-mindedness. The notion of sacrifice – that you can be moved in certain circumstances to sacrifice yourself – this is an idea which is unintelligible today. They haven't the faintest idea what you mean. They think you're insane.

EL: The New Age wants worship as part of 'spirituality,' in quotes. But Gandhi said, in his marvellous list of checks and balances, 'There can be no worship without sacrifice.'

SS: There's no sacrifice at all! Just personal, wonderful, personal *performing.* When I told people in New York I'd come back from a great deal of time in Sarajevo they'd say, 'But isn't it dangerous?'

I said, 'It couldn't be more dangerous!'

'Then why are you doing it?'

I said, 'Can't you ever imagine doing something dangerous because you felt there was a reason?'

———————

This interview took place in Ms Sontag's New York apartment early in 2000, and was assisted by a grant from the Literature Fund of the Australia Council.

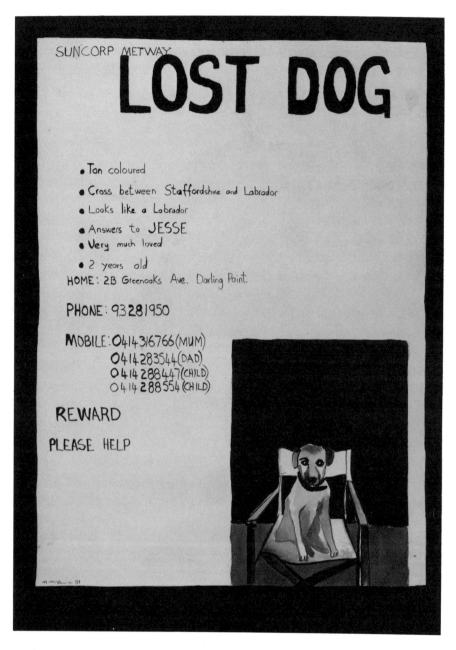

Noel McKenna is represented by Darren Knight Gallery, Sydney; Niagara Galleries, Melbourne; and Paul Greenaway Gallery, Adelaide.

Alexandra Pitsis

The terrain of his eternal amnesia

Thus I progressed on the surface of life, in the realm of words as it were, never in reality. All those books barely read, those friends barely loved, those cities barely visited, those women barely loved! I went through the gestures out of boredom or absent mindedness. Then came human beings; they wanted to cling but there was nothing to cling to, and that was unfortunate. For them. As for me, I forgot. I never remembered anything but myself.

ALBERT CAMUS, *The Fall*

A moment of inattention to his own grief and such a flighty expression – where did it come from, at what depths did it soil its wings, this expression – 'And Why Not?'

The first time he had considered socialising with her, he didn't think about what he was saying – he had no real opinion, it was neither here nor there. But at the core of it, there was the inkling that he didn't want to let go of her – not just yet.

His proposition was born from the moment. He was the one who suggested they go and see a movie to celebrate. This was the small step towards closing the lawyer-client relationship or obscuring that line, the way language is obscured in moments of opportunism disguised as scampering confusion. The mad scram – the psychic scuffle.

Her response to his suggestion summed her up quite well. No hint of cruelty, but something much more undefined and unknown. At that point he decided she was fleeting trouble, the consolation in the moment being 'fleeting'. For she didn't gracefully decline his offer, she was no demurrer, as they say. But she laughed in his face because she found the situation a laughing matter. Her crime was that she was full of innocent wit and sarcasm, which just spilt out in perfect formation with no ill intent. They were half-way through the game – life would appear to even out the scores one way or another.

What he didn't understand about her was, all this time she lived in a kind of reverie and in the realm of poetic gestures. He could only read her response to his childlike offer as a pathetic demonstration of her will and a shameless display of her naïvety.

So, he thought he'd try to invite her out a second time, 'And Why Not?' The same expression, but born out of what could only be described as an attempt to recapture the moment lost – to go back to where the adversarial monster lurks, bobbing its head up every now and then, whipping its tail against the polite mask every time they agreed to meet.

This agreement was hypothetical until transacted. And in the hypothetical realm he could afford to act as carefree as he wished, though in truth there was no one more incarcerated. And yet he acted as though he was untroubled and so true to the moment and true to his word. She couldn't understand this continual game of accepting and declining offers. But this was the ferocious creature unable to distinguish its desires from anti-desires. A strange predator, that abides by the laws about inflicting pain on other creatures in such an absent-minded manner.

So, on being asked to be more precise with his intentions through the use of language, to put someone out of their misery, he smiled like some mythical figure and came up with another one of those expressions...about him being in the moment and being in the moment as a lover of free and frank discussion.

When he laughed, it was difficult to gauge whether his laughter was stemming from conceit, or was it nervousness, or pleasure? She doubted that it stemmed from a cruel streak. He was another confused human being who had no idea what he was asking for and had even less intention to comply with any agreements, in the hypothetical or the real. He was what you might call a passive demurrer out of his depth.

They could have argued about the legal status of deception and its accomplices, illusion and expectation. What subclause it took up in an agreement scrawled on the heart of the matter.

On a wider scale they could have argued how deception is a form of confusion. Some might argue that deception is aligned with atrocities committed in history. Surely, to damage someone's soul, must amount to some type of crime.

Her eye caught sight of him walking towards her wearing a new suit. She remembered an expression where you asked the suit 'Where are you taking the gentleman?'

As he approached, he thought about all the phone calls he should be making, dealing with business, dealing with profitability not liability. Yet, he genuinely enjoyed the obscure un-nameable feeling he got from just talking to her.

But to be 'in the moment' requires an ability to commit yourself unconditionally to the future – Oh and what an ideal this is – divorced from reality and glittering away on a vast ocean. Who would be capable of this unconditional commitment to the essence of the future? What is the cost of being in the moment?

He had continually absented himself from any laboured thought about people. He had forgotten her, until now. The last time he had spoken to her they discussed intentions in such an allegorical way that they felt an illusory intimacy. Smiling and nodding as they agreed about indescribable matters and indefinable pockets of reality.

Had he put a moment's thought into the premise that 'intentions can only be inferred through words', she needn't have suffered at all. In a strange way, this was her plight, to take the *emotional misdemeanor* and turn it into an *identifiable act*.

Relegated to the terrain of his eternal amnesia...as if she were someone who gave him a bit of her innocence and he disdainfully smiled at how worthless even this small piece of innocence was.

Can such an act go unpunished? But it does – this is the micro-level where masculine and feminine relations are established so stupidly over eons. Was this never to change? If the act could be so removed from the soul – this is where the human animal can be likened to a robot. And if the act was examined most thoroughly, you would discover the gaping wounds that language can't absolve – the politics of intentions and misgivings.

So, who was this exquisite person who had been scared into being an automaton which came out with ready-made expressions and used quaint phrases, while she extended herself to engage with humanity, hovering between nobility and utter stupidity?

The little phrases he used were like a safety rail while all hell was breaking loose, the earth swallowing up people and fire descending from the skies. This was the voice of sanity and she came to depend on his presence, but to reach him was another matter all together.

It was as if she were to lure him out of himself – that place where he embedded himself – a place he put together over time – with perseverance, chance and deliberation, where he sat, where even his conceit was feigned. The moment she realised he was not a robot was when he smiled at the small green lizard brooch she wore.

Every now and then he was gripped by something you could call hope. But he thought, sadly, who would save him from this hope? His bad memory would save him, for everything eventually just slid off him. People were not worth the effort, for anything to do with people inevitably turned sour or brought him closer to the terror of being, that stinging feeling. This bad memory is the necessary fertile ground for ambiguities and equivocations. Amorality in the process of language.

When she laughed at the thought of socializing with him, it was an honest reaction. To her, he was another dead soul who had read too many law books and had calcified his brain.

She could remember that image of him in the corridors of the court, running from one person to the next, from one door to the next – like some infernal messenger, doomed, with no message – that soulless look on his face – he looked like the living dead – what could have killed his spirit like that? At what price did he decide his soul was worth so little? And what about her, on the other extreme, all soul and no where to go.

He was a bird hovering over a ship, waiting for the scavenging to commence. And what do these images indicate? Is he adept at getting what he wants? Probably not. He was just another tormented soul that had stopped asking questions about his passions. He had gathered momentum then extinguished this frightening force with vast amounts of oblivion, and oblivious thoughts.

He sensed her arrogance, that she thought so little of him. He found her irritating and interesting at the same time. Always about to say something meaningful. Coming out with some polite ambiguity that could be taken either way.

'Well I can relax, I haven't become a character out of a Kafka novel,' she said as he arrived at the table.

'No, there is no resemblance,' he responded. 'You didn't come anywhere near a Kafka character.'

'Oh yes I did – I felt the horror of the randomness of the institutional machine about to descend on me.'

'But you had me to represent you, to *look after your interests* – your legal counsel.'

'Then, tell me why I was convinced you would smile in your civil and polite way, and come up with one of those phrases like, *we'll see about that*. All the time I was sure that if I was in dire straits you'd say, *sorry I can't help you.*'

He smiled but was insulted that she had so little faith in him, although she was correct in her assumption.

From this little exchange he became acutely aware that she had

expectations, not of romance or frivolity, but something of a more serious nature, dealing with what she perceived to be his spiritual mess.
And she had no rights to any aspect of him, particularly his psyche.

'So you think I would *turn into a devil?*' he said, annoyed.

'No – I'd be more afraid you'd *be human.*'

With all her faith in the precision of language, despite this project
– the mission of precision in communication – being doomed to fail,
and her predisposition to ambiguities and ironies – the thing that
seized her in the middle of a rational discussion about banal topics, like
the energies between words and the effect these words have on the
psyche, was, when all is said and done it's all completed in civil polite
conversation. When all along, the thing that gripped her, locked her
into a labyrinth of misdiagnosed morality – the thing that she couldn't
fathom – was that he was in another realm and the only thing that
momentarily connected them was the illusion of language, and those
ready-made expressions criss-crossing the patches of oblivion.

She was convinced he had a beauty about him, a halo of martyr-
dom, you could call it. This halo was made of thorns worn tightly, but
looked like dainty white flowers spuriously held together with dis-
content. At least that's how it appeared from a distance.

He was like someone who had clambered through jagged mountains on bare knees to secure a deal. His unexplainable sweetness could
only be traced to his lack of ownership over his own persona, the part that
makes one true to one's word. That is why she couldn't ever hate him.

To not own oneself is a condemnation that only few suffer but
none as well as he does. That's what made him go on those fierce walks
that ended at some unknown point where he no longer had cognition
of his own self. That's what made him fly into those blind rages.

'And most people are a brick wall, look,' she pointed to some
imaginary part of his ether body. 'Here are the dents where someone
tried to reach you.'

He laughed at this. 'Well I should hope someone tried.'

He had the following thoughts about her: that she spoke of 'dents',
but of course – every person that came near to reaching him had to con-
tend with a greater rival – a greater contender that always won – that was
his fear cloaked as indifference, and his turmoil dressed in a new suit.

He was too polite to make it clear to her that his spirit had vacated long before that day he asked her to go and see a movie. If she wanted to engage in strange and frivolous activities embodying the superficial – he was her man. This was what his soul was asking for. Not undertaking the long and arduous task of finding a trail back from *Terra Internalis*.

She was trapped in some painful illusion that they knew each other. She sent him a few quotes from Chamfort, underlining the following – 'One is made happy or unhappy by a multitude of unseen things which one does not refer to and could not describe.' Although his favourite quote was, 'Considering that virtue is always dangerous or at least useless, and vice is always fortunate... what is a lofty soul to do? Take refuge in a sensible and unshakable pride, a sort of misanthropy which lets one love mankind in general yet holds individuals at bay, save those to whom he is attached by natural duty.'

She continued the ridiculous pursuit of trying to get him to redeem himself in a minor act, but for him it became crucial to continue the game. The most important weapon he possessed in this game was his politeness. The well trodden circular paths of politeness.

Surely people should be responsible for the way they use politeness. It's more deadly than cruelty and eats the soul of the offender more than the victim. This is the game that she so beautifully lent herself to.

All the time he agreed to meet her, but trailing behind him, some vague and lost ghost of his third-world poverty. A ghost draped with transient wealth.

If he closed his eyes momentarily, she reminded him of the lizards that ran briskly through the houses near the sea, in those humid afternoons of endless play and mystery, into the night and unaffected sleep. Instead of giving over to this, he used the words that made things tidy and distanced him from the past. This was a form of illusory control over his life. We create and depend on the tools that keep us standing up.

What are all the situations that crossed his path, what are the decisions he made – what well-carved paths had he trodden – what chaos had he avoided – what chaos subsumed him? – like everyone he wanted to feel alive – yet feared where life would hurl him if he stopped to think – what are all the choices he made along the way, and what are the choices he didn't make? Beaten into a type of spiritual submission, understood only by those who narrowly escaped the same fate.

The first time she saw who he was, much later in their acquaintance, she was astounded at her own awkwardness. She blithered on about misconceptions of historical events and race issues – this was no 'ready made' talk. It was pure nervousness at being touched by something unknown. And him, sitting across the table looking bewildered and pleased at the same time. Staring, unknowingly, into her soul.

At the end of their time together she was struck by something quite powerful. She was to realise later that it was the chaotic vacuum of him exiting from her life when she was only getting to know him.

She had feared becoming a character out of a Kafka novel when all the time she was suffering the effects of trying to commune with a character from a Camus novel – and one threatened with a kind of amnesia, at that.

It was like death's twin visiting without leaving a trace – each time he didn't keep an engagement she believed he was ill with some serious malady of the soul. And he was. Without a permit or agreement, he took his leave.

The words he uses are nothing but simulacra, he fills them with evasions, with equivocations, he turns them into wily devices, he uses them to play tricks... when he is lucky enough to come across someone like her who lends herself to it so beautifully to 'falling for it' every time.
NATHALIE SARRAUTE, *The Uses of Speech*

Alexandra Pitsis is currently working on a novel about science and aesthetics.

Peter Rose
Roman Fleuve

Graphic, if pointlessly moving,
re-reading that old volume of yours,
cracked now, yellow at the edges,
the autumn of our sophistry.
Student to your libertine,
I trace the dog ears of your fretfulness,
insomniac nights you tricked on their heads,
interrogating every certainty.
Whose inked spurs to the dialectic
snaking down the rancid page –
yours? mine? a third's?
Those epigrams were dying on a lip:
were they mine you edified, undid?
Your last bodement was all of a piece,
starkness worthy of a jabbing priest.
As then, I attend, say nothing.

Satellite

Somewhere, I suppose, a waking
is celebrated, wine poured,
assurances exchanged.

Here, a balloon eclipses morning,
hangs like an absorbed satellite,
golden, unmanned.

To Adelaide

Dawn flights weave eccentric routes,
veering as the land balds,
holdings scarred and beautiful.
Sunlight dawdles on a dam,
ignites the midget fauna.
Apologising for our tardiness
the pilot says we are bearers
of spare parts for a stricken jet.
'What sort of an excuse is that?'
bawls my Texan neighbour.
Below, the land is quilted
like a chequered past,
cosmetic, infinitely private.
The in-flight service is delayed
and I am glad, but not the Americans.
Just as the captain predicts
a smooth flight we hit the turbulence.

Peter Rose's latest collection of poems is *Donatello in Wangaratta* (Hale
& Iremonger, 1998). His family memoir, *Rose Boys,* will be published
by Allen & Unwin in 2001.

Christopher Pollnitz

Criticism, Biography and Les Murray

On Peter F. Alexander's biography *Les Murray: A Life in Progress* (Oxford University Press, 2000); with passing reference to David Ellis, *Literary Lives: Biography and the Search for Understanding* (Edinburgh University Press, 2000).

Grrr or *Shhh?* Is that the susurrus of gossip or the grinding of axes I can hear, as I sit down with the *Life* of Les Murray? Well before the re-issuing of this biography, withdrawn after the 1999 version had been threatened with at least one action of libel, whisperings were audible in the Australian literary community. They have risen to such a pitch in the past year that the question should be asked: is this cantankerousness and vituperation endemic in the community, or is it Murray himself, perhaps Murray's career, that inspires such animated defence from his assembled friends, and such naked animosity from the array of his enemies? It would be invidious to assign all blame to the community or the individual, but to raise the question at all suggests how much of a nettle, if not giant stinger, Peter Alexander seized in taking on the *Life* of Les Murray.

In *Literary Lives*, an attempt to theorise and even more to scrutinise the principles and practices of biographers in the last century, David Ellis deplores the standard of reviewing of biographies. Ellis profiles the ideal reviewer as one who has covered some of or the same ground as the biographer, since, as he brazenly declares, biographers 'sometimes cheat…there is so little danger of reviewers finding them out.' If that is admitted, imagine the clamant queue of potential reviewers for the *Life* in question! Few readers of these pages will not know a sheaf of Murray anecdotes; some will be first-hand. With such a public subject, Alexander has relatively little chance of cheating, or satisfying, Australian readers, most of whom are already entrenched in the side on which they stand – the *Grrr* camp, or the still-disconcerting *Shhh* persuasion.

To establish my qualifications, I had better come clean with my Murray story, having been disconcerted to find Murray, or should I say Alexander, has already recounted it as his Pollnitz story. In Alexander's biography the story is treated briefly and in appropriate proportion, and if I discuss it at greater length in this review, it is not to suggest it should be a *cause célèbre*, but because it is, for me, a convenient touchstone of Alexander's handling of his materials and of Murray's capacity to alienate and polarise acquaintances.

In 1989, Sydney University Press asked me to prepare a short critical study, targeted for secondary and tertiary students of Murray's poetry. Having other projects on the burner, I was reluctant at first, checked whether Murray himself was willing to give me a day or two of his time, and having obtained his consent ('Better you than some of those other wombats…'), correctly estimated that I could get the study written in a few months. I sent a first draft to Murray before travelling overseas, then a second to Murray and the publisher, on my return. Murray was seemingly troubled by the first draft, but his particular complaints related to the family history and discussion of poetic influences in the early chapters, most of which were cut for length reasons. His response to my second draft was to phone Oxford University Press which, in the interim, had taken over the press with which my study was originally contracted. With OUP, Murray had considerable influence. He 'prohibited' publication of my study; the verb I heard from an editor at OUP, who contacted me before Murray did to ask what Murray had taken exception to. At that stage, I knew no more than the editor. Murray's means for enforcing his prohibition was to instruct Tom Thompson, acting for Angus and Robertson, to deny copyright permission for any quotations. Of course, not even a powerful figure like Murray can prohibit criticism of his work – so the fair dealing provision in the Copyright Act seemed to guarantee, and so the publisher now in charge of my contract seemed to agree. OUP humoured me for a year, and then had me rewrite the preface a week before cancelling the study. At the time, I was more outraged by the press's perfidy than Murray's, though his going behind my back to the publishers remains a personal betrayal. What OUP did, so I surmise, was check the balance sheet for Murray's splendid anthology, the *New Oxford Book of Australian Verse*. The lesson handed out to me was one in economic principle, I suspect, that the bottom line can matter as much to 'university' presses as to commercial presses.

Murray did write to me, at length, explaining what he objected to in my book: it was the literary criticism. As inventions of the Enlightenment, criticism and critical interpretation were impediments to the function of poetry, namely, communication of the sacred. This had been the theme of some of Murray's essays in the eighties, both in verse and prose, but I found the tone of the letter in which he applied the theory to this particular case unpleasant – it recalled to me references Murray had made to his psychological difficulties, references that I should perhaps have construed as warnings – and I have filed rather than re-read it. Murray's claim to have rejected the study because it was criticism was too much a blanket explanation of his conduct. I had not disguised the book's purpose in raising it with him. As a practising critic, he ought to have been aware that readers turned to his criticism to compare their own critical readings with his. But however contradictory, his behaviour was not wholly inconsistent. Murray had cut me after my series of articles surveying his poetry appeared in *Southerly* in 1980–81. He was inclined to look upon such articles as academics making careers out of his creative work and seemed particularly to dislike attempts both to evaluate and discriminate; criticism as unalloyed praise might have passed unchecked. Some confirmation of this impression came from my editor at OUP, who said that the problem lay with the chapter on *The Boys Who Stole the Funeral*, in which I had suggested that the verse novel's sexual politics detracted from its readability. In darker hours, I suspected that Murray saw the role of the critic as that of a proselyte and proselytiser for the author's ideas. My abiding impression is that he prohibited the study because I had ideas about his poetry he had not had and did not want aired.

The story has two pendants. Murray did write to me again, after a review I wrote of *Translations from the Natural World*. He corrected me on some points, forgave me for having had to prohibit my book, and permitted me to go ahead and publish it. This did not seem an enormous concession, considering Murray's knowledge of how publishers operate, but who knows, one day my little study may have its day. I see a lurid cover with the blurb, *Now at last, the book Les Murray prohibited*. The second anecdote is that Peter Alexander rang me in 1994, asking my advice on whether to undertake the biography. In our only exchange on Murray, I warned him not to do it, adding that if he went ahead the very worst thing he could do was to show Murray drafts. How mistaken I was! Here is the biography in front of me, with footnotes referring to corrections Murray has made on Alexander's drafts, all bespeaking the complete amity between biographer and subject. Most intriguing is Alexander's account of how unreservedly Murray agreed to his project: 'I explained that I wanted complete access to everything – manuscripts, letters, diaries, accounts – that I could be interviewing them [Murray and his wife] over months, and that I would also be talking to family members, friends, ex-friends, enemies and literary rivals.' Murray's response to the proposal was 'You can publish anything you can find.' If Alexander's is not a warts-and-all life, it contains a variety of intimate details most writers would be reticent about disclosing, and I (were I ever to embark on a biography) would be reticent about asking. Is Murray's ego so much invested in his poetry that he doesn't care what people know of him, only what they think about his poems? There is much to be said for such a view of Murray as he emerges from this strange collaboration. But if there was one remark in Alexander's preface which whetted this reviewer's curiosity it was to learn the distinction in Murray's mind between a critical *reading* and a biographical *finding*. The answer was not what I foresaw.

Alexander elucidates the family history, the tangle of Murrays who migrated to the mid-north coast of NSW in the 1840s, then multiplied and intermarried in the river valleys between the Myall and the Manning. He draws a satisfying narrative circle to show how the descendants of emigrant Hugh Murray did not grow into a powerful, leisured squattocracy, but instead how Cecil, Hugh's great-grandson and the poet's father, fell in three generations 'to the level of tenant-at-will, which his ancestor Hugh had left Scotland to escape.' 'Born in a Biscay storm', Hugh's first son, John, missed out on being a currency lad, but won the title of first settler 'Bunyah Johnnie', when he married his cousin Isabella and moved south from his father's leasehold on the Manning, to take up land on the Wang Wauk River. A prodigy of generosity and fecklessness, Johnnie was able to leave only a small holding to his sixth son, Allan. Left to mimic his father's feats of generosity on a meaner scale with his drinking mates, Allan exploited the labour of his own sons, eventually neglecting to pass on to Cecil the farm he believed he was working to inherit.

Alexander outlines the family history firmly and for the right reasons – not because of any dotty theory of heredity, but because it forms the dramatic core of so much of Murray's poetry. Murray's fascination with family history offers clues to many of his poems, from 'The Widower in the Country' to the characterisation of Sam Mundine, the Jewish Aboriginal, in *Fredy Neptune*. Alexander's notes reveal that Murray's mother, Miriam, had one cousin, a Coolongolook Worth, who married an Aboriginal, and that ancestors of the Worths may have been Parisians and Jewish. The notes indicate that Alexander has followed rather than led Murray's research into ancestry, but the illumination of the poetry that becomes available through Murray's own impressions of his family tree makes the biography's explication of the research required reading. Without it, readers may overlook the explosive and changing mixture of celebration, defensiveness and satirical spleen with which Murray's portraits of 'simple' country life are loaded, a mixture that has enabled him to blow up the old conventions of Australian pastoral and start again with new foundations. It is of interest that Murray and Alexander see the bringing home of Lesley to a poverty-stricken shanty in terms of family drama rather than from a sociological perspective. Many Australian children grew up in shanties during the Depression and can relate to 'The Sleepout' and 'The Tin Wash Dish' because of it. Alexander may be right to point out that this was a difficult start for a poet, but Whitman in the nineteenth century and Heaney in the twentieth might at least vie with Murray in terms of educational disadvantage.

The proliferation of Murrays and other intermarrying Scottish families on the mid-north coast resulted, Alexander notes, in a Bunyah dialect, a local vocabulary and intonation that were predominantly Scots English but included some treasured (by Murray) Aboriginal borrowings. I can confirm this from personal experience. Standing on Broadmeadow station one day, I heard Murray's distinctive accents and, turning to say hello, was embarrassed to find myself addressing someone I had never met. No, he was not a Murray, he explained (my curiosity had got the better of me), but he did come from up the Myall Lakes. While offering a helpful glossary drawn from Murray's poetry and essays, Alexander betrays his own origins when he himself adds 'skillion', meaning a lean-to, to this regional dialect. 'Skillion' is not even East Coast; South Australian informants and the *Macquarie Dictionary* (which includes a citation from Henry Lawson) confirm that the dialect Alexander is dealing with here is Australian English. An Australian might also complain of a lack of tact in Alexander's treatment of the contacts between the Murray settlers and the Aboriginal people of the district, the Kattangal. Murray has expressed pride in his pioneer ancestry. In an early poem like 'Noonday Axeman', 'the dray-wheels' silence final in our ears,/ and the first red cattle spreading through the hills' makes the silence and hills sound suspiciously like *terra nullius*. While I know of no basis for disputing Alexander's historical assertions – 'in this new land, the Murrays prospered', partly because, it seems, 'Hugh Murray and his brothers found the Aboriginals no threat, and offered them no violence' – it is possible to miss any expression of regret at the shrinking and ghetto-ising of the Kattangal into the Purfleet settlement. Some will prefer Judith Wright's wistful account of first contact in her autobiography, *Half a Lifetime*, and in poems like 'Old House.'

To turn from family history to family romance, to the dynamics of Cecil, Miriam and Les in their Bunyah shanty, is to turn to that entry-way to a literary life where, David Ellis would say, a biographer must be largely dependent on his subject's witness, where the new materials Alexander has elicited from Murray and his family are indispensable, but where the requirement on him for detached and objective scrutiny of the evidence is at its most stringent. Alexander's narrative has a satisfying psychological complexity, the result of 'nice contradiction between fact and fact' which, in Robert Graves's words, 'makes the whole seem human and exact', but which also suggests he has not sceptically screened the testimony received. On the one hand, Murray as a child never had any friends to come around and play because his parents were ashamed to reveal the poverty of their home; on the other, he was dreamy, cocooned in his own world of words and sacred objects, socially inept and incurious. While the mother, with her nurse's training, was prim, efficient and 'untactile', by his own diagnosis Murray was semi-autistic as a child and unable to recognise or respond to parental affection. As a 'half-autie' he was also given to uncontrollable rages and destructive acts, which his parents attempted to manage with savage beatings, demanded by the mother and inflicted by the father: 'From about the time he turned two, Murray was smacked increasingly severely and often, intensifying to what he called "frequent harsh floggings for being a bad boy".' What credence can be put in this report? A child might remember being smacked at age two, but a routine of beatings at that age might rather be repressed. Given the vagaries of early memory, how would one know that the beatings had *begun* at the age of two? These are extraordinarily painful recollections. To deal with them in any other way than sympathetic acceptance may seem brutal, but their horrific content in itself must provoke doubts about their accuracy. A biographer might well be pleased to escape from such a nightmare atmosphere to the more historical and sociological question, of the effects of Murray's upbringing in that puritanical splinter sect, the Free Presbyterian Church. But Alexander gives little, in my opinion too little, attention to the effect of this on Murray's isolation, sense of guilt and fear of retribution.

Alexander's coup has been to reconstruct, from the testimony of other family members, an account different to Murray's own of the events leading up to his mother's death. Miriam Murray died of toxaemia in Taree hospital in 1951, after a miscarriage that left her haemorrhaging for some hours on the farm at Bunyah. In his poem 'The Steel' Murray blames the doctor at the hospital for refusing to send an ambulance. In Murray's version of events, the doctor was misled by social and professional snobbery: 'Did you often do/ diagnosis by telephone?' But since the countryside around was rich in Murray families with operational cars, Alexander deduces that no ambulance was sent because Cecil, ashamed of another pregnancy which might not go full term and which Miriam had been warned against, did not ring for one, but passed the fatal hours in a frenzy of shame and panic. If 'The Steel' remains undisturbed by this alternative narrative, it is because the poem is not primarily a meditation on professional ethics, but on a father and son coming to terms with their bereavement. How the status of 'The Steel' is affected is not an issue Alexander discusses, nor is the conclusion drawn that Murray's assaults on the educated do not always elicit his most self-aware writing. Alexander's account of the mother's death does help clarify Cecil's determination to fulfil his wife's dying wish, that Lesley should complete his education. Despite on-going financial hardship, quarrels and disappointments, it was Cecil whose resolve sent his son to Taree High, where he discovered there were such beings as Australian poets, and to Sydney University, where he became one.

In 1988, Murray's reading at a Rotary Club meeting in Taree led to his meeting former school acquaintances from Taree High, and the meeting in turn precipitated involuntary weeping, panic attacks and some six years of severe depression, which coincided with my 1989 visits to Murray. It is understandable, then, that Murray's self-diagnosis is that the two years at Taree High, specifically the sexual teasing meted out to him by some of the teenage girls, formed what David Ellis calls, after Freud, the 'primal scene', beloved of biographers for its explanatory power. It is less understandable that Alexander unquestioningly assents to this self-diagnosis, given the succession of other traumas to which Murray was subjected in childhood; indeed, that he, Alexander, attributes more explanatory force to this teasing than does Murray. According to Alexander, after being called 'fat names' by the girls, Murray, henceforward, 'would be always on the side of the outcast...It was Taree High that turned him decisively against conformity, intellectual gangs, particularly literary and academic ones, and the mob-persecution of any individual.' Here there is an unexpected transposition: from being the nerdy book-worm over-looked by silly girls, the adolescent Murray has become the common man singled out for persecution by an intellectual SS. I know at least one well-read contemporary of Murray's from Taree High who avers that the girls were not only *not* like this but not that bad. Why seize on this event to explain Murray's maverick intellectualism and defence of unlikely causes, at the same time as discounting the possibility that the teasing might have left Murray with some fear of, and hostility towards, women? Murray enjoyed the cadets at Taree High. At the University of Sydney, feeling excluded by the likes of Robert Hughes and Germaine Greer, though he got on well with Clive James and Bob Ellis, Murray clubbed together with younger undergraduates to form a group who called themselves the Four Colonels and went in for week-end-long, paramilitary bushwalks. During the Poetry Wars of the 1970s, Murray gathered around him a male cadre of poets whom he called 'the stable' of *Poetry Australia*. There are patterns here, but they are not the ones Alexander highlights. For Alexander, Murray's university days are a succession of friendships and pranks. He lacks the gift of an Andrew Riemer, to sum up the flavour of a period or the calibre of an institution in a single epiphany.

Alexander did well seizing the nettle and compiling this biography, which makes itself indispensable for those who want to learn more of the two major Australian poets (two, because Murray's interactions with Judith Wright are explored in detail) from the second half of the twentieth century. Extensive bibliographies go a long way to fill a pressing scholarly need. The chronology and the detailing of Murray's travels, from 1965 on, are useful, though Alexander, by insisting on the Australianness of the poems Murray wrote for *The Weatherboard Cathedral* during his time in Wales, misses pointing out that the way forward for Murray was through poems like 'The Fire Autumn', which position Australia in a global phantasmagoria. To have between boards Murray's account of the circumstances of composition of so many of his poems makes the book an invaluable resource. That Alexander has often played Boswell to Murray's Johnson means that we have some record of the second glory of the poet's verbal productions (I would set it equal with his essays), namely his conversation.

Yet the critical reception of Murray's poetry is not well handled, not because Alexander fails to go through volume by volume, quoting from selected reviews, but because he shows insufficient discrimination and independence of judgment. His usual procedure is to counter negative criticism and support laudatory reviews, with the result that Murray's entire oeuvre is evenly puffed – or would be, did Alexander not feel called on for a crescendo. So *Translations from the Natural World* is 'clearly' the work of 'a poet at the height of his powers', while *Subhuman Redneck Poems* demonstrates Murray's 'poetic output was rising to a peak', another peak presumably. In the case of the latter volume, Murray had already signalled to Alexander in an interview that Don Anderson's review, in which Anderson singled out ten per cent of the poems as 'vile', indeed vomitory, including it may be surmised those explicitly dealing with Taree High, was close to the mark. Murray himself did not rate these cathartic poems high on his list of achievements: 'I'm not interested in all that stuff now...I wrote that out directly in *Redneck*...Fred [i.e. *Fredy Neptune*] is the turning of it right up to the level of poetry.' I too can accept *Fredy Neptune* as the summit of Murray's achievement in the nineties, a recovery of the ground he had reached in *The People's Otherworld* and *The Daylight Moon*. But without the nod from Murray, would Alexander have found anything to endorse in Anderson's judgment? Then, in case he has not fully covered himself, Alexander goes on to reclaim the *Subhuman* Taree High poems as specimens of Swiftian, or Yeatsian, *saeva indignatio*. They are nothing of the sort. That accolade might be worth bestowing on the impersonal but deeply moving 'Dog Fox Field', but even here Alexander cannot resist quoting the couplet about the slaughter of the intellectually handicapped under the Third Reich – 'Our sentries, whose holocaust does not end,/ they show us when we cross into Dog Fox Field' – and relating it to the 'fashion police' and Taree High. It is offensive to those who lost their lives in the Holocaust or have been threatened with involuntary euthanasia since, and incidentally to Taree, to draw the belittling comparison. It is a detraction on Murray's poem. Lack of critical acumen is one reason Alexander's is not a critical biography.

Another is tied up with Alexander's almost Shavian propensity to offer stage directions for scenes at which he has not been present. Murray often produces an outrageous sally 'cheerfully' (indeed, he does), but when he faces one of his Taree High tormentors he delivers his one-liner 'evenly' – as indeed he might have, relating the encounter in interview, but how he did it at the time is Alexander's gloss. Alexander reaches for the purple when he seeks to engage a reader's full sympathy. While workshopping poems at the University of Sydney, Geoffrey Lehmann's 'dark, cold face would glow with triumph when he was about to annihilate one of Murray's efforts' – or so Alexander supposes, the style of reportage being his, not Murray's. This weighting of scales rises 'to a peak' in exchanges which are not even oral but epistolary, notably in Alexander's report on a series of letters between Judith Wright and Murray, initiated when Wright invited Murray to contribute to a manuscript exhibition being mounted in support of an Aboriginal Treaty. Murray sees the 'real menace' in Wright's initial letter, but his 'admirably sure-footed and elegant' reply leaves Wright 'clearly rattled by' its argument, and so on. An irritated reader learns to read against the grain of the superfluous commentary, but the result is to find it difficult to do justice to Murray's argument in this case, and to lament room was not found for more extensive quotation of a searching literary and political debate.

As against this distinguished exchange between well-matched adversaries, in which the text of the exchange is not in dispute, the biography enumerates a succession of what I could call 'Murray controversies' – quarrels which are high on acrimony, denunciation and hysteria, in which the substantive issues of the dispute have been lost in the dust of the conflict, and the clearest common factor has been Murray's involvement. Murray controversies include: Did Vincent Buckley disseminate the idea that the young Murray was 'a promising poet...but a terrible Nazi'? Were the poetry wars of the seventies any more than power struggles and Pyrrhic name-callings, in which Murray gave as good as he got? What manoeuvres and motives led to Murray's ousting as editor of *Poetry Australia*, as reader for Angus and Robertson, and as poetry editor of *Quadrant*? Did Manning Clark ever receive the Order of Lenin, and if so what significance had his wearing or not wearing the decoration? Alexander's venturing upon these questions only muddies the waters. While it is sometimes possible to read against his commentary, the over-reliance on Murray's testimony makes his adjudication of the controversies all but useless.

The first of the controversies exemplifies Alexander's approach to literary history. Alexander's source for Buckley having disparaged Murray's politics behind Murray's back is Murray, and again Murray. Alexander has interviewed Chris Wallace-Crabbe, but whether Wallace-Crabbe, for one, ever heard Buckley make such remarks is not a question Alexander has asked; or if he has, results of the enquiry are not included in the biography. My scrape with Murray is, as I said, a personal touchstone for Alexander's handling of his sources. Murray stopped my critical study, Alexander records, 'on the grounds that Pollnitz thought him a misogynist.' My initial response to this was one of relief (at last I knew Murray's real motive), followed by consternation (I hadn't directly called Murray a misogynist in either draft of the book, no such insult had been offered), followed by puzzlement (if Murray thought I thought he was a misogynist, on the basis of what I wrote about *The Boys Who Stole the Funeral*, he must himself have begun to re-read the book's anti-feminist rhetoric with something of the appalled embarrassment many readers had). The solution to the puzzle I found in the endnote: the source for what Pollnitz thought of Murray was the phone-call to me in which Alexander asked advice on whether to take on the biography. I suppose, speaking with Alexander, I may have used the word 'misogynist' to label some of my difficulties in conversation with Murray in 1989, or with reading *The Boys*. Though it would be more characteristic of me to say that I 'found the book's sexual politics intolerable', I am in no position to dispute the notes Alexander apparently took from our conversation. But why would a biographer ask Pollnitz for Murray's motivation for prohibiting a book, and not Murray himself, unless there were questions the biographer was frightened of asking his subject? Some questions Alexander felt he could only ask Murray about; some he felt he could never ask Murray about. Variant findings on such questions, Alexander seems to have felt, would have rendered his biography unacceptable to its subject.

Alexander's *Life* commits itself to saying far worse things about Murray than would have offended him in my drafts. Murray's attacks on the Literature Board in the nineties might, Alexander suggests, have been kept up out of a desire for publicity, and Murray's idea that the Board itself had been taken over by 'Tranterites' was paranoid. At least, Alexander does not use the word, writing instead how Murray believed 'cliques of his enemies were constantly plotting to do him harm', though this was 'largely imagination on his part.' Yet, within the page, Alexander is describing 'The Lecture Halls of the Fisher King', not as a collection of aphorisms whose vitriol has been distilled out of a troubled mind, but as 'one of [Murray's] most brilliant pieces.' This is a biographer unable to let his right eye see what his left hand has just written on the verso. David Ellis notes in *Literary Lives* that biographers of living subjects, like Norman Sherry on Graham Greene, may forfeit interpretative coherence, hoping to infect their readers instead with their own 'enthusiasm for information'. There is no dearth of intimate revelations or psychoanalytic interpretation, however, in Alexander's *Life* of Murray. Ugly truths about the subject are admitted in such oddly contradictory contexts in this *Life* because Murray has not spared himself. Very much as in *Subhuman Redneck Poems*, and to a lesser degree *Fredy Neptune*, Murray has conducted his autoanalysis with a genuine ruthlessness, and sent it forth, with all its confusions – not even Freud claimed to have completed his analysis of himself – in the form of Alexander's *Life*. If Murray has not spared himself, he's hardly been more considerate of Alexander who, while some of his contradictions verge on the disingenuous, never seems quite to twig that Murray has been ventriloquising a review of his psyche through his chosen biographer. Most of Murray's interviews with Alexander seem to have been completed by August 1998, when Murray wrote in 'The Lecture Halls of the Fisher King': 'Academics and authors despise each other most when each has it in mind to exploit the other.'

While I suppose I did gain a little self-respect when my study of Murray did not appear in 1990, I can't claim there was much pressure on me to bowdlerise that study and so appease its subject. Maintaining critical distance when writing literary criticism is not a matter of principle with me; I can't conceive of doing it another way. It seems from his preface that Alexander both personally admires and is daunted by Murray, but that what he was principally afraid of was Murray withdrawing the right to quote him. In his anxiety to please and his fear of not being allowed to publish, Alexander has produced a portrait that has this reader, for one, shivering with repudiation. It would take a remorseless foe to rejoice in retaining only the warts from this portrait, the larger outlines of which are so blurred with trepidation. Unlike the Ern Malley poems, *Les Murray: A Life in Progress* is not a hoax; the name on the cover is in some sense the author's; but like that hoax, this *Life* raises serious doubt about the calibre and confidence of Australian literary criticism. In the unlikely event of my ever being asked for advice again, I would encourage Alexander to keep all his preparatory notes and tapes. They will be of value for a future, critical biographer.

Christopher Pollnitz lectures in English at the University of Newcastle and is compiling a critical edition of D. H. Lawrence's *Poems*.

Fay Zwicky

Past and Present Worlds

Rosemary Dobson

Untold Lives & Later Poems (Brandl & Schlesinger, 2000)

Throughout a long, distinguished poetic career, Rosemary Dobson's capacity for protective self-scrutiny has always been balanced by aspirations to self-transcendence. Anchored in a sense of the present's dependence on the past, her best work has been characterised by exemplary clarity, restraint and tact. Predominantly elegiac in tone, mood shifts have rarely jolted her meditative, unpressured pace. Qualities I once described in a 1985 essay on her work as 'reclusive grace', distinctly unmodern in her considerate refusal to invade, 'wanting the light and sorry for the dark.'

In 1984, forty years after the publication of her first book, Rosemary Dobson brought out *The Three Fates* which contained surprising poems intimating the play of new possibilities: a less objec-tified engagement with the world, movement away from formal constrictions, and a willingness, albeit hesitant, to expose the lyric 'I' to the absence of closure. At the time I thought she had extended her range as far as she was ever likely to. *Untold Lives*, emerging in this her eightieth year, proves me wrong. The grace remains unchanged but awareness of its human context has broadened and deepened.

Divided into three sections, the book opens with 'Untold Lives',

a sequence originally published under that title in 1992 commemo-
rating 'unnamed people' known to the poet; 'untold' in the sense of
heroism unsung; 'untold' as in numberless, often implying regret as to
what should or should not have been 'told' by the narrator in life as in
art. Even understood as a pun on the tolling of a funeral knell, the
poems' complex potentialities are belied by their seemingly artless
structural simplicity.

An undercurrent of lament acknowledging the cost of human
loss and, more generally, time's sabotage of personal and collective
endeavour, breathes life into a *dramatis personae* drawn from the almost-
vanished world of Anglo-Australia some of us remember growing up
in and for which some retain residual nostalgia. The empathic affection
informing these vignettes for the voiceless, the inherent indebtedness
of the venture itself, reminded me of Edgar Lee Masters' ghostly re-
creation of an innocent homogenous community doomed to extinction
in his 1915 *Spoon River Anthology*. So, too, did the telling selection and
juxtaposition of detail bring Lowell's *Life Studies* to mind without his
chilly detachment.

The survival strengths and vulnerabilities of women, often
minimised or disregarded in the past, are here allowed memory's
unironic florescence. Their destinies, often hazy and unfocused in life
as wives, mothers, aunts, and sisters given to painful expiation of
impulses towards self-realisation, are contrasted with those of men of
the Victorian paterfamilias stamp. Such reliance on status and social
importance may have bolstered clear personal definition but it has
successfully and tragically impeded and crippled the growth of
emotional connective tissue. The waste, pathos, and sometime brutality in relationships between the unequally-equipped emerge in 'The
Major-General', for example, who 'kept the stoic phase/ Ready like a
revolver in his drawer' and 'beat the mischief from his younger son' as
his distressed wife stands speechlessly by. Surveying his 'well-kept
garden' every morning, he lays a cut flower for her on the breakfast
table 'like a threat', jamming another in his button-hole to meet
another day.

Frail masculine vanity conjures a wry satirical response in other
portraits like that of the becomingly-gowned academic whose shallow

concern for students is masked by an aura of ecclesiastical piety. In similar vein, an historian's five decorous daughters represent the arrested development consequent on parental tyranny, the dreadful shrinkage of their potential reduced to 'sewing small objects for the church bazaar.' In 'Chekhov's Sister', Dobson speaks on behalf of 'all those women and young girls/ Who gave or give their loyalty and love/ To men of genius', mourning the price of female submission more directly and dynamically than her earlier reticence has prepared us to expect.

Female vanity is as sharply observed but redeemed by more forgiving overtones. As in the sketch of once-charming, theatrical Kitty whose soul, 'like thinnest chiffon' of the scarves with which she once hid the 'tautened lives about her throat', floats free along with her laughter in an image of poignant, death-defying beauty, escaping the nemesis of a sidelined daughter ominously 'waiting in the wings.'

The true heart of the matter is revealed in poems touching on Rosemary Dobson's own family that reach beyond categories and stereotypes of gender and class to an innocent wartime world that left her mother early widowed to rear two gifted daughters. During Word War II, her uncle ('Too young for one war, too old for another') dies on stretcher duty in New Guinea, leaving letters from campaigns in Egypt and Crete recounting his eager untutored exposure to relics of classical antiquity. As potent a lure as Persephone's pomegranate seeds, the flower-seeds from Crete a young man once stuffed into his kitbag ensured, if not his return, at least his niece's future journey and allegiance to her uncle's enchanted underworld, to be later celebrated in many fine poems about ancient Greek civilisation.

We all carry the seeds of our parents' hopes and unfulfilled longings but their germination takes time. The seven year-old girl reading her first obediently-rhymed poem aloud to the rhythm of her mother pegging clothes on a line grows in the strength of her mother's encouragement and pride. 'The rhymes went "click" as rhymes, I knew, should go', a discipline – that 'I knew' is perfectly judged – eventually to yield the adult poet's liberation to hang free like the clothes, enabling fruition in late age of that child's vision of poetry, 'Blowing bright coloured, all about the world.' As fresh and immediate as the past and present worlds with which she now enriches us.

Poems in the middle section, 'The News and Weather', touch on present survival in an incorrigible world that 'will not be changed', a world where precious inner resources are modestly marshalled to meet what must be met. The consolations of art – paintings and poems that 'ring their own radiance round the everyday' ('The Green Years') – absorbed long ago by an idealistic young girl, now recur less consolingly in full knowledge of the price exacted by creation. In 'The Artist', the demon-haunted painter Arthur Boyd lectures, managing to speak 'with calm and courtesy' despite the nightmare slides propelled on the screen by his tormented imagination. Out in the street, amid the man-made horrors of a destructive metropolis, the great man is observed 'trembling at the pavement's edge'.

Small wonder that the poet turns for relief and nurture in two engaging acts of homage to George Herbert and his contemporary, Isaac Walton (who wrote the life of Herbert without ever meeting him), pacific filters to a transcendence that never abandons the earth and its 'stock of natural delights.' By example, however, they offer a comforting austerity willingly adopted in the following beautiful stanzas, humbling in their charged economy:

I move to bareness
A white-washed room

With a window telling
Of starlight, darkness
And pre-dawn pallor

And a white holland blind
To draw half down on
The full blaze of sunlight.

The book concludes with three very moving poems addressed to the poet's recently deceased husband, Alec Bolton, Printer, with whom she shared a 'calm content' and from whom she received the gentle reinforcement of a stoicism already possessed: 'Forgive, learn from the past. Press on.' Fortunately for us, she has done just that in a collection offering breathing space amid meaningless clamour, profundity, enlightenment, and a courageous reminder of the nearly-forgotten emotional resilience, and openness to change, of older age.

Fay Zwicky's collections of poetry include *Poems 1970-1992* (UQP, 1993) and *The Gatekeeper's Wife* (Brandl & Schlesinger, 1998).

Andrew Dowling

Truth and History

Peter Carey

True History of the Kelly Gang (UQP, 2000)

Peter Carey's last three novels have all been set in the nineteenth century. One can understand the poetic licence that Carey finds in history. Someone once said that 'the past is a foreign country', but the past is also a country that authors and readers will never actually visit. Aesthetically, history offers interesting pegs on which an author can hang a story. But politically, historical fiction also tries to give an authoritative voice and a 'true history' to the victims, the downtrodden, the forgotten of the past. There is, therefore, a contradiction between using history to create fiction and using fiction to reveal the 'truth' about history.

Carey's work reveals this mix of imagination and desire for 'truth.' His latest novel, *True History of the Kelly Gang*, is written in the first person and is meant to be Ned Kelly's account of his life, written for the daughter he will never see. The emphasis on 'truth' is evident in the first sentence:

I lost my own father at 12 yr. of age and know what it is to be raised on lies and silences my dear daughter you are presently too young to understand a word I write but this history is for you and will contain no single lie may I burn in hell if I speak false.

This is pure fiction. Ned Kelly had no daughter and certainly did not write any manuscript like this. Carey's title, *True History*, is thus very ironic. Carey has fun maintaining his claim to authenticity by describing in detail the manuscript from which the story was supposedly taken. Bibliographic details are included at the beginning of each chapter. The chapters are called 'parcels.' This tactic of emphasising an 'original' document draws on a long tradition that dates back to Defoe's *Robinson Crusoe* (1719). However, the reasons behind Carey's ruse are complex. There is a strong impulse here to make a version of history 'true.'

The epigraph to *True History*, from William Faulkner, reads, 'The past is not dead. It is not even past.' One meaning is that history repeats itself; another meaning is that past events reverberate in the present; however, a third meaning that is relevant for Carey is that real people lived in the past and what happened to them has significance for us today. The 'truth' about history lies in the passion and complexity of ordinary, forgotten people.

As Carey repeatedly stated on his promotional tour in Australia last year, his aim in resurrecting Ned Kelly was to discover the man behind the mask and to describe the inner life of that empty figure who stares out of Sidney Nolan's famous paintings – to capture the individual behind the icon. Carey describes with great skill the inner life of Ned Kelly. The plot is simple and we know it well. We have all heard of the boy who grew up under the constant tyranny of the law; who lived in poverty with his mother and siblings at Eleven Mile Creek in Victoria; who drifted towards a life of crime and became the leader of the Kelly Gang, which also included Joe Byrne, Steve Hart, and Dan Kelly; who killed a posse of police at Stringybark Creek; who constructed Australia's most famous suit of armour; and who was captured after the final shoot-out at Glenrowan and uttered 'such is life' before he was hung at the age of twenty-six. Carey brings these details to life with great skill.

However, the novel's great achievement lies in its ability to evoke a distinctive personality through a unique prose style. The plot is simple, but the narration of the novel is remarkable. Carey's prose recreates the style of a man with little formal schooling and it foregoes many standard grammatical features, such as commas. The effect is impressive. Thoughts and actions are yoked together in a single sentence so as to create a tremendous sense of narrative urgency. Every sentence has so much material squeezed into it that it seems ready to burst apart at the seams. Thoughts, feelings, and events all come in a rush. The following account of Ned Kelly's first crime at the age of ten, when he kills a heifer to feed his hungry family, illustrates this narrative urgency:

It were across this dry river bed that Mr Murray's heifer calf come calling out my name I were very hungry when I heard her and knew what I must do...Within the year I would of learned to kill a beast very smart and clean and have its hide off and drying in the sun before you could say Jack Robertson but on this 1st occasion I failed to find the artery. I'm sure you know I have spilled human blood when there were no other choice at that time I were no more guilty than a soldier in a war. But if there was a law against the murder of a beast I would plead guilty and you would be correct to put the black cap on your head for I killed my little heifer badly and am sorry for it still. By the time she fell her neck was a sea of laceration I will never forget the terror in her eyes.

This urgent style is also related to character. The sentences packed to capacity and bristling with energy develop the growing image of Ned Kelly as a man who can only barely contain his violence. Ned realises his own tendency to confrontation. At the age of seven, he stands by his mother when a policeman attempts to molest her and observes how his action contrasts with others in the room: 'Of a different disposition I begun to move towards my mother'. Ned also repeats the phrase 'he did not know me' to describe the violence that lurks within him and that often strikes out unexpectedly. This explosive fury is an essential part of Ned Kelly's character. What is brilliant is the way the prose reflects his personality through overflowing sentences that burst outward.

Carey's aim of uncovering the man behind the mask is developed through a language style that also evokes a particular idea of masculinity. Western masculinity is above all active, and is often represented as a flowing, internal force. Our culture's idea of masculinity is marked by both restraint and violence just as our ideal man is controlled yet always ready to spring into action. Masculinity is a performance that must avoid passivity on the one hand and brutality on the other. The traditional association of masculinity with discipline and the endurance of pain, for example, illustrates the idea that men need to be disciplined. Carey's prose illustrates and draws on this concept of manliness as a chaotic force in need of control.

In Sidney Nolan's paintings this image is dominant. Beneath Ned Kelly's rigid mask stares a mind locked away by steel and iron. Carey's aim is to probe beneath this image; and he does this very effectively through the counter-image of a man in a dress. Transvestism emerges as a theme in the first chapter of the book when we see the young Ned Kelly discover to his chagrin that reports of his father wearing a dress while riding about the countryside are, in fact, true. The dress is buried in a trunk in the Kelly's backyard. Ned brings this secret out of its earthen closet and in a fit of fury, he burns his father's hidden dress. His father does not acknowledge that the secret even exists and there results a growing separation between father and son. After burning his father's dress, Ned says:

I lost my own father from a secret he might as well been snatched by a roiling river fallen from a ravine I lost him from my heart so long I cannot even now properly make the place for him that he deserves.

Ned defines himself against effeminacy and secrecy. The reader knows, of course, that the rigid masquerade of a suit of armour awaits him at the end of the story. But by placing the dress in opposition to the suit of armour, Carey delves beneath the icons of masculinity that have traditionally defined Australia's most famous bushranger.

Later in the story, Carey explains away the theme of trans-vestism by saying that it was the custom of ancient Celtic warriors to ride about the countryside in a dress. Carey should not have done this. His 'explanation' is, in fact, the only moment when the narra-tive loses its urgency. The dress is an excellent metaphor for the fears against which manliness defines itself. It should have been left hanging, as it were, in opposition to Ned Kelly's suit of armour.

When Carey arrived in Australia last year to publicise *True History of the Kelly Gang*, he observed that 'the past is like science fiction to me.' Carey knows about science fiction. His early experiments in this genre in *Exotic Pleasures* created some of the brightest stars in the galaxy of Australian short story writing. But at his talk to the Art Gallery Society of NSW, he observed that his historical novels were just as fictional as science fiction. Carey was referring to the 'easy' aspect of historical fiction, that within certain acceptable limits it is completely made up. But the best science fiction manages to transport its readers to distant galaxies and also bring them closer to their own condition. Carey achieves this effect in *True History of the Kelly Gang*, where he creates a new world from the past in order to reveal a 'truth' about ourselves.

Faulkner's epigraph – 'The past is not dead. It is not even past.' – is thus very apt in that it describes the effect of Carey's reconstruction. Faulkner influences Carey not only in the rich figurative language that Carey uses, but in the way he gave voice to the rich thoughts of supposedly simple people. This is Carey's political function. Carey tries to humanise history's victims and show the complexity of the unknown and downtrodden. His aim of giving voice to the passions and feelings of forgotten people is evident, for example, at the end of *Oscar and Lucinda,* when the narrator describes a country thick with invisible stories:

My great-grandfather drifted up the Bellinger River like a blind man up the central aisle of Notre Dame. He saw nothing. The country was thick with sacred stories more ancient than the ones he carried in his sweat-slippery leather Bible. He did not even imagine their presence.

In a narrative of a nation's progress, all that is left of Oscar and Lucinda's own story are traces. Carey's political task is to give voice to the stories that are trampled by the grand narratives of history and civilisation. Carey thus creates history to reveal a deeper truth about history. This 'truth' is about the hidden depths of ordinary people; about the extraordinary in the ordinary and vice-versa.

Post-structuralist critics often claim that literature does more than simply 'reflect' life; that it 'constructs' life and pre-eminently, it constructs notions of personal identity. These critics claim that literature not only represents the inner life, it in effect creates the inner life. Ever since Samuel Richardson wrote *Pamela* (1740) and gave emotional depth and moral probity to a young servant girl the novel has created this sense of personal depth for common people. The novel as a genre is linked to democracy because it claims that complexity is a common legacy. Carey reveals this democratic impulse in most of his work, particularly in his novels set in the nineteenth-century – *Oscar and Lucinda* and *Jack Maggs*. He failed in *Jack Maggs* partly because he tried to attack something visible, Charles Dickens, and bring that famous author down a notch or two, instead of giving voice to something hidden. However, in *True History*, he returns to representing the inner life and succeeds admirably.

T. S. Eliot once claimed that 'the historical sense involves a perception, not only of the pastness of the past, but of its presence.' Carey's weaving of history and truth confirms this historical sense. In exploring the relationship between truth and history, Carey has moved from entirely imaginary characters (such as *Oscar and Lucinda*) to historical characters who are fictionalised (such as Charles Dickens as Tobias Oates in *Jack Maggs*) to real historical characters (such as Ned Kelly). Carey succeeds in *True History of the Kelly Gang* because his experimental narrative style works so well. However, it would be interesting to see the product of his imagination without any historical constraints. This is not to say that history is a crutch for Carey. Of course, it is always the case and will always be the case that poor novels and meagre tales are padded out by historical detail. This is not the case with Carey's historical fiction. Nevertheless, it would be interesting to see what Carey could accomplish with a contemporary tale, or perhaps even science-fiction.

Andrew Dowling is Research Manager in the Faculty of Humanities and Social Sciences at UTS; his study *Manliness and the Male Novelist in Victorian Literature* is to be published in 2001 by Ashgate Press.